Education and Social Inequality
in the Global Culture

Globalisation, Comparative Education and Policy Research
12-volume Book Series (Springer)

Series editor: Joseph Zajda (Australian Catholic University, Melbourne Campus)
http://www.springeronline.com/sgw/cda/frontpage

Book series overview

The *Globalisation, Comparative Education and Policy Research* book series aims to meet the research needs of all those interested in in-depth developments in comparative education research. The series provides a global overview of developments and changes in policy and comparative education research during the last decade. Presenting up-to-date scholarly research on global trends, it is an easily accessible, practical yet scholarly source of information for researchers, policy makers and practitioners. It seeks to address the nexus between comparative education, policy and forces of globalisation, and provides perspectives from all the major disciplines and all the world regions. The series offers possible strategies for the effective and pragmatic policy planning and implementation at local, regional and national levels.

The book series complements the *International Handbook of Globalisation and Education Policy Research*. The volumes focus on comparative education themes and case studies in much greater scope and depth than is possible in the Handbook.

The series includes volumes on both empirical and qualitative studies of policy initiatives and developments in comparative education research in elementary, secondary and post-compulsory sectors. Case studies may include changes and education reforms around the world, curriculum reforms, trends in evaluation and assessment, decentralisation and privatisation in education, technical and vocational education, early childhood education, excellence and quality in education. Above all, the series offers the latest findings on critical issues in comparative education and policy directions, such as:

• Developing new internal strategies (more comprehensive, flexible and innovative modes of learning) that take into account the changing and expanding learner needs
• Overcoming 'unacceptable' socio-economic educational disparities and inequalities
• Improving educational quality
• Harmonizing education and culture
• International cooperation in education and policy directions in each country

Book titles in the 12-volume series are listed at the end of this volume

Joseph Zajda • Karen Biraimah • William Gaudelli
Editors

Education and Social Inequality in the Global Culture

 Springer

Editors
Prof. Joseph Zajda
Australian Catholic University
Melbourne Campus, VIC
Australia
j.zajda@jnponline.com

Prof. Karen Biraimah
University of Central Florida
Orlando, FL
USA

Dr. William Gaudelli
Columbia University
New York, NY
USA

ISBN: 978-1-4020-6926-0   e-ISBN: 978-1-4020-6927-7

Library of Congress Control Number: 2007942177

Printed on acid-free paper

9 8 7 6 5 4 3 2 1

springer.com

Foreword

A major aim of *Education and Social Inequality in the Global Culture*, which is the first volume in the 12-volume book series *Globalisation, Comparative Education and Policy Research*, edited by Joseph Zajda and his team, is to present a global overview of the relationship of education, socio-economic status, and globalization. By examining some of the major education policy issues, particularly in the light of recent shifts in education and policy research, the editors aim to provide a comprehensive picture of the intersecting and diverse discourses of globalization, education, and policy-driven reforms. The spirit of dialogical encounter has very soundly directed editors' efforts in organizing this volume. The editors' task is to deepen, and in some cases open widely, diverse and significant discourses related to globalization, social stratification, and education.

The impact of globalization on education policy and reforms is a strategically important issue for us all. More than ever before, there is a need to understand and analzse both the intended and the unintended effects of globalization on economic competitiveness, educational systems, the state, and relevant policy changes—all as they affect individuals, educational bodies (such as universities), policy-makers, and powerful corporate organizations across the globe. The evolving and constantly changing notions of national identity, language, border politics and citizenship which are relevant to education policy need to be critiqued by appeal to context-specific factors such as local–regional–national areas, which sit uncomfortably at times with the international imperatives of globalization. Current education policy research reflects a rapidly changing world where citizens and consumers are experiencing a growing sense of uncertainty, and loss of flexibility. Yet globalization exposes us also to opportunities generated by a fast-changing world economy.

In this stimulating and important book, the authors focus on discourses surrounding three major dimensions affecting the equality/inequality debate in education and society: *hegemony*, *equity*, and *cultural capital*. These are most critical and significant concepts for examining and critically evaluating the dimensions of social inequality in the global culture.

Hegemony, as perceived by Antonio Gramsci, and other critical theorists, is the dominance of ideology and beliefs of powerful social groups built through implicit consensus. Here, poor and working class people, who have an unequal access to socially valued commodities, such as wealth, power, and education, participate in hegemonic relations, having consented to them.

Equity has come to mean that which, while upholding justice, is in the best interest of the individual and the community. As the editors argue, Aristotle's conception of equity is that of a corrective of justice, which sits within the law but allows for the interpretation of phenomena to uphold a greater good. According to Aristotle, an equitable person is someone who exercises a choice and does equitable acts, is not unreasonably insistent upon rights, but can accept less than his or her share. Such a notion of civil morality suggests that it is incumbent on all citizens, but especially those with means, to take less than they are entitled to so that others may have a sufficient amount.

Cultural capital, as coined by P. Bourdieu, defines dominant conceptions of what constitutes knowledge, knowing, and social value. Educational systems—schools, colleges, and universities, by upholding a single 'gold standard' of what it means to be knowledgeable, reinforce the differentiated achievement status of class groups, but also reward those who are conversant with implicit rules of dominant ideology. As such, cultural capital refers to success in schooling, largely dictated by the extent to which individuals have absorbed the dominant culture. As the editors explain, schools, in a sense, are markets wherein children enter with various stores of cultural capital that can be exchanged for enhancement of one's capital, and, thereby, their life-chances. Cultural capital, as a significant dimension of educational inequality, continues to shape and influence children's lives and destinies globally—as discussed in scholarly fashion in this book.

The book as a whole focuses on the issues and dilemmas that help us to understand in a more meaningful and practical way the various links between education, social stratification, and globalization. They include:

– The significance of the politics of globalization and development in education policy—their effects on cross-cultural perceptions of dimensions affecting the equality/inequality debate in education and society: *hegemony*, *equity*, and *cultural capital*
– The significance of discourses, which define and shape the nexus between education, social stratification, and globalization
– The encroaching homogeneity of global culture, which has the potential to reduce adaptability and flexibility, and reinforce the status quo
– The multidimensional nature of globalization dimensions of educational inequality

The perception of education policy research and globalization as dynamic and multifaceted processes clearly necessitates a multiple-perspective approach in the study of education and this book provides that perspective commendably. In the book, the authors, who come from diverse backgrounds and regions, attempt insightfully to provide a worldview of significant developments in education, hegemony, cultural capital, and equity. They report on schooling and policy changes in such countries as Brazil, Egypt, Guatemala, Nicaragua, Peru, and elsewhere. Understanding the interaction between education and globalization forces us to learn more about the similarities and differences in education policy research and associated reforms in the local–regional–national context, as well as the global one. This inevitably results in a far deeper and richer understanding and analysis of the globalization and education *Zeitgeist*.

Clearly, the emerging phenomena associated with globalization have in different ways affected current developments in education and policy. Globalization of policy, trade, and finance, for instance, has profound implications for education and reform implementation. On the one hand, the periodic economic crises coupled with the prioritized policies of the International Monetary Fund (IMF) and the World Bank (e.g., SAPs) have seriously affected some developing nations and transitional economies in delivering basic education for all. When the poor are unable to feed their children, what expectations can we have that the children will attend school? Children from impoverished families are forced to stay at home to help and work for their parents; they simply cannot afford to attend school. The policies of the Organisation for Economic and Cooperative Development (OECD), the United Nations Educational, Scientific and Cultural Organization (UNESCO), the World Trade Organization (WTO), and the General Agreement on Trade and Services (GATS) appear to operate as powerful forces, which, as supranational organizations, shape and influence education and policy, yet they also deny the access of the less privileged to the assumed advantages of an expanding global society. One might well ask what the corporate organizations are doing to enhance intercultural sensitivity, flexibility, and mutual understanding. And are those excluded by the demise of democratic processes really able to work together for the common good?

The editors and authors provide a coherent strategic education policy statement on recent shifts surrounding the major dimensions that affect the equality/inequality debate in education and society: *hegemony*, *equity*, and *cultural capital*. They offer new and exciting approaches to further explore, develop, and improve education and policy-making on the global stage. In the different chapters, they attempt to address some of the major issues and problems confronting educators and policy-makers globally. The book contributes in a very scholarly way to a more holistic understanding of the education and inequality nexus, and it further offers us practical strategies for combating educational inequality.

The book is rigorous, thorough, and scholarly. I believe it is likely to have profound and wide-ranging implications for the future of education policy and reforms globally, in the conception, planning, and educational outcomes of "communities of learning". The community-of-learning metaphor reflects the knowledge society, and offers us a very worthy insight into the way individuals and formal organizations acquire the necessary wisdom, values and skills in order to adapt and respond to change in these turbulent and conflict-ridden times. The authors thoughtfully explore the complex nexus between globalization, democracy, and education—where, on the one hand, democratization and progressive education are equated with equality, inclusion, equity, tolerance, and human rights, while, on the other hand, globalization is perceived (by some critics at least) to be a totalizing force that is widening the gap between the rich and the poor, and bringing domination and control by corporate bodies and powerful organizations. The authors further compel us to explore critically the new challenges confronting the world in the provision of authentic democracy, social justice, and cross-cultural values that genuinely promote more positive ways of thinking.

In this volume, the editors and authors jointly recognize the need for profound changes in education and society. They argue for education policy goals and challenges confronting the global village, which I think are critically important. Drawing extensively and in depth on educational systems, reforms, and policy analysis, both the authors and editors of this book focus on the crucial issues and policy decisions that must be addressed if genuine learning, characterized by wisdom, compassion, and intercultural understanding, is to become a reality, rather than rhetoric.

I commend the book wholeheartedly to any reader who shares these same ideals.

Vice-Chancellor   Peter W. Sheehan AO
Australian Catholic University

Preface

Education and Social Inequality in the Global Culture presents up-to-date scholarly research on global and comparative trends in education, social inequality and policy research. It provides an easily accessible, practical yet scholarly source of information about the international concern in the field of globalisation, access and social inequality. Above all, the book offers the latest findings to the critical issues in education, democracy and educational inequalities. It is a sourcebook of ideas for researchers, practitioners and policy-makers in education, globalisation and social inequality. It offers a timely overview of current changes in education and social stratification in the global culture. It provides directions in education, and policy research, relevant to transformational educational reforms in the 21st century.

The book critically examines the overall interplay between globalisation, social inequality and education. It draws upon recent studies in the areas of globalisation, educational inequalities and the role of the State (see also Zajda et al., 2006). It explores conceptual frameworks and methodological approaches applicable in the research covering the State, globalisation, social stratification and education. It demonstrates the neo-liberal ideological imperatives of education and policy reforms, and illustrates the way the relationship between the State and education policy affects current models and trends in education reforms and schooling globally. Various book chapters critique the dominant discourses and debates pertaining to the newly constructed and reinvented models of neo-liberal ideology in education, set against the current climate of growing social stratification and unequal access to quality education for all.

The book, constructed against this pervasive anti-dialogical backdrop, aims to widen, deepen and, in some cases, open discourse related to globalisation, and new dimensions of social inequality in the global culture. It is presented around three particular dimensions—hegemony, equity and cultural capital—as these continue to be most significant dimensions defining social inequality in the global culture.

The book explores the ambivalent and problematic relationship between the State, globalisation and social change. Using a number of diverse paradigms, ranging from critical theory to globalisation, the authors, by focusing on globalisation, ideology and social inequality, attempt to examine critically both the reasons and outcomes of education reforms, policy change and transformation, and provide a more informed critique on the Western-driven models of accountability, quality and school effectiveness. The book draws upon recent studies in the areas of equity, cultural capital and dominant ideologies in education (Zajda, 2005).

Equality of educational opportunity is difficult to achieve in highly stratified societies and economic systems. In 1975, Coleman (1975) and others have argued that education alone was not sufficient to overcome significant socio-economic status (SES) differences in the society divided along dimensions of class, power, income, wealth and privilege. The difficulty of attaining social justice in the global economy is explained by Rikowski (2000), who argues that sustainable social justice is impossible on the basis of capitalist social forms. Globalisation, in most developing countries (the majority of humanity), is articulated in the form of finance-driven policy reforms concerning efficiency and effectiveness. Their effect on education systems is likely to 'increase' educational inequalities and access (Carnoy, 1999).

Furthermore, a lack of emphasis on the relationship between policy, poverty and schooling, and the 'withdrawal of the state as a major provider in the field of education in many parts of the world' raise serious human rights and ethical questions (Soudien & Kallaway, 1999; Zajda, 2005). The growth of global education policy hegemony defining accountability, standards, quality assurance and assessment fails to respond to the changing relationships between the state, education and social justice in the global economy.

Equality of educational opportunities, labelled by Coombs (1982) as the "stubborn issue of inequality" (Coombs, 1982, p. 153), and first examined in comparative education research by Kandel in 1957 (Kandel, 1957, p. 2), is "still with us", according to Jennings (2000, p. 113). Furthermore, the prospect of widening inequalities in education, due to market-oriented schooling, and substantial tolerance of inequalities and exclusion, are more than real. Access and equity continue to be "enduring concerns" in education (OECD, 2001, p. 26). The policy shift away from the progressive and egalitarian vision of education that characterised the 1960s and the 1970s has serious implications for human rights, social justice and democracy.

The general intention is to make *Education and Social Inequality in the Global Culture* available to a broad spectrum of users among policy-makers, academics, graduate students, education policy researchers, administrators and practitioners in the education and related professions. The book is unique in that it

- Examines central discourses surrounding the debate of cultural capital and social inequality in education
- Explores conce ptual frameworks and methodological approaches applicable in the research of the State, globalisation and social inequality
- Illustrates how the relationship between the State and education policy affects current models and trends in schooling globally
- Demonstrates ideological imperatives of globalisation, neo-liberal ideology and the State
- Evaluates the ambivalent and problematic relationship between the State, education reforms and outcomes in education globally

- Provides strategic education policy analysis on recent shifts in education, and policy research
- Gives suggestions for directions in education and policy changes, relevant to democratic and empowering pedagogy in the 21st century

We hope that you will find *Education and Social Inequality in the Global Culture* useful in your teaching, future research and discourses concerning schooling, social justice and policy reforms in the global culture.

Australian Catholic University   Joseph Zajda
(Melbourne Campus)

References

Carnoy, M. (1999). *Globalization and educational reform: What planners need to know.* Paris: UNESCO, International Institute for Education Planning.

Coleman, J. (1975). What is meant by 'an equal educational opportunity'? *Oxford Review of Education, 1,* 27.

Coombs, P. (1982). Critical world educational issues of the next two decades. *International Review of Education, 28*(1), 143–158.

Jennings, Z. (2000). Functional literacy of young Guyanese adults. *International Review of Education, 46*(1/2), 93–116.

Kandel, H. (1957). Equalizing educational opportunities and its problems. *International Review of Education, 3*(1), 1–12.

OECD. (2001). *Educ ation policy analysis: Education and skills.* Paris: OECD.

Rikowski, G. (2000). Education and social justice within the social universe of capital. Paper presented at the BERA day seminar on "Approaching social justice in education: Theoretical frameworks for practical purposes", Faculty of Education, Nottingham Trent University, April 10.

Soudien, C. & Kallaway, P. (1999). *Education, equity and transformation.* Dordrecht, The Netherlands: Kluwer Academic.

Zajda, J. (Ed.). (2005) *International handbook of globalisation and education policy research.* Dordrecht, The Netherlands: Springer.

Zajda, J., Majhanovich, S., & Rust, V. (Eds.). (2006). *Education and social justice.* Dordrecht. The Netherlands: Springer.

Acknowledgements

We wish to thank the following individuals who have provided invaluable help, advice and support with this major research project:

Harmen van Paradijs, Publishing Editor, Springer

Marianna Pascale, Springer

Dorothy Murphy, Assistant Editor, *Educational Practice and Theory*, James Nicholas Publishers

Rea Zajda, James Nicholas Publishers

We also want to thank numerous reviewers who were prepared to review various drafts of the chapters. These include:

Helena Allahwerdi, University of Finland

Ari Antikainen, University of Helsinki

Alberto Arenas, University of Arizona

Jill Blackmore, Deakin University

Malcolm Campbell, Bowling Green State University

Paul Carlin, Australian Catholic University (Melbourne Campus)

David Gamage, University of Newcastle

Mark Hanson, University of California (Riversdale)

Yaacov Iram, Bar Ilan University

Erwin Epstein, Loyola University Chicago

Kyu Hwan Lee, Ewha Womans University (South Korea)

Kas Mazurek, University of Lethbridge

Marie-Laure Mimoun-Sorel, Australian Catholic University (Melbourne Campus)

Wolfgang Mitter, German Institute for International Educational Research

Gabrielle McMullen, Australian Catholic University (Melbourne Campus)

Jerzy Smolicz, University of Adelaide

Sandra L Stacki, Hofstra University

Margaret Secombe, University of Adelaide

David Wilson, OISE, University of Toronto

Rea Zajda, James Nicholas Publishers

We are particularly grateful to Harmen van Paradijs, Publishing Editor, Springer, who supported this project, and who took the responsibility for the book production process, and whose energy and enthusiasm ensured that the book was published on time.

Education and Social Inequality in the Global Culture

Edited by
Joseph Zajda
Australian Catholic University
Karen Biraimah
University of Central Florida
and
William Gaudelli
Teachers College Columbia University

Contents

Introduction: Education and Social Inequality in the Global Culture

Karen Biraimah[1], William Gaudelli[2], and Joseph Zajda[3]

1 Dimensions of Globalization

1.1 Globalization as a Construct

Globalization is not an easy term to define. There are numerous competing and contested definitions of globalization. The problem lies not so much in defining globalization, but in understanding and critiquing its intended and unintended consequences on nation-states and individuals around the world. Nearly 3,000 definitions of globalization were offered in 1998 alone, as noted in the *Globalisation Guide* (2002):

> One can be sure that virtually every one of the 2822 academic papers on globalisation written in 1998 included its own definition, as would each of the 589 new books on the subject published in that year. (http://www.globalisationguide.org/sb02.html).

Definitions of globalization have varied from one author to another. Some have described it as a process, while others a condition, a system, a force, or an age. In the past few years, there has been a virtual explosion of interest in globalization by comparative education scholars and policy analysts (Appadurai, 1990; Giddens, 1990, 1996; Robertson, 1992; Arnove & Torres, 1999, Sklair, 1999; Carnoy, 1999; Stromquist & Monkman, 2000; Welch, 2001; Crossley & Jarvis, 2001; Carnoy & Rhoten, 2002; Sen, 2002; Dale & Robertson, 2003; Biraimah, 2005; Rhoads, 2005; Ritzer, 2005; Zajda, 2005, 2006; Clayton, 2006; Zajda et al., 2006).

There still is no consensus, from the literature, as to what constitutes its essential characteristics or core processes. Amongst the most influential scholarly definitions of that term, we can include Anthony Gidden's statement that it is "the intensification of worldwide social relations which link distant localities in such a way that local happenings are shaped by events occurring many miles away and vice versa" (Giddens, 1990). To Leslie Sklair (1999) globalization refers to the "emergence of

---

[1] *University of Central Florida*
[2] *Teachers College Columbia University*
[3] *Australian Catholic University*

a globalized economy based on new systems of production, finance and consumption" (Sklair, 1999, p. 146). Some scholars, including Amartya Sen (2002), argue that globalization affects the expansion of markets, and imposes neoliberal policies, but it also impacts positively on human rights and democracy:

> Globalisation has contributed to the progress of the world, through travel, trade, migration, spread of cultural influences, and dissemination of knowledge, and understanding (including of science and technology). To have stopped globalisation would have done irreparable harm to the progress of humanity. (p. 11)

In most cases, scholars bring their own critical approach to the intersection of globalization and their particular discipline and methodology. One could argue that under the influence of the World Trade Organization and other multilateral institutions, policy makers in Europe, and elsewhere, have adopted remarkably similar strategic policy goals and reform initiatives, in order to reform universities as entrepreneurial institutions, which appear to be symbiotically connected to the global economy.

In recent years, the construct of 'globalization' has become a ubiquitous signifier in education and social sciences and there is a need to analyze the paradoxical complexity and ambiguities surrounding connotations and denotations attached to the term by different individuals who employ a rich diversity of perceptions, disciplines, and methodologies. By finding some common features and differences we may be able to provide a more meaningful paradigm in policy and pedagogical discourses surrounding globalization, the global economy, and the global culture.

Globalization has been referred to as 'the most over-used term in the current political lexicon'. It refers both to the compressions of the world in such a way that local happenings are shaped by events occurring many miles away and vice versa *and* the "intensification of the consciousness of the world as a whole" (Simon Bromley, Feature Article, *New Political Economy* March 1996, p. 120).

What is 'globalization'? Is it a market-driven process, propelled by forces of consumerism that imposes a neoliberal economic regime of trade relations, and which represents the ubiquity of global capitalism? If so, is it spearheaded by multinational conglomerates? Is it connected to the discourse about modernity (Giddens, 1991; Robertson, 1992; Zajda, 2006)? Is it also driven by intensified modes of competition that compresses 'the time, and space aspects of social relations' (Giddens, 1990; Robertson, 1992)? These are some of the questions arising from a critical perception of multidimensional globalization. In general sense, the phenomenon of 'globalization' refers to individuals and institutions around the globe being more connected to each other than ever before, to a quantum-like pace of the international flow of communication, capital, knowledge, and other socially valued commodities, to consumer goods and services produced in one part of the world, and being increasingly available in all parts of the world, and to shifts in political and economic systems influenced by forces of globalization.

The term 'globalization', like postmodernism, is used so widely today in social theory, policy, and education research that it has become a cliché (Held et al., 1999; Zajda, 2005). As a construct, 'globalization' has acquired considerable emotive force among pro- and anti-globalization researchers. Some scholars view it as a process that is beneficial—a key to future world economic development—and also inevitable and irreversible. Others regard it with hostility, even fear, believing that it increases inequality within and between nations, threatens employment and living standards and thwarts social progress. Economic 'globalization' is a historical process, the result of human innovation and technological progress. It refers to the increasing integration of economies around the world, particularly through trade and financial flows. The term sometimes also refers to the movement of people (labor) and knowledge (technology) across international borders.

As demonstrated above, globalization appears to be a conundrum. As it offers new venues for participation beyond national boundaries, it has exacerbated the socioeconomic divide of means and access to this participatory space. While it creates dialogical terrain to engage others about diverse ways of living, it stigmatizes certain identities as impediments to global progress. Though globalization hints of cooperation among international powers towards peaceful ends, it has given rise to deep schisms in the global body politic and has wrought atrocious violence. As it promises a richer, more diverse dialogue about our global futures, it forecloses public discourses about the myriad problems it has created. Environmental effects, social dislocation, and labor degradation are all directly related to the commingling of profit and progress that is part and parcel of the global age. The voices that attempt to draw attention to emergent social problems produced by globalization have themselves become faint whispers in a deafening chorus of tacit obedience to a new social contract of neoliberalism *qua* democracy that holds certain principles beyond debate: that market forces are always in the best interest of most people, that accumulating wealth is the good life, and that education must support these ends.

Do advocates of globalization desire participation, opening dialogical space, promoting cooperative power, or social equality? Evidence on this question resides with the former. Globalization has come to be associated with exacerbating social inequality, exemplified in the proverbial race to the bottom. In this race untethered capitalists seek to perfect a socially toxic formula that maximizes production and profit while minimizing worker and environmental protection. Popular and scholarly dialogue generally focuses on these events, whether it is the outsourcing of labor from developed countries, the in-sourcing of capitalism that exploits local people and ecosystems, or the subsequent trade issues that emerge from these global outflows and inflows. Increasingly what is needed, however, is study of the systemic complexities associated with these relationships in light of the myriad examples in the social world, rather than myopic attention to a case or detached theorizing about an abstract trend. Progress in understanding globalization will certainly be made when the macro and micro can be viewed in light of each other, each analysis working towards emergent and tenuous theories about globalization. To know something of globalization is to look carefully, closely, and locally at its manifestations, uncovering some element of its meaning, unearthing some dimension of its effects. While such an archaeological method of knowledge development is tediously slow, hampered by the shifting qualities of globalization itself, it provides some basis on which to extend an analysis of what globalization is and what it portends.

George Ritzer (2005, p. 3) offers a useful analytical lens through which to view the macro and micro areas of globalization. He argues that globalization is a category of *nothing*, or "a social form that is generally centrally conceived, controlled, and comparatively devoid of distinctive content". *Nothing* he contrasts with *something*, or that which is "indigenously conceived, controlled, and comparatively rich in distinctive substantive content" (Ritzer, 2005, p. 7). Ritzer avoids casting social phenomena blithely into this dichotomy, recognizing the potential faultiness of his argument in its apparently oversimplistic logic. Yet he maintains that establishments such as weekend markets, craft fairs, and the corner pub are fundamentally different than the behemoths of corporate globalization, such as Wal-Mart, McDonalds, and Microsoft. The former embrace their individuality and distinctive character while the latter seek uniformity, consistency, and, thus, portability.

Ritzer (2005) examines how manifestations of *something* and *nothing* move and thereby alter one another, processes he refers to alternatively and oppositionally as *glocalization* and *grobalization*. Glocalization is the intermingling of the global and the local such that a hybrid is formed. Eating in a Vietnamese restaurant in Brazil while talking on a Japanese cell phone through a US satellite network to someone in Indonesia about the purchase of land in Russia is an illustration of what has become commonplace and has led to the hybridization of cultural artifacts. Hybridization has brought kosher pizzas, matrioshka dolls (originally a Russian folklore artifact) manufactured in Mexico, and Starbucks coffee, masquerading as a local café in Romania. While such glocalization stirs excitement in the possibilities of a small planet for some, others are dismayed at what they see as the bastardization, commodification, and exploitation of the local. Put another way, is the ubiquity of commodification familiarity an illustration of rationalization, Americanization, and restriction or freedom, diversity, and cultural synthesis (Ritzer, 2004, p. 80)?

Advocates of glocalization see these new syntheses as progress, an effect being people identifying as one. Opponents like Ritzer, however, characterize these same changes as illustrations of grobalization. Grobalization minimizes and trivializes the differences among people and places, affords them less ability to adapt and innovate, directs social processes that are deterministic and dominant, and represents people in commodified ways (p. 77). Heuristically, grobalization *others* people in the world such that they are no longer agents of and for themselves, but are acted on by the ominously large and rationalized order of a global world.

We introduce this vocabulary here since it informs much of the scholarship developed in this volume. Though the authors generally do not use these terms to illustrate their work, the contestation of glocalization and grobalization theory underlies much of what they offer. Alexander Wiseman's piece about education in Islamic states (see chapter 11) illustrates the ways in which socially diffused commitments to maintaining religiously based Islamic schools are often opposed to market-oriented Western education, thus creating tensions about the nature of schools. His is a nuanced study, however, in that he suggests that intra-national differences among Islamic states and their allocation of resources to education largely illustrates why these countries have been marginalized. Diane Hoffman and

Guoping Zhou's work about how hegemony of Western early childhood discourse undermines traditional Chinese parenting (see chapter 1) suggests that grobalization is at work through popular parenting magazines, presenting dissonant maxims for child-rearing as revealed truth.

2 Dialogical Encounters and Globalization

The scholarship of globalization that has emerged in the last two decades is remarkably lacking in its dialogical quality, social critique, and reflections, so typical of classics that have withstood the test of time. Globalization has facilitated the incredible proliferation of pulp literature and coffee table books that has reached a broad audience. Perhaps there is no better example of this than the bestseller *The Lexus and the Olive Tree* by Thomas Friedman (2000). Written in a journalistic style, at times in a sensationalistic manner, Friedman attempts to paint the world in broad strokes, relying heavily on his own extensive travel experiences. While this style may be highly readable and engaging, it is severely deficient with respect to theoretical depth and foundation. The author is not aware of himself in the book, presuming that his worldview is simply *what is* and seeks to explain *what ought to be* in these terms. His description of the "electronic herd" or what he refers to as rapid shift of capital away from a country/region when corporations feel there is political or social trouble afoot is a prime illustration (see Friedman, 2000, chapter 12). An elite view pervades this example, and the book as a whole, as he writes as if the means of social development, such as capital, are ends in and of themselves rather than means to further aims.

What is most troubling in considering discourse about globalization in the social mainstream is the general failure to explore its incongruities and, worse, the opposition to engage dialogue about presumptions embedded in globalization. Like Friedman's electronic herd, globalization and its neoliberal attachments have been reified as *how things are* without a careful examination and subsequent debate of *both* (1) the ontological claims, diverse perspectives on what is happening, and (2) its broad, social effects, along with views about possible alternatives to the current state of affairs. China's recent economic boom offers a cogent case in point. As China is in the midst of a period of economic growth that has threatened to overheat and collapse due to its pace, it has done so without regard to the consequences of growth. Employing an unsustainable program of development based largely on a Western model of rapid capital accumulation, diminutive environmental standards, and strident effort for comparative advantage internationally, China's growth is threatening on many levels. Environmental degradation, disregard for urban and rural poor, and labor exploitation are just a few of the many problems such development causes. What is significantly lacking has been a vigorous debate in China about the processes and direction of their economic growth. Rather, they have largely emulated Western-style development, illustrated by their most recent move to begin mass production and exportation of automobiles, not unlike their neighbors in Japan and South Korea (Bradsher, 2005, June 28). China's development, illustrated briefly here, is in a real sense an offspring of globalization, with a local twist. The market for goods, the availability of resources, the fixation on consumer goods and technology, and foundational nature of trade are all directly related to the economic interconnectedness that globalization has created.

What globalization has failed to create, in the case of China and many other societies who are major players in this economic system, however, is a robust dialogue about the nature, effects, and alternatives associated with its growth. Relying on what is narrowly *true*, in particular the principles of unsustainable market economics, globalization has jeopardized social stability, such as a safe environment, equitable access to resources, and protection of human labor, in the quest for greater profits. What is perhaps most disconcerting about this trend is not the effects that such obedience to often implicit principles has caused, as if these were not disturbing enough, but the concomitant subverting of free, open, and diverse discourse about the processes at work and their aims. As meetings such as the G-8 Summit and World Trade Organization occur in locations isolated from the din of protest and discourse, those committed to the free and fair interplay of another marketplace, that of ideas, cannot help but be alarmed.

The task of this volume, set against this pervasive anti-dialogical backdrop, is to widen, deepen, and in some cases open discourse related to globalization, social stratification, and education. While we are aware of significant work that comes before ours (see Robertson, 1992; Appadurai, 1996; Carnoy, 1999; Gabbard, 2000; Stromquist & Monkman, 2000; Mittelman, 2000; Stiglitz, 2002; Sklair, 2002; and Daun, 2004), we hope that what is offered here will extend and deepen this scholarship. We have organized this discourse around three particular issues—*hegemony*, *equity*, and *cultural capital*—as we believe these are the most critical concepts in examining the social inequality of globalization.

3 Hegemony

Hegemony, as articulated by Antonio Gramsci (see Forgacs, 2002; and Clayton, 2006), is the fairly static dominance of social groups built through implicit consensus. For Gramsci, whose conceptualizations of hegemony developed through his struggles and imprisonment as an Italian communist leader during the 1920s and 1930s, dominance was not a purely Machiavellian method where the powerful were consciously and purposefully orchestrating the oppression of the oppressed. Rather, poor and working class people participate in hegemonic relations when they have consented to them, have gained something from them, or otherwise assist in their perpetuation (Forgacs, 2000). In terms of this book, hegemony refers to the exploited worker in an economically disadvantaged situation who seeks a *good life*, usually defined in economic terms, at the expense of his/her coworkers and community. This desire to improve their situation leads them to internalize the image of the oppressor and seek their power. As Paulo Freire (2001) suggested writing in the context of Brazil, land-deprived peasants see the "new man" that they wish to become not as someone born with freedom, autonomy, and responsibility to enact land reform, but "to acquire land and thus become landowners—or, more precisely, bosses over other workers" (p. 46). Gramsci and Freire's tact differed from Marx in that he did not believe social change and class consciousness would emerge spontaneously among the oppressed out of cataclysmic events, but only through a dialectical process that leads to their political agency and action.

Hegemony is a significant idea within this volume. Diane Hoffman and Guoping Zhou's piece on the domination of Western childhood models in Chinese popular culture (chapter 1) places hegemony front and centre, as they contend that Western notions of individualization and youth agency, as opposed to parental authority, are implicated in much of what parents read about in *how to* parenting journals. Caroline E. Parker (chapter 2) analyzes school attendance patterns in Nicaragua comparing urban and rural populations. While the heuristics of low-income families, being a girl, and living in rural areas predict that less access to education has merit, she finds the phenomenon is more complex. In particular, her study examines how living in certain rural areas and in the capital city of Managua confounds such generalizations. Mary Holbrook (chapter 3) also develops and problematizes hegemony as she explores the way in which Mayan culture interactively shapes and is shaped by global discourses within and outside Guatemala. Her work presents a strong emphasis on making the global contributions of Mayans, representing the global South, visible. Such analysis allows readers to move beyond the simplistic dualisms of oppressor/oppressed in analyzing changes in Mayan culture to reach a deeper understanding of how hegemony works to involve the oppressed in their own exploitation. In a similar vein, Victoria Miquel-Marti and Tere Sorde-Marti (chapter 4) explore another group frequently ignored in global discourses, the Roma of Europe. They recount the history of the Roma people, associating their frequent movement and cultural dispersion with current forces of globalization. Rather than presenting the oppressed nature of Roma people as those acted upon, Miquel-Marti and Sorde-Marti explore how Romani, particularly women, are using the tools of globalization such as the Internet as a means to participate on their own terms and to advance community goals within this framework.

4   Equity

Aristotle's conception of equity is that of a corrective of justice which sits within the law but allows for the interpretation of phenomena to uphold a greater good.

As he wrote in *Rhetoric*: "It is equitable to pardon human failings and look to the lawgiver and not the law, to the spirit and not to the letter … to the whole and not to the part" (I: 13). From these early iterations, equity has come to mean that which is in the best interest of the individual and community while upholding justice, though not in a tight and narrow sense (see also Zajda et al., 2006). The equitable man "is one who chooses and does equitable acts, and is not unduly insistent upon his rights, but accepts less than his share" (Aristotle, cf. Beever, 2005). Such a notion of civil morality suggests that it is incumbent on all citizens, but especially those with means, to take less than they are entitled to so that others may have a sufficient amount.

Rather than a principled, rights-based argument that fixes justice solely on what one is due by right, equity tempers justice by considering what all is due through a larger, moral criterion than what is fixed in law. Equity is what fills the gap between where the law or civil society is ambiguous, silent, or even nonexistent, as a means of weighing what actions will promote justice and serving the best interests of the community and the individuals within it. Equity discourse is vital since those who advocate social equality in an era of globalization rely on appeals to equity, justice, and fairness rather than codified law. Education scholarship, particularly within multicultural education, often invokes equity as both a pedagogical principle and a rationale for public education. Christine Bennett (2003) differentiates equity from equality, as the latter requires identical treatment and the former "different treatment according to relevant differences" (p. 16). Gloria Ladson-Billings (1996) refers to equity pedagogy as insuring equal access to knowledge for all students, which requires an intimate knowledge of the child (p. 196).

Randall Zimmerman's work (chapter 5) about higher education in Eastern Europe describes the way in which fair access to postsecondary education has taken shape in the years following the breakup of the Soviet Union. Focusing on the prevalence of class in determining access to higher education, he finds that countries with both a commitment to equity and the resources to service this goal have a broader representation of all social classes in higher education. Marta Luz Sisson de Castro and Janaina Specht da Silva Menezes (chapter 6) examine how policy efforts intended to rectify educational inequities in Brazil often exacerbate the situation they were intended to correct. The municipal government of Rio Grande do Sul implemented a transportation and nutrition program that, while intended to provide access to poor students and thereby promote justice, drained direly needed funds away from efforts to improve teacher quality, develop curriculum, and purchase educational materials. Access to educational resources is also a primary concern of Mariana Alfonso (chapter 7) in her work on education reforms in Peru. She describes a quasi-privatization policy that is designed to augment funding through parental resources. Through a detailed analysis of demographic and expenditure data, she argues that such policies seek to undermine equitable access to education, disenfranchising poor children, particularly those from the Quechua ethnic minority.

The macro-level analyses of equity are well-complemented by the micro/qualitative pieces included herein. Kara Janigan (chapter 8) takes a micro-level analysis of equity, studying Eritrean adolescents who managed to succeed in secondary education despite longstanding limitations about educating girl children in sub-Saharan Africa. She finds that the justice that these young women sought by becoming educated was due in part to their personalities and personal attributes, family resources, and parents' educational achievement. Nagwa Megahed (chapter 9) also takes a focused look at issues of equity with respect to recent educational reform in Egypt, choosing to interview secondary and postsecondary teachers about their interpretations of these efforts. Teachers were somewhat varied in their reactions to these policies, as those whose background included working in the private sector were less optimistic about the possibility of achieving equity of opportunity than those who had always been teachers and saw education as a great equalizing force.

5 Cultural Capital

Cultural capital refers to dominant conceptions of what constitutes knowledge, knowing, and social value. By upholding a single standard of what it means to be knowledgeable, educational systems both reinforce the differentiated achievement status of class groups while rewarding those who are conversant with implicit rules of dominant ideology (see Saha, 2005). Sociologist Pierre Bourdieu is widely recognized for his groundbreaking work on cultural capital. In *Distinction* (1979) Bourdieu argues that children develop from their parents a *habitus*, or unconscious orientations towards ways of being that fit their class position and thus reproduce social classes. He argues that these outlooks are cast at birth and even attempts to *add on* cultural capital later in life will convey the sense that the child is an outsider. Schools, in a sense, are markets wherein children enter with various stores of capital that can be exchanged for enhancement of one's capital, and thereby their life-chances. Children who lack the *habitus* of educated parents, or the working or poor classes, are simultaneously viewed as devoid of valued knowledge and filled with useless or detracting family baggage, or what Bourdieu described as an organic culture.

Jane Roland Martin (2003) has shifted this emphasis, seeking to explore the educative forces of society that transcend schools. Rather than employ Bourdieu's category of cultural capital, which generally focuses on that which is explicitly passed on by schools, she refers to this broader emphasis as cultural stock. She suggests that in order for a democratic society to thrive, there needs to be a commitment to examine what in our cultural stock is an asset and what a liability. This vision of cultural socialization, or education as a reproductive institution, is challenged by conservative educators such as E. D. Hirsch (1988) who, in the tradition of Emile Durkheim, insist that culture, and thereby acculturation, is *the* rationale for public education and needs to be done rigorously and with focused attention on continuation of what has come before.

Educational discourse, particularly which involves globalization, often invokes cultural capital in spirit, if not letter. Most of the chapters in this book, and arguably the volume as a whole, develop from an unstated commitment to providing access to high-quality education for all, though there will surely be disagreement about how this ought to proceed. Cultural capital troubles this path, however, as it defies facile explanation, focusing instead on the important matter of socialization into ways of being that are necessarily local, yet emerging within a larger global culture. This is perhaps most evident in Gillian Hampden-Thompson, Lina Guzman, and Laura Lippman's work (chapter 10) addressing cultural capital internationally. Using two massive international datasets, they use statistical analyses to examine how in nine countries increasing cultural enrichment activities led to academic improvements. While their results are not predictive, they do indicate that in all countries, student literacy achievement increased when participation in cultural events was in evidence. Alexander W. Wiseman (chapter 11) also studies the effects of Western-style education being imposed on four Southwestern Asian (or Middle Eastern) countries. He argues that while this systemic imposition has contributed to the marginalization of these states in the global arena, the persistence of class inequalities within nations is of greater significance than the external forces when analyzing the failure of education to provide opportunity for all of its members.

6   Conclusion

While we have foreshadowed what this volume is about in broad terms, we hesitate to make such assertions without a few cautionary notes for the reader. In selecting these chapters for inclusion in the work, we have purposely included studies that are not only constructive, engaging, and scholarly, but also representative of diverse people, regions, and institutions *while* promoting a lively debate about the nature of the relationship between globalization and education. While we and the authors clearly have views about this relationship, we invite the reader into a dialogical encounter about their views and with those with whom they live and work. Our task in this encounter is not necessarily to persuade or convince an audience, and never to present a hypocritically monolithic sense about *what is*, but to extend, inform, and critique assumptions about the relationship of education, social stratification, and globalization. This spirit of dialogical encounter has directed our efforts in organizing this volume and we invite you into this space towards these uncertain ends.

7   References

Appadurai, A. (1990). Disjuncture and difference in the global cultural economy, *Theory Culture and Society, 7*, 295–310.

Appadurai, A. (1996) (Ed.). *Modernity at large: Cultural dimensions of globalization*. Minneapolis, MN: University of Minnesota Press.

Apple, M. (2004). *Ideology and curriculum* (3 ed.). New York: RoutledgeFalmer.

Arnove, R. & Torres, C. (1999) (Eds.). *Comparative education: The dialectic of the global and the local*. Lanham, MA: Rowman & Littlefield.

Beever, A. (2004). Aristotle on equity, law, and justice. *Legal Theory, 10*, 33–50.

Bennett, C. (2003). *Comprehensive multicultural education: Theory and practice*. Boston, MA: Allyn & Bacon.

Biraimah, B. (2005). Achieving Equitable Outcomes or Reinforcing Social Inequalities? *Educational Practice and Theory, 27*(2), 25–34.

Bourdieu, P. (1999). *Distinction: A social critique of the judgment of taste*. London: Routledge.

Bradsher, K. (2005, June 28). China economy rising at pace to rival U.S. *New York Times*, A6.

Carnoy, M. (1999). *Globalisation and education reform: what planners need to know*. Paris: Unesco IIEP.

Carnoy, M. & Rhoten, D. (2002) (Eds.). The meaning of globalization for educational change [Special issue]. *Comparative Education Review*, *46*(1).

Clayton, T. (2006). *Rethinking Hegemony*. Melbourne: James Nicholas.

Crossley, M. & Jarvis, P. (2001) (Eds.). Comparative education for the twenty-first century: An international response [Special issue]. *Comparative Education*, *37*(4).

Dale, R. & Robertson, S. (2003) (Eds.). *Globalisation, Societies and Education*, *1*(1).

Daun, H. (2006). How does educational decentralization work and what has it achieved? In H. Daun (Ed.), *School decentralization in the context of globalizing governance. International comparison of grassroots responses* (pp. 27–54). Dordrecht, The Netherlands: Springer.

Forgacs, D. (2000). *The Antonio Gramsci reader*. New York: New York University Press.

Freidman, T. (2000). *The lexus and the olive tree: Understanding globalization*. New York: Anchor Books.

Freire, P. (2001). *Pedagogy of the oppressed*. New York: Continuum Books.

Gabbard, D. (2000). *Knowledge and power in the global economy: Politics and the rhetoric of school reform*. Mahwah, NJ: Erlbaum Associates.

Giddens, A.(1990). *The consequences of modernity*. Oxford: Polity Press.

Held, D., McGrew, A., Goldblatt, D., & Parraton, J. (1999). *Global transformations: Politics, economics and culture*. Stanford, CA: Stanford University Press.

Ladson-Billings, G. (1996). Lifting as we climb: The Womanist tradition in multicultural education. In J. A. Banks (Ed.), *Multicultural education: Transformative knowledge and action* (pp. 179–200). New York: Teachers College Press.

Martin, J.R. (2003). *Cultural miseducation: In search of a democratic solution*. New York: Teachers College Press.

Mittelman, J. (2000). *The Globalization syndrome*. Princeton, NJ: Princeton University Press.

Ritzer, G. (2005). *The globalization of nothing*. Thousand Oaks, CA: Sage Publications.

Saha, L. (2005). Cultural and social Capital in global perspective. In J. Zajda (Ed.), *International handbook of globalisation and education policy research* (pp. 745–755). Dordrecht, The Netherlands: Springer.

Sen, A. (2002). Does globalisation equal Westernization? *The Globalist* (accessible at: http://www.theglobalist.com/DBWeb/StoryId.aspx?StoryId=2353).

Sklair, L. (1999). Competing conceptions of globalization. *Journal of World-Systems Research*, *5*, 143–162.

Sklair, L. (2002). *Globalization: Capitalism and its alternatives*. Oxford: Oxford University Press.

Robertson, R. (1992). *Globalization: Social theory and global culture*. London: Sage.

Stiglitz, J. (2002). *Globalisation and its Discontents*. London: Penguin.

Stromquist, N. & Monkman, K. (2000) (Eds.) *Globalization and education: Integration and contestation across cultures*. New York: Rowmand & Littlefield.

Welch, A. (2001). Globalisation, post-modernity and the state: Comparative education facing the third millennium. *Comparative Education*, *37*, 475–492.

Zajda, J. (2002). Education and policy: Changing paradigms and issues. *International Review of Education*, *48*, 1–2, 67–91.

Zajda, J. (2005) (Ed.). *International handbook of globalisation and education policy research*. Dordrecht, The Netherlands: Springer.

Zajda, J. Majhanovich, S., & Rust, V. (2006) (Eds.) *Education and Social Justice*. Dordrecht, The Netherlands: Springer.

Chapter 1
Global Convergence and Divergence in Childhood Ideologies and the Marginalization of Children

Diane M. Hoffman[1] and Guoping Zhao[2]

1   Introduction

The global diffusion of knowledge and practice concerning children's development, early education, and welfare is today among the more remarkable phenomena that can be linked to the emergence of global information networks. Much of this knowledge has come to constitute a normative discourse about early childhood with firm roots in the development of child psychology in Western Europe, Russia, and the United States during the first part of the 20th century. Even a cursory glance at early childhood education and development programmes in universities and educational training institutes around the world reveals a startling emphasis on a few major theorists such as Piaget, Dewey, and Vygotsky, whose theories fill relatively standardized courses in child development in which the true nature and characteristics of a universal child are disseminated.

Best practices in early childhood care and education are increasingly represented in popular media as converging around models of developmentally appropriate practice. Indigenous views of children and appropriate early education are being increasingly challenged by what is represented by childhood experts around the world as more current, progressive notions of childhood. The diffusion of theories and ideologies about child-rearing across cultural borders is normal and natural in a global age. Despite the apparent homogeneity of thinking about raising children, local knowledge often remains robust, forming an integrative base for incorporation of new ideas. Yet, childhood ideologies may be particularly susceptible to the uncontested and implicit normativity inherent in both scholarly and popularized views of child needs emanating from media-powerful countries such as the United States.

[1]University of Virginia

[2]Oklahoma State University

J. Zajda et al. (eds.), *Education and Social Inequality in the Global Culture.*
© Springer 2008

2   The "Indigenous Foreigner"

In a competitive global environment where questions of national power, prestige, and progress are critical for many nations, early education has a particularly significant symbolic role to play. This connection is noted by Popkewitz (2000), who discusses the centrality of the "indigenous foreigner" in early childhood education programmes of study and policy-making in many countries around the world:

> The names of foreign authors, for example, appear as a sign of social, political, and educational progress of the national education debates. The turn of the century American philosopher John Dewey and the Russian psychologist Lev Vygotsky, for example, have become icons in the educational reforms that circulate among many countries. Dewey and Vygotsky appear as universal heroes to explain the "new" principles of pedagogy in South Africa, Spain, the Scandinavian countries, and the United States, among others (p. 10).

Popkewitz observes that the indigenous foreigner is (1) an effect of power; (2) a manifestation of universal categories that order interpretations and possibilities of practice; and (3) an illustration of the interactive dynamic of local and global discourses that legitimize emancipatory projects supposedly associated with them.

This study extends Popekewitz's observations concerning the symbolic and legitimizing role of the indigenous foreigner to the domain of parenting and childcare. Given the widespread global appeal of certain themes concerning childhood education that focus on values such as freedom, democratic education, and child-centredness (see Cannella, 1997), it would seem plausible that parenting, too, might also be influenced by cultural discourses that transcend national borders. The hegemonic discourse of Western-based assumptions concerning the child's self, such as values like individualism, autonomy, and choice, is linked to the emergence of transnational global capitalism (Stephens, 1995; John, 1995).

The diffusion of educational ideals and models is central to the history of education around the world. Various scholars have discussed the adoption of educational discourses, models, and values directly from such centres of power as the United States and Australia. Johnson and Gaiyabu (2001) describe Maria Gaiyabu's observations of Fijian early childhood education and teacher preparation—coursework full of the requisite number of hours of Piaget—alongside a plethora of education materials upholding Western values:

> How we have easily come to crave and embrace Westernized educational menus as part of our daily nourishment never ceases to amaze me. Unbelievably, we seek afar for a "model" Early Childhood Program from Brisbane, Australia, at the advice of a special curriculum consultant (who was here for a week.) Certainly he was a great salesperson, for he scored an annual market from many infant teachers and of the course the responsible minister for education at the time! (p. 287).

Shon (2002) similarly describes how Korean early childhood education has been directly influenced by American missionaries who introduced various so-called progressive practices such as *hands-on activities* and *child-centredness* that were presented to Korean teachers as superior to native cultural practices. She claims that such Western beliefs about children and education continue to dominate the Korean early childhood landscape (p. 47). In the case of Indian early education, Viruru (2002) writes:

> In the preschool in India, and in my interactions with the school teachers, I could not help feel how our "voices" were contextualized by the dominant perspectives, which I, from a quasi-Western background, was seen as representing. Getting people to talk about things like the curriculum or multilingualism without comparisons to "Western countries" being invoked was difficult, and usually these comparisons resulted in Indian ways being seen as deficient or lacking. For example, Indian schools were usually criticized for being too academically oriented, since they did not have enough "play" (p. 153).

Extant scholarship about the interactive and hegemonic Western discourse in early childhood education is remarkably similar in many developing nations.

Indigenous critiques of Western dominated discourse in education, specifically early childhood, do exist, however, as illustrated by the previous references. The existence of such critiques indicates that ideological hegemony is never total as space remains for local agency and voice. Thus, while it is critically important to examine the convergence across many contexts on certain ideas about childhood and early education in the world today, it is equally important to recognize that divergence is present as well. The situation is further complicated by the fact that perceptions of similarity and difference often depend on the level of abstraction through which one examines them. Terms such as individualism, for example, can mask fundamental differences in understanding when used in a different cultural context. Further, the use of terms such as "Western", "American", or "Chinese" can result in unwarranted generalization, leading to monolithic comparisons that erase internal differences. We use these terms with awareness of the dangers of ignoring intra-cultural variation, yet with a belief that they are useful as heuristic devices to illustrate broad cultural contrasts.

3   Parenting in China

Popular parenting magazines represent a window into contemporary perspectives about childhood. Drawing on the analytical tool of discourse hegemony examined at the outset, this chapter examines lessons on child-rearing from some Chinese parenting magazines. Thematic commonalities and discontinuities with dominant discourses on parenting in the United States are explored. This study recognizes that many of the fundamental presumptions about the nature of children and their enculturation are shared between popularized parenting beliefs and practices and early childhood education. In both China and the United States, parenting magazines represent one important source of diffusion of professionalized, expert-based knowledge about childhood to parents.

The Chinese magazines examined for this analysis target educated, urban, middle to upper middle-income parents. This stratum by no means represents the full spectrum of ideas on child-rearing present in contemporary Chinese society. The case of Chinese parenting is a particularly interesting and complex one in which to explore the theme of globalized discourses on child-rearing, given the recent economic changes and subsequent creation of an affluent middle class whose values are also undergoing changes. There also exists a legacy of communist ideology alongside what might be identified as more traditional approaches to child-rearing embedded in long-standing culturally based ideals. Given the emergence of new departments and fields of study in China concerned with early education, a growing cadre of early childhood experts with knowledge of Western practices, and increased exposure to Western media, along with large numbers of Chinese studying abroad, there would seem to be ample opportunity to explore the diffusion of non-Chinese ideals and practices in the Chinese child-rearing landscape.

4   Method and Research Questions

Two major Chinese parenting magazines, *For Children* and *Parents Must Read*, for the years 2000 and 2001 (24 issues) were read and analysed thematically by the second author, Zhao. These magazines were chosen because they were fairly popular in China and readily obtainable. Similar studies had already been conducted by Hoffman (2001; 2003) that examined American parenting advice magazines during the same time frame, which provided the authors with some level of comparability[1]. During the analysis, articles were grouped in topical categories, such as disciplinary concerns, health and well-being, parent–child relationships, and education. Each article was then read and its major points noted. The analysis focused on identifying themes (such as individualism) that seemed to represent non-traditional Chinese ideas that might be more closely identified with Western and/or American traditions. Judgement of significance was made not on the basis of frequency of a given theme, however, but on how much the idea was developed or elaborated in the text and the extent to which it reflected points of similarity or difference from authors' previous knowledge and familiarity with parenting ideas common in Western discourse.

The basic questions that provided focus for the analysis revolved around consideration of how popularized discourses of child- rearing in China might reflect non-indigenous child-rearing ideas. Such questions included:

1. Is there evidence for Western or American influence on Chinese child-rearing ideas? What themes appear similar?
2. On what points do Chinese values and practices continue to appear to diverge from American views?

---

[1] This study was not intended to be a point by point comparison between Chinese and American parenting advice, but an exploration of how some basic themes identified by Hoffman (2001, 2003) and Zhao (2004) in previous work were reflected in the Chinese context.

3. What are possible outcomes in terms of themes of cultural resistance, hybridity, and hegemony?
4. Does a concern for child needs indeed have promise for promoting children's welfare, or is it one that risks further marginalizing children both within and across national boundaries?

5 General Themes

5.1 Parenting and Social Class

Social class differences should be considered in any analysis of parenting and child-rearing as they have often been linked to value differences, particularly with regard to autonomy and conformity in children's behaviour (Biraimah, 2005). Xiao (2000) illustrates this pattern in China as younger parents in small families and those of higher socio-economic status tend to prefer autonomy as a child-rearing goal, while older parents in larger families with lower social class status prefer conformity. In the present analysis, it is the young, urban, educated mother that is the focus, and one cannot overlook that some of the articulated ideals and practices for child-rearing are thus influenced by aspects of social position and political economy specific to the Chinese case, and not only by ideas directly imported from outside China.

Since the 1980s, parent education programmes have expanded dramatically around the world, as Bennet and Grimley (2001) point out. In China in 2001 there were about 240,000 parent schools falling into four different types, including schools run by research institutes to disseminate information about child development, hospital-based schools, community schools, and schools run by departments of education (Bennet & Grimley). These parent schools were carefully evaluated by UNESCO in 1995 in terms of their effects in promoting increased knowledge about parenting and child-rearing among parents and improved school learning outcomes for children (p. 125). Parent schools, family education books and publications, and even a prime-time TV lecture series have contributed to an increased level of social consciousness about what constitutes good parenting since the 1980s.

5.2 Expertise and the Role of Scientific Knowledge

The voices of experts who promote scientific knowledge are prominent in parent schools and magazines. The parenting magazines analysed in this study strongly legitimized expert opinion in their discussions of children's education and socialization. Experts were those with background in child development psychology, educators, psychiatrists, and medical doctors. The parallels with US childcare advice literature in this area are striking (see Harkness et al., 1996; Harkness et al., 1992; Hoffman, 2001; 2003). It appears that the role of experts is linked to deeper assumptions about the relationship between science and culture, particularly the idea that scientific knowledge can ameliorate ordinary behaviours and interpretations that are guided by mere, or worse, obsolete, cultural traditions. It is also likely that scientific knowledge—as opposed to culture or tradition—represents a more legitimate, professionalized perspective, and is thus more appealing to an educated or socially conscious parent.

There appears to be a conflict between expert knowledge and cultural tradition in the context of China. The following example illustrates how the conflict between expert knowledge and cultural practice was experienced by one Chinese mother:

> After Yueyue learned to walk, she was very curious and insisted on exploring everyday. I was so worried I followed her like a bodyguard. When she fell and hurt herself, I would immediately run to her and hold her, ask if it hurts and only after that would I tell her, "It's all right, get up yourself. Yueyue is brave." Then I would do something that I know is not necessary. Whatever hurt Yueyue I would pretend to spank it and say, "Mommy hits it back!" as if only by doing that I was my daughter's most trustworthy, able-to-protect Mommy, although I know this is wrong: the child could grow up irresponsible and blaming others (Jai, 2001, p. 7).

The mother is struggling with her learned cultural response (the saying "mommy hits it back" is very popular in China) and what she knows the experts say about personal responsibility and blaming. The expert view obviously conflicts and de-legitimizes traditional cultural practice.

This tension raises concern about whether the appeal of science for both American and Chinese parents stems from the same sources, and/or whether or not there is anything really new in this. In the United States the appeal of scientific models for education and child development has a long history, beginning with G. Stanley Hall's child study movement. It is difficult to say whether the appeal to expertise in the Chinese case *per se* reflects any outside influence, for it may simply reflect the convergence of indigenous cultural traditions (Confucian in origin) of respect for teachers, experts, and educated persons with a newer admiration for modern knowledge. Expertise may be valued simply because it is implicitly assumed that the expert is the representative of what is most modern, up-to-date, and/or scientific whether or not such knowledge is empirically derived. There is good reason to believe that the culture–science opposition is in reality overdrawn, particularly when it comes to childcare and education. What experts tell parents is usually not just research-based science but a mixture of research and implicitly held cultural assumptions and scripts (Young, 1990). This tension notwithstanding, the appeal of expert opinion is powerful in both the Chinese and American contexts.

5.3   Independence and Individualism

What kinds of ideals are valued and what kinds of interpretations are made of these? Among the most important values often noted in the literature on contemporary best practice is the importance of a child-centred approach where children's needs and assumed developmental competencies are prioritized. Along with this is an implicit reverence for the child's autonomy, choice, and self-expression. These ideas are central to constructivist/progressive models of childcare, learning, and development as they have evolved in Western developmental psychology and are in opposition to what are viewed as authoritarian/traditionalist ideas of child-rearing that treat children as empty slates dependent on adults whose goal is to create social conformity (see Cannella, 1997; Cannella & Viruru, 2004). A number of critiques have emerged, however, of developmental appropriateness and child-centredness (see Walkerdine, 1984, 1988) that illustrate how values such as individualism, independence, autonomy, choice, and the like are imbued with particular cultural and political ideologies that are by no means universal. Such scholarship contends that much of what is taken as developmentally desirable in contemporary early childhood education is in fact ethnocentric. It is interesting to note that measures of parental authority, such as authoritarian, authoritative, and permissive, have been very influential in studies on parenting and social class (Baumrind, 1967, 1989), as higher social class and educational attainment is typically associated with a preference for autonomy over conformity (see also Xiao, 2000).

Non-traditional ideals of independence and self-direction appear to be receiving increasing attention from parents and educators in China. Independence appears to have a particular Chinese interpretation, focusing on nurturing a child's natural will:

> Independence is the core of a person's character. … But how to nurture independence in young children? … At a young age, children's wills and desires are very strong and often expressed through acts. When their desires and wills are impeded by adults, this psychological frustration would be transformed into their emotions. They would express restlessness, easily get upset, and even lose appetite and have unsound sleep. If they are prevented by adults from doing things that they see no wrong in, they will act rebelliously or develop emotional resistance. As time goes on the relationship between parents and child would become disharmonious. … Nurturing independence in children should use the rule of 'following the natural trend.' The job of caregivers is to figure out the natural trends of the children in order to guide them to develop. … Adults' control and undermining of their resistance would smother independence (Lee, 2001, pp. 13–14).

This view of independence as rooted in the positive power of a child's natural will diverges rather radically from the negative interpretation of children's wilfulness that dominates US parenting literature. The mainstream American parenting magazines, while typically valuing independence, paradoxically paint adult–child relationships as a contest of wills that parents *must* win; what are called *power struggles* are a central, uncontested trope of American child-rearing (Hoffman, 2001; 2003).[2] This reflects an assumption that the child's natural will—so positively valued in the Chinese case—is viewed in the United States as a potential source of misbehaviour and social deviance, requiring adult redirection in socially appropriate ways. The American and Chinese interpretations of children's natural tendencies are almost

---

[2] The American parenting discourse values independence mainly when it means ability to take care of one's own needs and to be self-directed in daily life. It is dissociated with will in this sense, for the child's will is seen negatively as a potent source of opposition to adult control and rules.

diametrically opposed in this area, leading to very different views of what constitutes child-rearing for independence.

The idea of developmental stages is a central organizing theme in American childcare magazines, where it functions to explain children's behaviour as well as to define expectations for normalcy and deviance (Hoffman, 2001, 2003). Stages do not have any intrinsic, natural value but they do work to explain puzzling behaviour for parents and to allow parents to know how to act toward the child in supposedly age-appropriate ways. In Chinese magazines, while stages are mentioned, these are given much less attention and do not appear to have the same significance as schemas for determining normalcy or deviance as they do in American discourse. Rather, they are interpreted as reflections of the child's natural tendencies toward imagination which must be respected:

> Children of this age like to imagine all kinds of things. This is the way the child imagines how this world works, and what kind of roles he is playing in it. Many children have to go through many stages, imagining they are superheroes, policemen, or ballet dancers. Some of them imagine being the opposite sex. It is fun to dress up differently and try something new. Usually this is a short period (Shi, 2000, p. 14).

The popularized Chinese discourse appears to value what is assumed to be natural interests and imagination within the child such that the natural aspects of the child's self should be nurtured and preserved since they are inherently of value. Chinese child-rearing has certainly been influenced by the use of a terminology of independence and individualism, but these terms are interpreted differently from the American context, suggesting a process of cultural hybridization is occurring.[3]

5.4   Empathy, Emotions, and the Development of Character

Chinese expert advice emphasizes the need for parents to see things from the child's point of view and to empathize with children's inner feelings by putting themselves in their children's shoes. A central value is placed on maintaining a sense of emotional harmony between adult and child—a clear contrast with articles in American parenting magazines where it is assumed that interactions between parents and children will often be filled with negative emotions such as anger and frustration (see Hoffman, forthcoming; 2004). Other scholars, such as Boler (1999), Dunn and Brown (1991), and Lutz (1990), have also argued through comparative studies that negative emotions and their management play an especially significant role in discourses on education and social relationships in the United States. In

---

[3] The question of ideological dominance thus remains very much unanswered, or, rather, that the answer is both "yes" and "no." One could interpret the use of a discourse of independence as a symbolic (and empty) bow toward appearances and desires for social mobility and international status; one could also interpret it as a genuine diffusion of an idea that takes on nuances and meanings from a new context and is thus hybrid. It is then correct to claim diffusion in any real sense? It is beyond the scope of this paper to examine the complexities of the issues underlying this question.

contrast, the Chinese appear to be very concerned about the consequences of adult behaviour that may foster negative emotions, such as frustration. Lee (2001) notes in the Chinese parents' magazine previously quoted that frustration will result from parents impeding the will of children (pp. 13–14),

In another example, a mother wrote for advice concerning her daughter's use of a mechanical pencil. She did not want her daughter to use the pencil and took it away from her, making her daughter very disappointed. The Chinese expert replies:

> Maybe we adults think that the mechanical pencil is nothing and it's not necessary to have one, but it's not the case with children. We all have had the experience that when we were little sometimes we just wanted something terribly. We longed for it without knowing the reasons. ... I think this is human nature and nothing is wrong about it. Why did Xiaowan want the pencil? Maybe she liked the shape, the colour, or just the feeling of using it, or she wanted to compete with the other kids. We don't know but we don't have to know. Maybe she couldn't explain it herself. We should allow this ambiguity of feelings and it may not be wise to crystallize and rationalize it. ... Xiaowan is a human being with emotions. Mom was too focused on the technical aspects of this and ignored the child's emotions (Wang, 2001, p.35).

In American discourse, parents may reason with a child and in fact are often advised to get a child to label his or her emotions and to explain his or her feelings, if possible, and they are even told to label children's emotions for them if they have trouble doing it themselves (Hoffman, 2001; forthcoming). There are also many examples of parents advised to obtain compliance from children simply by using the appeal to rules and even mechanical devices such as timers. Emotional identification with children is not recommended; negative emotions need to be handled or managed by using a kind of parent–child talk therapy in which parents identify the child's negative emotions but insist all the same on the child's compliance with rules.

Although spoiling appeared to be a major concern of Chinese parents and educators in the 1980s and early 1990s, of the issues reviewed for this study, it is hardly mentioned. It appears that spoiling has been subsumed to some extent in a generalized concern for character development. Indeed, since the demise of Communist ideology in the reform era in China, there has been much discussion of a lack of systematic and explicit guidance for children's moral education. As a result, during a national education conference in June 1999, the Chinese government announced a decision to promote character education, borrowing terminology from the United States as a central theme for educational reform.

There appear to be differences in the Chinese and American understandings of character education, however. In the United States, character education may be regarded as the process of instilling desired qualities and moral orientations in children who lack them or whose natural tendencies are undesirable, but in China it is more often seen as developing the tendencies that are already present in children that are seen as fundamentally good:

> To understand character education, we can start from unpacking the meaning of the two words, 'su zhi.' [Character education is called 'su zhi jiao yu.'] Literally, 'su' means plain, white, original, constant; therefore 'su zhi' means the original and stable qualities of the person. Hence, su zhi education should be understood as the educational process of targeting a person's original qualities to stabilize and develop the good qualities (Shi, 2001, p. 8).

Transforming or educating people always starts from recognizing and working with what are seen as positive natural human feelings and qualities in the Chinese case. In contrast, the child's nature in the American parenting magazines is more often portrayed negatively (e.g., manipulative or wilfully pushing parents' buttons) and is treated as the source of negative outcomes unless it is clearly transformed by adults acting on children to contain and break down those negative natural tendencies. Children, in this sense, are adult products in a moral sense—they do not reflect a natural flourishing of innate goodness but rather the action of adult caregivers upon fundamentally undesirable natural tendencies.[4]

6 Points of Convergence and Divergence

6.1 Similarities and Differences in Chinese and American Advice

While there are clear similarities in Chinese and US parenting advice concerning the status and value of expert opinion ostensibly grounded in scientific child development knowledge, character education, and developing children's independence, Chinese interpretations of these concepts still differ from those in the United States. In some sense they remain localized and integrated with ideas of personhood that emphasize the child's fundamentally positive inner nature and the need for harmonious emotional inter-subjectivity between parent and child. It is difficult to tell with certainty, however, whether and how these similarities and differences reflect an adoption of certain aspects of a more Western-influenced discourse of child development and education in a Chinese context or whether these ideas reflect more an indigenous emergence responding to the conditions of the Chinese situation. Without an in-depth historical analysis, it is difficult to determine if, for example, the ideal of harmonious parent–child emotional interactions is a new one that has arisen as a response to lack of these relationships, or an idea grounded in a different cultural psychology, one that is at the same time shaped by the exigencies of national political economy.

In a recent study of changing perspectives among Chinese early childhood educators, Hsueh and Tobin (2003) raise important questions regarding changes in views of what is appropriate and good practice in early childhood. Among in-service teachers and early childhood experts, a dramatic change was noted in the ways educators talked about the need to respect the child and nurture the child's individuality. The authors note that this emphasis on respecting the child was "unheard of and perhaps even unthinkable in China 17 years ago" (p. 83), illustrating a changing ideological landscape in Chinese views of children and early education.

---

[4]Clearly, partial explanations for these differences are to be found in long-standing religious and philosophical traditions that have shaped views of children and children's natures, as well as nature in a more general sense and mankind's proper relationship to nature.

Certainly it cannot be demonstrated that there has been a direct importation of early childhood ideology from the United States, but there is a likelihood of transnational circulation of an early childhood ideology. Hsueh and Tobin (2003) suggest in their analysis of changing beliefs about early childhood in China that the roots of such changes indeed lie in the greater influence of Western notions of child development in China since the 1990s:

> The People's Republic of China, long resistant to capitalism, decided a decade ago to switch strategies and become a major player in the global economic system. China's assimilation of western child development and early childhood educational values and strategies is seen by many Chinese experts to be an essential step toward preparing a citizenry suited to compete in such a global system. ... In recent years, university researchers trained in western ideas of early childhood education have become increasingly influential in the development of research agenda, curricula, and standards for preschool education. ... An American approach to preschool curriculum is becoming increasingly popular among Chinese early childhood educators (p. 87).

Hsueh and Tobin also found, paradoxically, the younger cohort of pre-service teachers they studied tended to have more traditional, non-Westernized views of early childhood care. One explanation is that they have not yet been socialized into the new more Westernized views held by veteran teachers and experts. The new normative view is also alien to the younger teachers' own experiences when they were preschoolers in the 1980s.

6.2 Hybridity as Response

Hybridity offers another plausible explanation for the apparent migration and intermixing of Western child development knowledge with local norms. As Wollons (2000) illustrates in her volume on the kindergarten as diasporic institution, child-rearing ideals are frequently global in their identification but local in their implementation. Thus, the situation in China herein described cannot be read simply as a case of Western cultural dominance. A more accurate interpretation is probably hybridity: a merging and reformulating in which the foreign idea or practice is recontextualized and reinvented in locally relevant and meaningful terms. Certainly this explains best the extent to which the discourses of individualism and independence as well as the persistence of indigenous Chinese interpretations of the child's nature are present in the parenting advice examined.

Notions of hegemony, resistance, and hybridity are complicated by the question of universality. From one perspective, perhaps, what we are looking at globally in terms of policy and culture is not so much American or Western ideas but ones that science has now revealed to be universal and applicable to all children everywhere. Certainly this is at least in part one of the underlying assumptions behind the spread of child development knowledge and notions of developmentally appropriate care and education socially diffused today. We cannot ignore the fact that for some social actors, particularly those concerned with global competitiveness, the appeal of certain Western child-rearing ideas lies precisely in the fact that they are associated with the more developed societies. China is not the only place in which the identification of a practice or idea as *American* or *Western* is part of its appeal, at least for some (Hsueh & Tobin, 2003).

A third, more critical interpretation of the findings herein highlights the ethnocentric bias that may be inherent in the definition of universal goods and values in the field of early childhood. This view conflates universal with whatever happens to be developed and/or discovered by Americans working with American children. Research purports to discover the best thinking and knowledge about children everywhere, though such a positivistic stance fails to account for the real and limiting effects of cultural diversity that extend deeply into the conceptualization of childhood socialization and research related to it. The role of the United States in all of this is complicated. It is not the case that flows of ideology are always unidirectional from the United States to other countries. One can simply point to the case of Reggio Emilia which has attained worldwide influence and almost cult status in the world of early childhood education:

> The popularity of Reggio Emilia has been phenomenal the world over, for as a program model it continues to *the rage* in early childhood today. Intriguing as it is, well over 10,000 international educators have visited Reggio, early education conferences are devoted specifically to Reggio, and "Reggio Emilia" is now a thematic content strand in many national and international conferences (Schiller, 1995; quoted in Johnson & Gaiyabu, 2001, p. 282).

Hsueh and Tobin (2003) also found several Chinese experts mentioning Reggio Emilia and developmentally appropriate practice in their comments. This does not negate the possibility that the United States and other first-world nations may play a greatly legitimizing role in worldwide flows of early childhood ideology, particularly through processes of publicizing, marketing, and commodification of early childhood programmes. In this sense, issues of power and domination depend not so much on point of origin but on control and dissemination of educational ideas and products.

7 Emancipation or Marginalization?

The field of early childhood pedagogy is influenced by the acceptance of a missionary role of science in society as a whole and with particular national/cultural processes of governmentality that regulate the inter-shaping of self and social order. This pattern was cross-nationally evident in studies conducted by Dahlberg (2000) in Sweden and Bloch and Blessing (2000) in Eastern Europe. If discourses in early childhood development and care are firmly linked to multiple economic and political agendas, the question of children's welfare and needs may be overlooked in deference to a superordinate economic agenda. Educators and those concerned with social welfare need to ask continually whether the convergence of particular models of child development and care in effect privilege children's selves or a social order that is less concerned with child welfare than with globally competitive market economies.

Despite the appeal to values such as independence, individualism, character, and developmental appropriateness that appear to promote democratic, emancipatory, and child-centred education, the underlying ideals of selfhood that inform them may be grounded in culturally particular traditions associated with developed, market economies of the West (Cannella, 1997; Leavitt, 1994; Polakow, 1992; Tobin, 1995; Walkerdine, 1988). It may be that parenting itself has become a form of symbolic capital and it is this meaning of parenting that underlies a process of worldwide convergence on a professionalized, expert-driven approach to child-rearing. As de Carvalho (2001) observes, parenting in the global world order has become a science with normatized, standardized, and expert-prescribed contents. Parent-producers are responsible, through active exercise of the right skills, to generate specific competencies in their children; indeed, children are treated as parent products, honed and shaped to fill desirable social positions (p. 104).

Progressive, reform-minded child-rearing ideology in the United States and around the world appears, at least on the surface, to be child-centred and supportive of individuality. Such commitments belie their subtexts, wherein social status, instrumentality, productivity, and institutional prerogative are implicit and generally remain unchallenged. A convergence around the world on ideals and practices that ostensibly support independence, for example, masks very real differences that continue to exist across cultural contexts in the meanings and values associated with such terms. More critically, though, it allows and encourages a kind of ignorance of children's daily lived experiences because of the already-assumed legitimacy of expert and scientific views that dictate how parents and others conceptualize their relationships toward children. Children's perspectives risk marginalization, paradoxically, through the very discourses and practices that claim to support them. It would be dangerous to assume that childrens' or parents' voices and identities are or should be at the top of the list of things education and child-rearing ought to support. These concepts, too, can be part of a dominant colonialist discourse that privileges Western assumptions about others and fails to inquire about, or truly appreciate, local values and practices and their social relevance (see Viruru, 2002).

It is difficult to claim with certitude that Western notions of science and child psychology, supported by an internationalized discourse of early childhood education, are currently undermining local cultural traditions of parenting and care without further research. Most of the evidence examined in this chapter suggests an emerging hybridity in China, where a discourse of individualism and child-focused care is clearly emerging, but is grafted onto or integrated with local cultural traditions. As hybridization evolves, we may expect to see even more fundamental changes in Chinese thinking. Examining parental discourse in other countries, both Western and non-Western, about early childhood education and child-rearing would contribute to what is known about this phenomenon.

The question as to whether local or imported practices are better remains open, for the definition of better is highly dependent on a range of goals and values that are variously determined. Regardless of how one evaluates models of childcare and education, however, the arguably greater need is to be able to uncover and inquire about the assumptions that lie behind particular practices. This requires a habit of critical awareness among educators, parents, and all those concerned with child welfare that encourages, and even demands, critical engagement with the ways in which ideals and values are realized—or fail to be realized—in practices. In this regard, societies that acknowledge a gap between their ideals and practices offer the best models. For example, in the 1990s in Japan new categories of parenting advice have emerged that recognize that the ideal of the all-sacrificing mother is sometimes a far cry from reality (Tsuneyoshi, 2001). Yet, the professional early education and childcare establishment in the United States generally fails to engage in self-criticism regarding its basic commitments and, more importantly, whether its commitments conflict with its practices.

8   Conclusion

While postmodern perspectives deconstruct the natural child or a child's innate nature—a positive development in many cases—we cannot ignore the fact that children have views of their own nature and needs that often diverge from adult interpretations. The only truly defensible global childhood ideology is one that privileges children's own understandings of their lives and relationships and remains circumspect with regard to the globalizing reach of ideologies, no matter how well-intentioned. Some cultures and societies around the world are already more attuned to, and respectful of, children's lived experiences than others, perhaps because they have cultivated the habits of mind that encourage self-examination and attention to the gaps that inevitably exist between appearances and realities. What really matters is that parents, experts, and educators alike be capable of genuine inquiry: to be able to see where ideals diverge from practices, and to be able to generate the kinds of critiques that lead to transforming what is into what might be.

References

Baumrind, D. (1967). Childcare practices anteceding three patterns of preschool behaviour. *Genetic Psychology Monographs, 75*, 43–88.

Baumrind, D. (1989). Rearing competent children. In W. Damon (Ed.), *Child development today and tomorrow*. San Francisco, CA: Jossey-Bass.

Bennet, J., & Grimley, L. (2001). Parenting in the global community: A cross-cultural/international perspective. In M. Fine & S. W. Lee (Eds.), *Handbook of diversity in parent education* (pp. 97–132). San Diego, CA: Academic Press.

Biraimah, K. (2005). Achieving Equitable Outcomes or Reinforcing Societal Inequalities in Education? *Educational Practice and Theory, 27*(2), 25–34.

Bloch, M. & Blessing, B. (2000). Restructuring the state in Eastern Europe: Women, childcare, and early education. In T. Popkewitz (Ed.), *Educational knowledge: Changing relationships between the state, civil society, and the educationalcommunity* (pp. 201–220). Albany, NY: State University of New York.

Boler, M. (1999). *Feeling power*. New York: Routledge.

Canella, G. S. (1997). *Deconstructing early childhood education: Social justice and revolution.* New York: Peter Lang.

Cannella, G. S. & Viruru, R. (2004). *Childhood and postcolonization: Power, education, and contemporary practice.* New York: RoutledgeFalmer.

Dahlberg, G. (2000). From the "People's Home"—Folkhemmet—to the enterprise. In T. Popkewitz (Ed.), *Educational knowledge: Changing between the state, civil society, and the educational community.* Albany, NY: State University of New York.

De Carvalho, M. E. P. (2001). Rethinking family-school relations: A critique of parental involvement in schooling. Mahwah, NJ: Lawrence Erlbaum.

Dunn, J. & Brown, J. (1991). Becoming American or English? Talking about the social world in England and the United States. In. M. H. Bornstein (Ed.). *Cultural approaches to parenting* (pp. 155–172). Hillsdale, NJ: Lawrence Erlbaum.

Harkness, S., Super, C., & Keefer, C. (1992). Learning how to be an American parent: How cultural models gain directive force. In R. G. D'Andrade & C. Strauss (Eds.), *Human motives and cultural models* (pp. 163–178). Cambridge: Cambridge University Press.

Harkness, S., Super, C., Keefer, C., Chemba, R., & Campbell, E. (1996). Ask the doctor: The negotiation of cultural models in American parent-pediatrician discourse. In S. Harkness & C. Super (Eds.) *Parents' cultural belief systems* (pp. 289–310). New York: Guilford.

Hoffman, D. M. (2004). How (Not) to feel: Culture and the Politics of Emotion in the American Parenting Advice Literature. To appear in Discours: Studies in the Cultural Politics of Education. Unpublished manuscript.

Hoffman, D. M. (2003). Childhood ideology in the United States: A comparative cultural view. *International Review of Education, 49*(1–2), 191–211.

Hoffman, D. M. (2001). Enculturating the self: Person, relation, and the discourse of childrearing in the American family. In B. Wong (Ed.), *Family, kin, and community: A contemporary reader* (pp.97–115). Dubuque, IO: Kendall-Hunt.

Hoffman, D. M. (forthcoming). How (Not) to Feel: Culture and the Politics of Emotion in the American Parenting Advice Literature. To appear in Discourse: Studies in the Cultural Politics of Education.

Hsueh, Y., & Tobin, J. (2003). Chinese early childhood educators' perspectives on dealing with a crying child. *Journal of Early Childhood Research, 1*(1), 73–94.

Jai, Y. (2001). Parents Must Read, *224*, 7.

John, M. (1995). Children's rights in a free-Market culture. In S. Stephens (Ed.), *Children and the politics of culture* (pp. 105–137). Princeton, NJ: Princeton University Press.

Johnson, R. T. & Gaiyabu, M. (2001). Resisting normative representations in the Pacific Islands: Domestic enemies meet over coffee. In J. Jipson & R. T. Johnson (Eds.), *Resistance and representation: Rethinking childhood education.* New York: Peter Lang.

Leavitt, R. L. (1994). *Power and emotion in infant-toddler day care.* Albany, NY: State University of New York.

Lee, W. (2001). *Parents Must Read, 223*, 13–14.

Lutz, Catherine. (1990). Engendered emotion: Gender, power, and the rhetoric of emotional control in American discourse. In C. Lutz & L. Abu-Lughod (Eds.), *Language and the politics of emotion* (pp. 69–91). Cambridge: Cambridge University Press.

Polakow, V. (1992). *The erosion of childhood.* Chicago, IL: University of Chicago.

Popkewitz, T. S. (2000). Globalization/regionalization, knowledge, and educational practices: Some notes on comparative strategies for educational research. In T. Popkewitz (Ed.), *Educational knowledge: Changing relationships between the state, civil society, and the educational community.* Albany, NY: State University of New York.

Shi, J. (2000). *For Children, 217*, 14.

Shi, J. (2001). *Parents Must Read, 223*, 8.

Shon, M. R. (2002). Korean early childhood education: Colonization and resistance. In G. S. Cannella & J. L. Kincheloe, (Eds.), *Kidworld: Childhood studies, global perspectives, and education* (pp. 138–149). New York: Peter Lang.

Stevens, S. (1995). Children and the politics of culture in "Late Capitalism." In S. Stephens (Ed.), *Children and the politics of culture* (pp. 3–48). Princeton, NJ: Princeton University Press.

Tobin, J. (1995). Post-structural research in early childhood education. In J. A. Hatch (Ed.), *Qualitative research in early childhood settings* (pp. 223–243). Westport, CT: Praeger.

Tsuneyoshi, R. (2001). *The Japanese model of schooling: Comparisons with the United States.* New York: RoutledgeFalmer.

Viruru, R. (2002). Postcolonial ethnography: An Indian perspective on voice and young children. In G. S. Cannella & J. L. Kincheloe, (Eds.), *Kidworld: Childhood studies, global perspectives, and education* (pp. 151–160). New York: Peter Lang.

Walkerdine, V. (1984). Developmental psychology and the child-centered pedagogy: The insertion of Piaget into early education. In J. Henriques, W. Holloway, C. Urwin, C. Venn, & V. Walkerdine (Eds.), *Changing the subject: Psychology, social regulation, and subjectivity* (pp. 153–202). London: Methuen.

Walkerdine, V. (1988). *The mastery of reason: Cognitive development and the production of rationality.* London: Routledge.

Wang, X. (2001, February). *Parents Must Read, 224,* 35.

Wollons, R. (2000). Introduction: On the international diffusion, politics, and transformation of the kindergarten. In Wollons, R. (Ed.), *Kindergartens and cultures: The global diffusion of an idea* (pp. 1–15). New Haven, CT: Yale University.

Xiao, H. (2000). Structure of child-rearing values in urban China. *Sociological Perspectives, 43*(3), 457–471.

Young, K. T. (1990). American conceptions of infant development from 1955 to 1984: What the experts are telling parents. *Child Development, 61,* 17–28.

Chapter 2
Measuring Inequities in Secondary School Attendance: The Probability of Attending Secondary School for Primary School Graduates in Nicaragua

Caroline E. Parker

1 Introduction

Alvaro[1] began first grade when he was 7 years old. Even though he began later than he should have, as do many Nicaraguan children, he completed primary school (sixth grade) without repeating any grades. His neighbourhood, made up of squatters who had settled on abandoned land in Managua, did not have a public school, and so Alvaro's parents put together the bus fare from their sporadic work to make sure he got to and from the nearest school safely every day. When he graduated from the sixth grade, he enrolled in a public secondary school that required a daily 45-minute bus ride. He had to register for afternoon classes because of overcrowding at the school. He failed seventh grade because of a prolonged absence (due to a broken leg). On his second try, now 14 years old, he failed two classes that he had passed previously, in part because he chose to stay home and care for younger siblings rather than attend identical classes a second year in a row. Forced to repeat a third time, he registered at a different school, but dropped out halfway through this third attempt because he was harassed by gangs on his way to and from school. Two years later he tried again, but was frustrated by teacher strikes. At age 18, Alvaro had still not passed seventh grade.

Nicaragua's education system has long been characterized by inequities which affect students like Alvaro. Poor-quality education, overcrowding, overwhelming bureaucracy, and lack of safety affect poor students far more than wealthy students. Alvaro registered for seventh grade four times, but not many youth have his persistence. Only 31.3% of Nicaragua's high school age population attends secondary school, and only 16.5% of Nicaraguans have earned a high school diploma. Those poor students who do attend high school tend to enrol in lower quality schools, have lower graduation rates, and be less likely to attend university (Interamerican Development Bank (IDB), 1999;

Education Development Center, Inc.

---

[1] Not his real name.

J. Zajda et al. (eds.), *Education and Social Inequality in the Global Culture.*
© Springer 2008

Filmer, 1999a; Economic Commission for Latin America and the Caribbean (ECLAC), 2000; Global Education Database (GED), 2000).

Yet, despite the acknowledged crisis, young people continue to persevere, and those who complete primary school are likely to continue and attend secondary school. Who are these students in Nicaragua who complete primary school and continue their studies in secondary school? Is attendance influenced by household wealth, other household characteristics, repetition, urbanicity, or gender of the student?

Using survey data from a 1997 Demographic and Health Survey (DHS) of 11,567 Nicaraguan households, this study specifically looks at the effects of household wealth, gender, the schooling gap,[2] urbanicity, departmental characteristics, and household size on the probability that 12- to 17-year-old primary school graduates attend secondary school.[3] Results show that household wealth and the schooling gap interact in predicting secondary school attendance, that urbanicity and departmental variation do matter, and that while girls are more likely to have graduated from primary school, girls who have graduated from primary school are no more likely to be attending secondary school than are boys.

2   Factors Predicting Secondary School Attendance

What are the factors that contribute to educational access, particularly access to secondary school education, in resource-poor countries like Nicaragua? As one of the areas of the world with the greatest levels of inequality between the rich and the poor, education in Latin America has traditionally been seen as a way to promote social mobility. In the 1990s, some Latin American countries succeeded in narrowing the gap in educational attainment between the rich and the poor for basic education, but large gaps remain at the secondary level (IDB, 1999; ECLAC, 2000; Buchmann & Hannum, 2001). Latin Americans have, on average, fewer years of education than would be expected given the GDPs of the countries (Cariola, 2000), but this differs by country. Tedesco and Lopez (2002) divide the countries of Latin America into four groups, based roughly on per capita GDP and demographic characteristics. Nicaragua falls into the fourth group, with the smallest GDP and the smallest percentage of youth currently in secondary school. In addition, Nicaragua has the greatest within-country disparities in three categories: girls are more likely than boys to be in school, urban youth more likely than rural, and wealthy youth more likely than poor. The literature review below summarizes some of the key factors that have been found to contribute to educational access in studies of other

---

[2] "Schooling gap" is defined as the difference between a student's expected grade level for their age and their actual grade level: total education / (age – expected age at beginning of schooling).

[3] I chose primary school graduates because they are the group that is eligible for secondary school, and chose 12- to 17-year-olds because they are the appropriate age for secondary school. This choice is discussed further below.

Latin American countries: household wealth, urbanicity, household characteristics, the schooling gap, and gender.

2.1 Household Wealth

Studies that measure access to education generally include some measure to represent household wealth. Household wealth is consistently found to be a critical predictor of basic education attendance. Ilon and Moock (1991) link household wealth to opportunity costs of education while Filmer (1999b) and Bracho (2000) note that wealthy children are more likely to attend school. Behrman et al. (1999) show that they are more likely to be at the appropriate grade level (see also Behrman & Wolfe, 1987; Patrinos & Psacharopoulos, 1996; Filmer & Pritchett, 1998a; Filmer, 1999b). All of these studies, however, look at the effect of household wealth on basic education attendance, and do not distinguish between basic and secondary education. The study herein looks at how secondary attendance patterns differ for wealthy as compared to poor students. In addition, looking at interactions between household wealth and other factors, especially repetition rates and geography, contributes to an understanding of how wealth is mediated by other factors.

2.2 Urbanicity

Studies that have included urbanicity find that children living in urban areas are more likely to be in school than those in rural areas (Behrman et al., 1998; Filmer & Pritchett, 1998a; Bracho, 2000). Most studies limit urbanicity to defining whether or not respondents live in rural or urban areas, but this dataset permits further disaggregation in two ways. First, urbanicity is divided into four categories, looking separately at the capital (Managua), cities, towns, and the countryside. This permits an examination of the characteristics particular to the capital, and an opportunity to see if there are differences between smaller towns and cities. Second, school attendance is observed by departments. Nicaragua is divided geographically into 17 departments, and this study allows an examination of community characteristics that contribute to school attendance rates that are not captured by the dichotomous urban/rural variable.

2.3 Household Characteristics

Some studies have found that characteristics associated with wealth, like parental education or household size, are independent predictors of attendance, while others have found that household characteristics are strongly correlated with wealth and do not help to explain more variation in attendance. Parent education levels are some-times included as measures of household cultural capital (Behrman & Wolfe, 1987; Dellapiane, 1994; Bracho, 2000). Studies focusing on household characteristics find that the mother's education interacts with household wealth to prevent school fail-ure (Schiefelbein & Wolff, 1992; Gargiulo & Crouch, 1994). In this study, it is not possible to measure parent education levels or sibling relationships because of the structure and content of the dataset. In order to account for household characteris-tics that may have an impact on secondary school attendance rates, three factors are included that measure household characteristics: household size, number of chil-dren under 5 years in household, and gender of the household head.

2.4 Repetition

Repetition has been found to be most serious in early primary grades and in rural areas, contributing to the eventual abandonment of schooling. Schiefelbein and Wolff (1992) argue that 40% of repetition rates in primary school are due to poor-quality schooling. Repetition patterns are linked to school quality and teacher qual-ity, with repetition being more prevalent in lower-quality schools (Schiefelbein & Heikkinen, 1991; Camargo et al., 1992; Bedi & Marshall, 1999). In Nicaragua, repetition has been associated with family influence, type of school, teacher dedica-tion, the general economic situation, and teacher experience at the first grade level (Ministry of Education (MED), 1996; De Franco, 1998).

Few studies consider the effects of early repetition on secondary school attend-ance, as it tends to be linked with dropout rates before completing primary school. Throughout the region, there is almost no data available on repetition and dropout rates at the secondary level (Schiefelbein & Wolff, 1992; UNESCO, 2001). By focusing on secondary school attendance, this study shows the longer-term effects of repetition on secondary school attendance. Does being overage for grade level contribute negatively to secondary school attendance rates, or does the negative effect of overage lessen for secondary school students?

2.5 Gender

Unlike other areas of the world, Latin American countries tend to have a small gender gap, and in many cases the gender gap is closely associated with being indigenous (Ilon & Moock, 1991; Caillods & Maldonado-Villar, 1997; Patrinos, 1997; IDB, 1999; Filmer, 1999b). Previous studies of gender and access in Nicaragua have found that being a girl is positively associated with school attend-ance (Filmer, 1999b). Although girls are as likely or more likely to attend school in Nicaragua, no study has broken down school attendance by level. By looking at gender in secondary school, this study will show whether the pattern found in primary school continues in secondary school, that girls are more likely than boys to attend and graduate. Among primary school graduates, are girls more likely than boys to attend secondary school?

Previous research illustrates that household wealth is one of the most important predictors of school attendance and that attendance rates vary by urbanicity. Extant research further suggests the importance of looking at repetition rates, and at differential secondary attendance rates by gender. Few studies have looked at secondary school attendance patterns in countries like Nicaragua or at the ways these may differ from primary education attendance patterns. This study provides a more careful investigation of the relationship between different factors, for example, how the effect of household wealth operates differently depending on the student context, whether it be geography, being at the appropriate grade level, or household characteristics.

3   A Brief Description of Nicaragua

In Nicaragua before 1979, high schools were primarily intended for the wealthy. There were only 23 secondary schools in all of Nicaragua in 1947, with a total of 3,445 students (Ebaugh, 1947). The secondary population had grown to some 7,000 students by 1965 (Pallais, 1965). With the Sandinista revolution in 1979, there was a massive outpouring of support for the national literacy campaign that focused on adult literacy. Urban high school students left their homes and travelled throughout rural Nicaragua teaching adults in rural communities to read. This emphasis on education continued throughout the 11 years of the Sandinista government, but so too did the interruptions to schooling. Youth were called upon to participate in the coffee and cotton harvests, and with the military draft beginning in 1983, young men aged 16 and older were drafted. While education was declared a national priority and many new schools were built, the political and social situation did not promote the development of processes to improve the quality of secondary schools, and youth were not necessarily receiving more or better education.

Since 1990, Nicaraguan youth have experienced a radical political shift and have been subjected more and more to the economic forces of globalization. Nicaraguans need increased education levels in order to participate effectively in the global economy, and the government has responded to this pressure by promoting education in both rural and urban areas. At the same time, there have been counter-forces operating at the secondary level. The government-sponsored decentralization programme known as autonomy was seen by many as a step toward privatization, and the battle in 1995 to reform the constitution to say that the right of free basic education extended only through sixth grade rather than through high school raised the question of who has the right to secondary education (under the Sandinistas, all education was free, from primary school through university). If public education is not free, then who can attend? Certainly not the poorest. The resulting tension in education during the 1990s posited globalization demands and the need for a more highly educated work force against the government's decree that free education only extended through sixth grade. Those who attend high school must have enough resources to be able to pay. In addition, while globalization demands more education, the Nicaraguan economy cannot guarantee better jobs to more educated youth. Nicaragua, as one of the poorest countries in Latin America, has yet to find its niche in the global economy.

In 1998, 47.9% of Nicaraguans were living in poverty, and 17.3% in extreme poverty. While there was a gross increase of 22,000 jobs from 1990 to 1997, 17,000 of those jobs were in the Free Trade Zones, offering piecework at very low salaries. Government reports showed a slight decline in unemployment after 1994 and cited open unemployment at 13% in 1997, but only 47% of the workforce was fully employed (Dijkstra, 2000). Nicaraguan teenagers thus make their schooling decisions in the context of economic fragility and job scarcity. Primary school graduates in Nicaragua who hope to attend secondary school face many challenges: an unstable and weak economy without a defined job market for high school graduates, changes in funding structures that require them to pay monthly fees,[4] a lack of commitment by the national government toward secondary schools, and long-standing weaknesses in quality of instruction. Educational inequities at the primary level mean that primary school graduates tend to be wealthier than teens who have not graduated from primary school, they are more likely to be from urban areas, and they are more likely to be girls. This research looks at how these economic and demographic trends are intensified or changed by secondary school attendance.

3.1   Characteristics of Nicaraguan Primary School Graduates

Forty-two percent of Nicaragua's 5.3 million citizens are of school age. The average age of Nicaraguans is 22 years, which has been rising for the last 10 years, but still ranks it as the youngest population in Latin America. The average total education for Nicaraguans is 4.6 years. Adult illiteracy rates range around 33% while 36.8% of the adult population does not have a complete primary education. Sixty percent of teenagers are not in the educational system. Of the poor, only 16.4% attend secondary school (Ministry of Education, Culture and Sports (MECD), 2003). Only 4.7% of the adult population have university degrees.

Nicaraguan youth who have completed primary school and who are part of the cohort eligible for secondary school have different characteristics from youth who have not completed primary school. They differ in terms of household wealth, urbanicity, and gender. Primary school graduates tend to be wealthier than their counterparts who have not completed primary school. There are more primary school graduates from urban areas, and more of them are girls.

Of the 12- to 17-year-olds in the DHS survey, 44% have graduated from primary school, while 56% have not. Of those who have graduated from primary school, 77%

---

[4] Although secondary schools are not required to charge, charging monthly fees has become the norm in both non-autonomous and autonomous secondary schools.

are attending secondary school. (Of those who have not graduated from primary school, more than half are still attending school in first through sixth grade.) While fewer than 50% of teens have graduated from primary school, among those who have, many continue on to secondary school rather than stop formal schooling.

In Nicaragua, if students have not repeated or missed any years, they complete their 5 years of secondary education from 12 to 17 years of age. Students sometimes begin later than the standard 6 years, and they often repeat grades, and so many secondary students are overage. Overage students (over 17 years) are not included in the study because they may have a fundamentally different experience of schooling that is more like adult education. While limiting the sample to 12- to 17-year-olds may bias it toward the less poor population (because poor students tend to be further behind), older students face schooling conditions that differ enough from the younger cohort that they merit a separate study.

The most striking difference between those who have graduated from primary school and those who have not is their household wealth. Almost half of primary school graduates (1,953) come from the richest 25% of the population. Only 26.6% of primary school graduates come from the poorest 50% of the population. The sample for this study, the 12- to 17-year-old primary school graduates, tends to be wealthier, although there is still a sizable group from the poorer strata of society.

A greater proportion of youth in the countryside have not graduated from primary school. Only 25% of youth in the countryside are primary school graduates, while between 60% and 65% of youth in towns, cities, and the capital have graduated from primary school. Though there are more rural than urban youth in the DHS sample, the cohort of primary school graduates is skewed toward the urban sector. While 49% of 12- to 17-year-old girls have graduated from primary school, only 41% of boys have completed the cycle, and so there are more girls than boys in the cohort qualified to attend secondary school.

Primary school graduates tend to be wealthier than their counterparts who have not graduated from primary school, there are more graduates from urban areas, and more girls graduate from primary school. And yet, even within this sample, 20% of primary school graduates are among the poorest 25 % of Nicaraguan 12- to 17- year-olds, and 27% are from rural areas. Although primary school graduates are less poor and more urban, poor and rural students do make up a sizable part of the cohort.

4 Research Design

4.1 Dataset and Sample

The Demographic and Health Surveys (DHS) are nationally representative household surveys carried out in many developing countries with large sample sizes of about 5,000 households. The 1997–1998 Nicaraguan DHS provides data on educational issues. Forty-five DHS datasets from 35 countries have been used to compare educational attendance and attainment cross-nationally (Filmer & Pritchett, 1998b). The Nicaraguan DHS survey used 1995 census information to establish a national probability sample, stratified at department level by urbanicity. The questionnaires were administered in 1997–1998 to one randomly chosen woman of childbearing age within households. The analysis used data drawn from women's reports on all youth in their households aged 12 through 17 who have graduated from primary school (completing sixth grade). Of the 9,945 12- to 17-year-olds in the dataset, 4,467 were reported to have completed sixth grade and information about their current school status is provided, and are thus included in the sample.

4.2 Descriptive Statistics

This section describes each of the key variables used to look at the probability of secondary school attendance.

Wealth The Demographic and Health Surveys do not collect income or spending information, but they do collect information about household characteristics. Principal components analysis, as described by Filmer and Pritchett (1998b), was used to create a composite that describes household wealth. Table 2.1 (see **the Appendix**) shows that among primary school graduates, students who are in school have a higher mean standardized wealth than students who are not in school. This study looks at whether wealth is an important predictor of secondary school attendance for the relatively more affluent students who have completed primary school.

Total education and Age for grade Grade repetition is a critical problem in Latin American schools, and Nicaragua is no exception. Some studies have used repetition as an outcome variable, looking for the factors that contribute to repetition (Patrinos & Psacharopoulos, 1996; Behrman et al., 1999). For this study, both total education and being behind grade level (the schooling gap) are used as predictor variables, in order to understand how being behind contributes to the probability of being in school.

The variable to represent the schooling gap (age grade) is a function of age and total education, expressed in the following formula:

$$age\ grade = total\ education\,/(age-6)$$

where 6 is the expected age at first grade. Teens with an age grade value of 1 are at the appropriate grade level. In this study, the lowest possible value of age grade is 0.545, a 17- year- old who has only completed sixth grade (primary education). Poor students tend to be farther behind than wealthier students, and teens who are in school tend to be closer to their appropriate grade level than teens who are out of school.

By the time youth reach secondary school age, both late starts and repetition make it less likely they will be at the secondary level, and even less likely for poor youth. The schooling gap is due both to high repetition rates and late starting rates. While 34% of 6-year-olds are not in school, that rate drops to 22% for 8-year-olds. Students both begin school late and repeat grades. The age at which children begin school is a function of household wealth. While 88.3% of 6-year-olds from the richest quartile are in school, only 61.6% of 6-year-olds from the poorest quartile attend school. For 8-year-olds, 94 % from the richest quartile are in school as compared to 76.6% from the poorest quartile.

Urbanicity While most studies use two categories to divide urban from rural households, this study uses an urbanicity variable that divides communities into four categories: the capital (Managua), cities, towns, and countryside. Managua may have characteristics that differentiate it from cities and towns. Managua's attendance rates are slightly lower than that of cities and towns (81% for Managua compared to 85% for cities). Attendance rates in the countryside are notably lower—only 64% of rural primary school graduates attend school.

Department Nicaragua is divided into 17 departments, which have different levels of economic development and infrastructure and different cultural traditions. Looking at school attendance by department allows an identification of those departments that have particularly high or low secondary school attendance rates while controlling for other variables. This allows a consideration of the effects of regional variation on school attendance. Table 2.2 (see **the Appendix**) shows primary school completion rates for selected departments. Managua has the highest primary completion rate, and can be expected to have a similarly high secondary attendance rate.

Household Composition Variables Numerous studies have shown the importance of household wealth in school attendance, and other household level variables have also been shown to be predictors of school attendance (Behrman & Wolfe, 1987; Dahan & Gaviria, 1999; Bracho, 2000; Buchmann & Hannum, 2001). While many of the variables are closely correlated with household wealth, such as parent educational attainment, the variables are also found to have an impact when controlling for wealth. Three household variables are included in this study: number of household members, number of children under 5 years in the household, and gender of the household head.[5]

Gender As shown above, more girls than boys in the DHS survey have graduated from primary school. Yet, even though a higher percentage of girls than boys have completed primary school, the same percentage of girls as boys attends secondary school (77.7% and 77.3%). Gender is used in this study to see if it contributes to the probability of secondary school attendance, and to see if the effect of gender on school attendance is different in primary school than in secondary school.

---

[5] In this survey, parent education had too many missing variables to be included.

4.3 Statistical Analysis

The purpose of this chapter is to identify the predictors of secondary school attendance among primary school graduates. The descriptive variables indicate that among primary school graduates, those who are poorer, overage for grade level, or living in rural areas are less likely to attend school. By using logistic regression, where school attendance status is the dichotomous outcome variable, even more of the complexity of school attendance can be understood. In particular, interactions between variables can, for example, identify the difference in probabilities of secondary school attendance for poor teens at grade level as compared with wealthy teens at grade level.

A taxonomy of fitted logistic regression models was built describing the probability that Nicaraguan primary school graduates attend secondary school. The gender of the teen does not affect the probability of secondary school attendance, and thus was dropped out of the model. Additionally, the three household characteristic variables (household size, number of children under five, female headship) were omitted because they do not contribute to explaining secondary school attendance. Two-way interactions were tested between all of the variables in the model, and two interactions were found that contribute to predicting secondary school attendance: the interaction between wealth and total education, and the interaction between urbanicity and total education.[6] The implications of these interactions are explored below. The final regression model is thus:

$$P(inschool = 1) = 1\Big/ {1+e}^{-(\beta_0 + \beta_1 AGE + \beta_2 TOTALED + \beta_3 AGEGRADE + \beta_4 STWEALTH + \beta_5 MANA + \beta_6 CITY}$$
$$+ \beta_7 TOWN + \beta_8 (16) REGION + \beta_9 TOTALED * WEALTH + \beta_{10} TOTALED * MANA$$
$$+ \beta_{11} TOTALED * CITY + \beta_{12} TOTALED * TOWN^7$$

5 Findings

5.1 Geography: Where You Live Matters

Studies are increasingly recognizing the importance of the effects of community wealth on schooling attendance patterns. This study looks at two factors: urbanicity and regional location. Urbanicity is divided into four categories: rural remains the same, but the urban category is divided into the capital, small cities, and towns. This

---

[6] Because AGEGRADE is a function of total education, it is also part of the interaction with wealth and urbanicity.

[7] I have not listed the 17 departments in order to conserve space.

breakdown of the urban variable reveals an interesting phenomenon about Managua. The probability of being in school shows the greatest negative change by age, controlling for total education and age for grade. While 13-year-olds in Managua have a 90% probability of being in school, 17-year-olds in Managua have only a 79% probability of being in school, as compared to 89% and 85% probability for 17-year-olds in cities and towns, respectively. It appears that there are characteristics of living in smaller cities or towns that make it more likely that older primary school graduates attend secondary school than those living in the capital.

The situation in the countryside is particularly interesting. Thirteen-year-olds from the countryside are the least likely to be in school, but 17-year-olds from the countryside are the most likely to be in school, *if* the level of grade retention remains the same. For students who are only 1 year behind, 17-year-olds in the countryside are more likely to be in school than 17-year-olds in towns or cities.

Figures 2.1 and 2.2 both show secondary school attendance by urbanicity. Figure 2.1 looks at students 1 year behind grade level, while Fig. 2.2 looks at students who are at the mean grade level for their age. In both of the figures, while the situation of cities and towns follows an expected trend (lower attendance rates for older students), Managua and the countryside show interesting phenomena. In Managua, for youth who are 1 year behind grade level, the probability of being in secondary school is lower at all ages than for almost all other youth, and the difference between 13- and 17-year-olds is the largest among all urbanicities. In Managua something among the older teens is contributing to a decreased probability of school attendance.

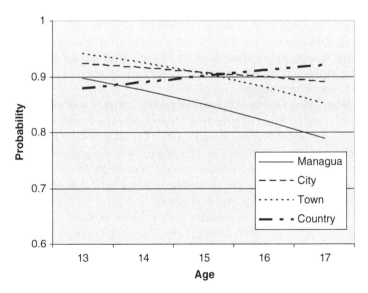

Fig. 2.1 Probability of being in secondary school for primary school graduates by urbanicity, one year behind grade level (n=4467)

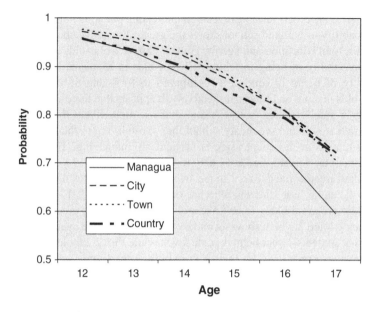

Fig. 2.2 Probability of being in secondary school by urbanicity (mean wealth and mean total education for age) (n=4467)

In the countryside, both figures show that while 12- and 13-year-olds are less likely to be in school than their counterparts in towns or cities like Managua, this changes for older students. Older rural students who are only 1 year behind in school (Fig. 2.1) are *more* likely to be in school than their counterparts in all other areas of the country, and for those students who are at the mean grade level for their age, living in the countryside makes them more likely to be in school than those living in towns or in Managua.

Rural youth often face the challenge of finding secondary schools close enough to their home, and so issues of poverty are compounded by issues of access (Downs, 1989; Burki & Perry, 1997; di Gropello, 1997; Castillo, 1998). Only 316, or 26%, of rural primary school graduates in the sample are at the appropriate grade level. Of those, 91% are currently attending school. In contrast, 28% of primary school graduates in the countryside are more than 2 years behind their grade level. Of those, only 24% are currently attending school.

Most studies find that rural students are less likely to attend school than urban students (Burki & Perry, 1997; Zhang, 1998; Filmer & Pritchett, 1998a; Filmer & Pritchett, 1998c; Bracho, 2000). This study shows that appropriate grade level mediates the effects of urbanicity. The interaction between being at grade level and urbanicity suggests that policymakers should focus on issues of the schooling gap and school quality among the poor, rather than focus on poverty or urbanicity as reasons for school failure. Living in urban areas does not automatically make it more likely that youth are attending secondary school, and living in the capital can actually be detrimental to secondary schooling.

In addition to urbanicity, the department one lives in also has an effect on the probability of secondary school attendance. Some departments fit the patterns that would be expected of them: Carazo, the department with the second highest mean wealth coefficient, has the highest probability of school attendance. Río San Juan, the second poorest department in the country, has the lowest probability of secondary school attendance. There are also some departmental surprises—namely, the North Atlantic Autonomous Region (RAAN) and Managua. Table 2.3 (see **the Appendix**) and Fig. 2.3 show the probability of attending school in selected departments.

Higher attendance rates in Managua were anticipated due to household wealth, but this did not prove to be the case. The coefficient for Managua represents unexplained characteristics of living in that department. These unexplained characteristics deserve further exploration. Managua is a large, sprawling city. Many people live in outlying settlements that have grown up recently, and do not have schools nearby. If a teen wants to attend high school, he or she often must use crowded public transportation for over an hour each way. In addition, the anonymity of the capital means that the teen may have no personal connection to the high school. Other issues may include the effects of the autonomy policy (fee charging), a programme which has been concentrated in the capital, informal sector work options,

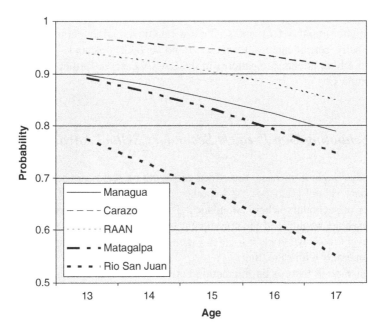

Fig. 2.3 Probability of attending secondary school by region for primary school graduates, one year behind grade level (n=4467)

and immigration from the countryside. No studies to date have looked specifically at characteristics of cities like Managua that are negatively associated with school attendance.

In the RAAN region, on the other hand, far lower attendance rates would be expected given the mean household wealth. It is the poorest department in the country, and its levels of total education and age for grade are also among the lowest. In this study, all of these factors are associated with lower school attendance. And yet in the RAAN, 15-year-olds who are 1 year behind in their schooling have an 88% probability of attending secondary school, the sixth highest probability (the same probability as 15-year-olds from Managua who are 1 year behind). The RAAN region covers the north-eastern portion of the country. It has a different history than much of the rest of Nicaragua, beginning with colonization by the British rather than the Spanish, with resulting Moravian rather than Catholic traditions. The population is majority Miskito Indian, and schools conduct classes in both Spanish and Miskito. It is one of the least densely populated departments of the country and its infrastructure is among the least developed. For much of the 1980s and 1990s, the roads to the RAAN were only open during the dry season. Together with the South Atlantic Autonomous Region (RAAS), the RAAN has suffered from institutional neglect and abuse by leaders in the capital, and it has an antagonistic history with the central government.

Only 30% of teachers in the RAAN have teaching certificates, compared to 65% in Managua. The RAAN has one of the lowest percentages of autonomous schools in the country, which throughout the 1990s meant that it received less attention and less external funding (Castillo, 1998). On the other hand, autonomous schools charge higher monthly fees, and so the low rate of school autonomy in the RAAN may actually permit more students to attend secondary school. The higher than expected school attendance patterns in the RAAN deserve further investigation in future studies.

5.2   Schooling Gap Predicts Secondary School Attendance

This study sought to measure the effects of wealth on secondary school attendance for primary school graduates. As hypothesized, household wealth is an important predictor of secondary school attendance. The interaction between total education and household wealth, and the consequent importance of being at the appropriate grade level (since age grade = totalled/(age − 6)), suggests one important way that wealth interacts with schooling.

In this model, there is an interaction between total education and wealth. This means that the effect of total education on the probability of being in school varies by wealth. For poor students, higher levels of total education have a stronger effect on the probability of being in school than for wealthier students. Primary school graduates who are poor are more likely to be behind in grade level. Students who are behind are more likely to leave school, and poor students who are behind are even more likely to do so. Those poor students who are not behind, however, are more likely to stay in school. Among older students, poor students at grade level are actually more likely to be in school than wealthy students at grade level. As shown in Table 2.4 (see **the Appendix**), among the poorest 40% of primary school graduates, 90% of those at grade level are in school, but only 27% of those 2 or more years behind are in school. Only 387 (23%) of the poorest 40% of primary school graduates are at grade level.[8]

Figure 2.4 shows the probability of being in secondary school for primary school graduates at the appropriate grade level for their age, separated by household wealth.[9] While middle and wealthy 12-year-olds are more likely to be in school than their poor counterparts, middle and wealthy 17-year-olds at grade level are *less* likely to be in school than their poor counterparts.[10] This could mean that while among the poor fewer make the transition from primary to secondary school, once they do, and if they remain at grade level, they are unlikely to drop out of school. Table 2.5 (see **the Appendix**) shows how few poor students are enrolled at grade level.

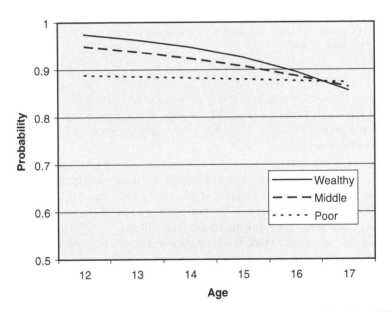

Fig. 2.4 Probability of being in school for primary school graduates, at grade level (n=4467)

[8] Throughout the rest of this study, I refer to the poor in the sample of primary school *graduates*, which as I have shown, tends to be wealthier than the sample of all 12 to 17-year- olds.

[9] For all graphs in this paper, wealthy = 90th percentile, middle = 50th percentile, and poor = 10th percentile.

[10] General linear hypothesis tests confirm the statistical significance of this finding. The difference between wealthy, middle and poor 13-year-olds is statistically significant. For 17-year-olds, poor youth at grade level are more likely to be in school than their middle or wealthy counterparts, but this difference is not statistically significant.

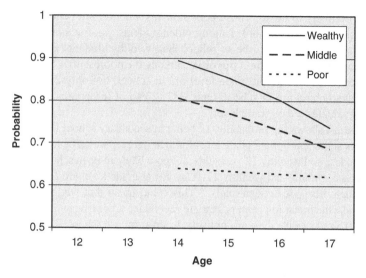

Fig. 2.5 Probability of being in school in Managua for primary school graduates, two years behind grade level (n=4467)

Among the wealthy, the probability of being in school is lower for older youths even if repetition is not an issue. This means that for poor students, not falling behind is a greater predictor of staying in secondary school than it is for students from wealthier families.

Students at grade level tend to be wealthier than other primary school graduates. Older students at grade level tend to be wealthier than younger students. That is, wealthier students tend to be on grade level, while poorer students tend to be farther behind. While 27% of the sample are rural primary school graduates, only 17% of those at grade level are from the countryside. Figure 2.5 illustrates students in Managua 2 years behind grade level, and shows that the probability of attendance is lower for all students regardless of wealth. Once again, the gap between the poor and wealthy is smaller for 17-year-olds than for 14-year-olds.

These findings encourage further research looking at the relationship between school quality, household wealth, repetition rates, and secondary school attendance, in order to untangle the complex relationship between being poor, attending poor-quality schools, repeating grades, and dropping out.

5.3   Girls Do Better in Primary School

This study demonstrates that while more girls than boys do attend secondary school, being a girl does not contribute to the likelihood of attending school. A slightly higher percentage of girls than boys who have graduated from primary school attend secondary school (77.7% of girls attend secondary school, as compared to 77.3% of boys). While gender does not predict secondary school attendance, it *is* a significant predictor of primary school completion. Girls are more likely than boys to complete primary school, but they are no more likely to attend secondary school. Similarly, this study also found that the number of people in the household and the number of children under 5 years are not significant predictors of secondary school attendance. Those household variables, however, *are* significant predictors of primary school completion, as is gender. The effect of gender appears to operate only during the primary school years, not in secondary school. This raises interesting questions for further study. Even though girls are more likely to complete primary school, why are they no more likely to attend secondary school?

6   Analysis

Most educational access literature in developing countries has focused on basic education. This is a logical area to focus on, particularly in countries like Nicaragua, which has a reported net attendance rate in elementary schools of 73.1% and a repetition rate in primary school of 14.8%, one of the highest in the region (GED, 2000; UNESCO, 2001). The literature has reflected a similar policy emphasis on basic education, which in Nicaragua has focused on improving access to, and quality of, basic education. But this study found that of 4,467 primary school graduates between the ages of 12 and 17, 77% are currently in school, indicating that those students who do finish primary school look to secondary school for continued studies.

This study looks at each age group and how being enrolled at the appropriate grade level contributes to the probability of being in school. It looks specifically at the relationship between household wealth and being at the appropriate grade level in order to understand the way that wealth mediates the schooling experience. Both urbanicity and department are included as geographic variables, allowing an analysis of the different probabilities of attendance for students living in towns as opposed to the capital city. Most studies limit geography to delineating between urban and rural status; separating urban into three categories of the capital, cities, and towns permits exploration of the variation in greater detail. The inclusion of department as a separate variable allows for the exploration of the variation among them and provides a finer-grained analysis than urbanicity alone. Finally, this study examines to what degree gender parity, or in Nicaragua's case the gender advantage for girls, also holds for secondary education. Do girls maintain, increase, or decrease the gender advantage that has been reported for basic education? By looking in detail at the factors that contribute to secondary school attendance in Nicaragua, this study moves beyond the general conclusion that household wealth positively predicts secondary school attendance and contributes to an understanding of the particular characteristics of the neglected area of secondary education in Nicaragua.

This study of secondary school attendance patterns by 12- to 17-year-olds in Nicaragua has shown that being poor distorts the schooling experience. As shown in the descriptive statistics, more than 50% of primary school graduates come from the richest 25% of youth, and only 20% come from the poorest 25%. Wealth continues to be an important predictor of secondary school attendance, but the difference in secondary school attendance across income groups varies depending both on the age of the student and the student's schooling gap. Poor 16- and 17-year-olds who have not repeated grades are thus as likely or more likely than their middle and wealthy counterparts to be in school. This finding is counter to conventional wisdom that poor students tend to drop out of school, and raises a critical issue for further study: what school characteristics are associated with poor students maintaining age-appropriate grade levels and staying in school?

This study cannot unpack the reasons why poor youth are more likely to be behind in school, but other studies have looked at opportunity costs, health and nutrition, and school absences (Behrman & Wolfe, 1987; Ilon & Moock, 1991; Munoz Izquierdo, 1994; Dahan & Gaviria, 1999; Bracho, 2000; Buchmann & Hannum, 2001). As shown above, while the official age for first grade is 6 years, many students begin the schooling process at 7 or 8, and poor students tend to begin schooling later than wealthier students. In Nicaragua, the Ministry of Education recognized the seriousness of falling behind when it required that all first graders be automatically promoted to second grade. The law did not solve the problem, however, because teachers found other ways to hold back first graders who they felt were not ready for second grade (Castro Cardenal, 1998). This study indicates that repetition continues to be a serious problem that affects secondary school attendance as well as primary school attendance, although it cannot identify different impacts of repetition in primary school as compared with repetition during secondary school.

The differences in secondary school attendance by wealth and by schooling gap might reflect differences in school quality, both at the secondary level and earlier, at the primary level. Further research must incorporate school-level variables in order to understand both school effects *and* the interaction between school effects and individual characteristics. Measuring school quality presents challenges, but some school effects that merit further consideration include school type (public non-autonomous, autonomous, semi-private, private), teacher education levels, teacher salaries, infrastructure, availability of quality educational materials, teaching methodology, class size, links to parents and the community, and finally, school culture.[11]

This study also revealed unexpected departmental variation. In particular, teens in the capital, Managua, are less likely to be in school than their counterparts in other cities, towns, or the countryside when controlling for all other variables.

---

[11] Another important issue to consider for further study is the appropriate dependent variable for a study of school quality. Some variables include grades, standardized tests, post-schooling job status or income.

Disaggregating urbanicity reveals the challenges facing the nation's capital. Although the capital has more primary school graduates and higher household wealth levels, these two factors do not contribute to proportionately higher secondary school attendance. This finding has implications for further research both in Nicaragua and in other countries in the region. In Nicaragua, further research should focus on the particular experiences of youth in the capital. Can it be explained by Managua's awkward geography, which means that students often must travel over an hour to get to school? Is it related to immigration from the countryside or the presence of the informal labour market? This finding has implications for regional research as well. Most studies divide urbanicity into urban and rural, joining the capital together with other cities. In countries like Nicaragua, where the capital has characteristics that set it apart from other cities, it should be studied separately from other urban areas.

While Managua emerged as a city with lower than expected secondary school attendance, the RAAN emerged as a department with higher than expected secondary school attendance. This departmental variation highlights the need for further research that incorporates community characteristics. Why does the RAAN, a community which has been geographically, politically, and socially isolated, which suffered inordinately in the 1980s war, and which has a different cultural history and present than the rest of the country, have higher than expected secondary school attendance rates? Finally, this study finds that while girls are more likely than boys to graduate from primary school, they are no more likely to attend secondary school. The gender advantage is concentrated in attending and completing primary school, but there is no gender advantage for girls in attending secondary school. The study does not examine *why* this is the case. It does not appear to be related to household size, number of children under five, or gender of the household head. Further research should investigate more carefully the gendered experiences of schooling in order to identify whether this difference results from factors that negatively affect teen girls or from factors that positively affect teen boys. Other variables that could be considered are parent education levels, distance to schools, and opportunity costs. The ways that girls and boys experience both primary and secondary school cultures also deserve further investigation.

7 Conclusion

In general, studies of school attendance patterns find that household wealth and urbanicity predict schooling, both in primary and secondary schools. This study has looked more carefully at these patterns, and has found a more complex story. Living in the large capital city of Managua is different than living in smaller cities, and counter-intuitively, youth at similar levels of wealth are less likely to be in school in Managua than in other cities. Certain rural areas, like the RAAN in northern Nicaragua, have higher than expected attendance rates given their urbanicity and average household wealth. In addition, being wealthy by itself does not guarantee secondary school attendance; poor students who are at grade level are more likely to be in school than their wealthy counterparts. These findings outline a more complex framework for describing secondary school attendance in developing countries like Nicaragua.

Alvaro, the youth who began seventh grade four times, continues to struggle to get through secondary school despite his family's poverty. Many factors have contributed to his struggle—some of those measured in this study include poverty, and living in Managua. But other factors also need to be considered in Alvaro's case, as in the case of all Nicaraguan youth—the quality of his past education, the quality of the secondary school he attends, the community characteristics that encourage or discourage studies, and the economic prospects he sees for the future, among others. This study has shown that Alvaro's experience is typical of primary school graduates; he is one of many Nicaraguan youths who are unable to develop their talents fully through the education system.

8   References

Bedi, A. & Marshall, J. (1999). School attendance and student achievement: Evidence from rural Honduras. *Economic Development and Cultural Change, 47*(3), 657–682.

Behrman, J. (1987). Schooling in developing countries: Which countries are the over and underachievers and what is the schooling impact? *Economics of Education Review, 6*(2), 111–127.

Behrman, J., Birdsall, N. & Szekely, M. (1998). *Intergenerational schooling mobility and macro conditions and schooling policies in Latin America*. Washington, DC: Inter-American Development Bank.

Behrman, J., Duryea, S. & Szekely, M. (1999). *Schooling investments and aggregate conditions: A household survey-based approach for Latin America and the Caribbean*. Washington, DC: Inter-American Development Bank.

Behrman, J. & Wolfe, B. (1987). Investments in schooling in two generations in pre-revolutionary Nicaragua: The roles of family background and school supply. *Journal of Development Economics, 27*.

Bracho, T. (2000). *School attendance in Mexico, poverty and inequality*. Paper presented at the meeting of the Comparative and International Education Society, San Antonio, TX.

Buchmann, C. & Hannum, E. (2001). Education and stratification in developing countries: A review of theories and research. *Annual Review of Sociology, 27*.

Burki, S. & Perry, G. (1997). *The long march: A reform agenda for Latin America and the Caribbean in the next decade*. Washington, DC: World Bank.

Caillods, F. & Maldonado-Villar, M. (1997). *Temas asociados a la educación secundaria de América Latina*. [English Translation]. UNESCO-OREALC.

Camargo, M., Charria, M. & Uribe, C. (1992). *La repitencia escolar en la escuela básica primaria oficial colombiana*. [English Translation]. Santafe de Bogota: Ministry of Education.

Cariola, M. L. (2000). *Tendencias y Perspectivas de la Educación Media*. [English Translation]. Ciudad de Panamá: Universidad de Panamá.

Castillo, M. (1998). *La Descentralización de los Servicios de Educación en Nicaragua*. [English Translation]. Santiago de Chile: Naciones Unidas Comisión Económica para América Latina y el Caribe. (Serie Reformas de Política Pública).

Castro Cardenal, V. (1998). *Understanding grade retention in the light of teachers' beliefs in Nicaragua primary schools*. Unpublished doctoral dissertation, Harvard Graduate School of Education.

Dahan, M. & Gaviria, A. (1999). *Sibling correlations and social mobility in Latin America.* Washington, DC: Interamerican Development Bank.

De Franco, S. (1998). *Repitencia, deserción resultados escolares en Nicaragua.* [English Translation]. Managua: Ministry of Education.

Dellapiane, S. (1994). *Relaciones entre el rendimiento en primer año escolar y el acceso a la educación inicial en zonas carenciadas.* [English Translation]. Montevideo: Universidad Católica del Uruguay.

di Gropello, E. (1997). *Descentralización de la Educación en América Latina: Un análisis comparativo,* CEPAL. [English Translation].

Dijkstra, G. (2000). *Structural adjustment and poverty in Nicaragua.* Paper presented at the meeting of the Latin American Studies Association, Miami, FL.

Downs, C. (1989, May). Politics, design and results: Regionalisation and decentralisation in Nicaragua and Haiti, 1982–1986. *Third World Planning Review,* 11.

Ebaugh, C. D. (1947). *Education in Nicaragua.* Washington, DC: Federal Security Agency, US Office of Education.

ECLAC. (2000). *Social panorama of Latin America.* Santiago: Author.

Filmer, D. (1999a). *Educational attainment and enrolment profiles: A resource book based on an analysis of demographic and health survey data.* Washington, DC: World Bank.

Filmer, D. (1999b). *The structure of social disparities in education: Gender and wealth.* Washington, DC: World Bank.

Filmer, D. & Pritchett, L. (1998a). *The effect of household wealth on educational attainment around the world: Demographic and health survey evidence.* World Bank.

Filmer, D. & Pritchett, L. (1998b). *Estimating wealth effects without expenditure data–or tears: An application to educational enrolments in states of India.* Washington, DC: World Bank.

Filmer, L. & Pritchett, L. (1998c). *Educational enrolment and attainment in India: Household wealth, gender, village, and state effects.* Washington, DC: World Bank.

Gargiulo, C. & Crouch, L. (1994). *Nicaragua: Escolaridad, Repetición y Deserción Escolar: Resultados de una encuesta nacional.* [English Translation]. Washington, DC: Research Triangle Institute/USAID.

Global Education Database. (2000). *Global education database 2000.* Washington, DC: USAID.

Inter-American Development Bank. (1999). *Facing up to inequality in Latin America.* Washington, DC: Inter-American Development Bank. (Economic and Social Progress in Latin America: Annual report).

Ilon, L. & Moock, P. (1991). School attributes, household characteristics, and demand for schooling: A case study of rural Peru. *International Review of Education, 37*(4), 429–451.

MECD. (2003). *Estado de la formación de la ciudadanía y recursos humanos: La Educación en Cifras.* [English Translation]. Managua: Ministry of Education, Culture and Sports.

MED. (1996). *Causas de deserción y repitencia en escolares rurales de primer grado.* [English Translation]. Managua: UNICEF, Ministry of Education, Ministry of Social Action.

Munoz Izquierdo, C. (1994). *Determinantes de las desigualdades educacionales con énfasis en los grupos de menor desarrollo socioeconómico.* [English Translation]. Oaxaca, Instituto estatal de educación pública de Oaxaca.

Pallais, M. (1965). *Análisis de la situación educativa de Nicaragua.* [English Translation]. Managua: Oficina de Planificación del Ministerio de Educación.

Patrinos, H. (1997). Differences in education and earnings across ethnic groups in Guatemala. *Quarterly Review of Economics and Finance, 37*(4).

Patrinos, H. A. & Psacharopoulos, G. (1996). Socioeconomic and ethnic determinants of age-grade distortion in Bolivian and Guatemalan primary schools. *International Journal of Educational Development, 16*(1), 3–14.

Schiefelbein, E. & Heikkinen, S. (1991). *Guatemala, acceso, permanencia, repetición y eficiencia en la educación básica.* [English translation]. Santiago: Oficina Regional de Educación para América Latina y el Caribe.

Schiefelbein, E. & Wolff, L. (1992). *Repetition and inadequate achievement in Latin America's primary schools: A review of magnitudes, causes, relationships and strategies*. The World Bank. (A View from LATHR).

Tedesco, J. C. & Lopez, N. (2002). Desafíos a la educación secundaria en América Latina. [English Translation]. *Revista de la CEPAL, 76*.

UNESCO. (2001). *Situación de los países en relación con los objetivos y componentes del proyecto principal de educación*. [English Translation].

Zhang, Y. (1998). *The determinants of enrolment in basic education in rural China: Evidence from three provinces*. Unpublished doctoral dissertation, Harvard Graduate School of Education.

Appendix

Table 2.1 Mean of standardized wealth by in school status (*n* = 4,467)

	Mean standardized wealth
In school	0.151
Not in school	−0.522

Table 2.2 Primary school completion rates by department among 12- to 17-year-olds (*n* = 9,945)

Managua	63.8%
Carazo	58.1%
Madriz	39.3%
Matagalpa	38.7%
RAAN	29%
RAAS	27.9%
Río San Juan	23.7%

Table 2.3 Cohort size, mean standardized wealth, age for grade, total education, and probability of secondary school attendance for five departments (*n* = 4,467)

	Mean st wealth	Total # in cohort	Mean age for grade	Mean total ed	Overall probability of being in school (15-year-old in town)
Carazo	0.04 (4th)	269	0.88	7.67	0.93 (1st)
RAAN	−0.77 (17th)	160	0.77	6.94	0.88 (6rd)
Managua	0.61 (1st)	757	0.87	7.59	0.88 (6th)
Matagalpa	−0.07 (8th)	278	0.84	7.28	0.79 (15th)
Río San Juan	−0.53 (16th)	79	0.82	7.16	0.61 (17th)

Table 2.4 In school status among the poorest 40% of sample by grade level (standardized wealth < −0.34) (*n* = 1,690)

	At grade level (%)	One year behind (%)	Two years behind (%)	More than 2 years behind (%)
In school	349 (90)	286 (81)	317 (69)	134 (27)
Not in school	38 (10)	69 (19)	143 (31)	354 (73)
Total	387	355	460	488

Table 2.5 Students enrolled in secondary school at grade level among the poorest 25%

12	64
13	44
14	33
15	18
16	19
17	12
TOTAL	190

Chapter 3
Religion, International Aid, and Used Clothing: Globalization and Mayan Literacy Revival in Guatemala

Mary Holbrock

1 Introduction

The indigenous languages and cultures of Guatemala are currently experiencing revitalization efforts as is the case with many of the indigenous languages of the Americas and other parts of the world. This study examines Mayan literacy revival in Guatemala, broadly defined to include a range of cultural literacy practices, and the involvement of globalization in that phenomenon. Globalization is most commonly thought of as the imposition of so-called "Northern" or "First World" culture and economics at the expense of the "South" or "Third World". But in the case of Mayan literacy revival, the direction of the movement of global forces is more complex. This chapter suggests that there are three ways in which globalization is involved in Mayan literacy revival. Two effects are related to forces coming in to affect literacy. Some of these, such as religion, mass media, and used consumer goods, take on culture-suppressing forms, while others, such as the women's movement and the work of international aid organizations, take on culture-sustaining forms. Yet Mayan literacy in the form of alphabetic print, glyphs, and traditional clothing and folklore is also moving from inside Guatemala to the outside world by way of migration, the Internet, and tourism.

Globalization is commonly thought of as the export of Western culture to the rest of the world. A definition given in a 1995 lecture by Martin Khor states this concept nicely: "Globalisation is what we in the Third World have for several centuries called colonization or imperialism" (as cited in Baylis & Smith, 1995, p. 15).

Although there is certainly truth to this definition, globalization is more complex. A definition by Giddens (1990) which defines globalization as "the intensification of world wide social relations which link distant localities in such a way that local happenings are shaped by events occurring many miles away and *vice versa*" (p. 64, emphasis added) captures the true complexity of this phenomenon. It is the "vice versa" part of this definition which challenges the traditional point of view.

University of Illinois

J. Zajda et al. (eds.), *Education and Social Inequality in the Global Culture*.
© Springer 2008

What is interesting about the Mayan literacy revival situation is that both "import" and "export" aspects of globalization are present. The Mayan language literacy revival movement is shaped by events occurring far away, but, in turn, it is shaping, or at least its products are appearing, in distant locales. Outsider influence is present in the movement, but Mayan literacy is also appearing abroad.

This chapter discusses aspects of globalization involved in a Mayan literacy revival movement which is taking place in Guatemala. It is based on qualitative research conducted mainly during 2001. Research methods followed an instrumental case study model in which Mayan literacy revival was investigated by focusing largely on two research sites, Santa Eulalia, Huehuetenango, and San Pedro la Laguna, Sololá. The Mayan languages spoken in these two villages are Q'anjob'al and Tz'utujiil, respectively. Data-gathering methods included qualitative interviews with 60 participants, observations of primary school and adult literacy classes, and homestays with Mayan families. In reporting quotes from the interviews in this chapter either a pseudonym or the actual name of the interviewee is used according to the wishes of each interviewee. The symbol * indicates a pseudonym.

2   Context

Ferdman (1999) notes that a "sociocultural approach" to literacy conceptualizes it "as a cultural construction that has meaning only in a specified cultural context" and a "power approach" takes into consideration the social hierarchy surrounding literacy (p. 97). In Guatemala, Mayan literacy revival is taking place in the context of a larger movement of indigenous language and culture revitalization (Fischer & Brown, 1996; French, 1999; Garzon, Brown, Richards, & Simon, 1998; Jiménez Sanchez, 1998). The revitalization efforts are in response to language and culture suppression which have been part of the subjugation of the Mayan people and their culture since the time of the Spanish invasion. This revitalization movement is sometimes referred to by scholars as the Maya movement or the Pan-Maya movement.

Similar movements in which language shift is being counteracted by language revitalization and empowerment are occurring among indigenous peoples around the world. Many native North American Indian communities have begun language revitalization projects and several such projects are described, for example, in Reyner et al. (1999). Furthermore, Hinton and Hale (2001) discuss language revitalization projects around the world in countries such as Australia, New Zealand, Great Britain, and the United States.

Literacy in particular can be used as a strategy for language and culture revitalization. This topic is discussed in five of the articles in Reyner, et al. (1999) while Hornberger's (1997) edited collection discusses reversing language shift and revitalizing culture through the use of literacy in traditionally unwritten indigenous languages of the Americas. The volume includes case studies of indigenous literacy in several countries including Mexico, Guatemala, Peru, and the United States. The studies in the Hornberger volume demonstrate the usefulness of native literacies for increasing indigenous language status, for extending the domains of use of the language, and for empowering indigenous language speakers. Importantly, the studies also remind us that context is key when making decisions about using a written code.

I deem the use of literacy in the Maya movement a revival because the Mayas have an ancient literary tradition. Although in recent history the Mayan languages have been used mainly as oral languages, the Mayas created one of the earliest, most developed writing systems in history. The historical literary tradition that the Mayan languages enjoyed is described briefly by England (1996). She notes that Mayan hieroglyphic writing was "the only true writing system developed independently in the Americas" (p. 181) and it was still in use at the time of the Spanish invasion. At this time hundreds or perhaps thousands of Mayan books were destroyed by the Spaniards. In the 16th century, using a Spanish-based alphabet, the Mayas wrote "some of the most important world literatures" (England, p. 181) such as the *Pop Wuj* (*Popol Vuh*) and the *Annals of the Kaqchikels*.. In the 19th century the *Books of the Chilam B'alam* were written in Yucatan and the *Xajooj Tuun* (*Rab'inal Achi*) was written in the highlands (England). Between that time and the present era little was published and the use of Mayan languages for writing fell largely into disuse.

Recently, over the past several decades, a number of events have contributed to a resurgence of Mayan literacy. The Summer Institute of Linguistics started creating alphabets and publishing small booklets on religious, health, and cultural topics in the 1970s. Other events that could be categorized as part of the Maya movement include the 1987 officialization of an alphabetic script for the Mayan languages (known as the "Unified Alphabet"), the establishment of the Academy of Mayan Languages of Guatemala (ALMG) which works on Mayan language standardization, and the creation of Maya-staffed, linguistics, non-governmental organizations (NGOs) such as the Proyecto Linguistico Francisco Marroquin (PLFM) and Oxlajuuj Keej Maya' Ajtz'iib' (OKMA) which have created dictionaries, grammars, and bilingual literacy instructional materials (French, 1999; Jiménez Sánchez, 1998). A number of Mayan presses such as Cholsamaj, Nojib'sa, and Saqb'e publish materials written by OKMA and other NGOs (Jiménez Sánchez). Mayan language published materials include children's stories, novels, newspaper articles, and translations of official documents. The Guatemalan government has also played a role in Mayan literacy revival, with the 1996 Peace Accords allowing for wider use of the Mayan languages. Working with the United States Agency for International Development (USAID), the Guatemalan Ministry of Education has produced literacy instruction materials in ten Mayan languages, as well as bilingual education materials in four Mayan languages (Richards & Richards, 1997).

3   Literacy Defined

Street (1999) notes that

> '[l]iteracy is always practiced in social contexts. ... [This] notion is ... profound in that it
> has significant implications for our understanding and definitions of what counts as liter-
> acy' (p. 37).

According to the findings of this study, literacy in the Mayan world is intricately
linked with culture. Besides reading, writing, and numeracy, literacy encompasses
oratory skill and oral language expression, meanings associated with symbols and
patterns on traditional clothing, and traditional rituals, gestures, and behaviours.
Thus, in this chapter literacy in the Mayan context is not only defined as representations of language in alphabetic and pictographic form, but is also broadened to
include customs, traditions, and cosmology.

Critical literacy theory views literacy as an "ideological practice" (Street, 1999,
p.1). Examining the relationship between literacy and development, Street notes:

> An 'ideological' model of literacy begins from the premise that variable literacy practices are
> always rooted in power relations and that the apparent innocence and neutrality of the 'rules'
> serves to disguise the ways in which such power is maintained through literacy (p. 13).

In the case of the Mayan literacy revival in Guatemala, global forces from the outside were culture threatening, and, as such, presented a challenge to literacy revival.
Returning to the discussion of global forces in Mayan literacy revival, this chapter
first discusses external forces, such as those implied in the first definition of globalization by Martin Khor (as cited in Baylis & Smith, 1995, p. 15). Khor's definition paints a picture of a culture suppressing force and the replacement of diverse
cultural traditions by mass-marketed Western commodities.

4   Culture-Suppressing, Global Forces from the Outside

4.1   *Religion – The Summer Institute of Linguistics and the Alphabet Controversy*

Religion is one of the global forces involved in Mayan literacy revival. According to
many interviewees in this investigation, Protestant/Evangelical Christian religion
threatens Mayan language and culture by imposing foreign ideology. For example,
the Summer Institute of Linguistics (SIL), a Christian missionary organization, creates grammars and alphabets for oral languages around the world in order to translate
the Bible into these languages. SIL has worked in Guatemala for several decades,
publishing Christian religious materials as well as booklets and posters about health
topics into the Mayan languages. The involvement of SIL in Mayan literacy revitalization is complicated. On the one hand, SIL has created an alphabet system and published many Mayan language booklets. Thus, this organization could be seen as a

pioneer in the modern day Mayan language literacy revival movement. However, as noted by Street (1999), SIL literacy programmes, like all literacy programmes, are not "neutral", but rather have an ideological agenda. The alphabet system used by SIL in their published materials and the ideology of Evangelical Christianity are controversial.

The alphabet controversy revolves around two competing alphabet systems. One system is comprised of the alphabets which were created and used by SIL. The other is called the Unified Alphabet. The SIL alphabet system is older, while the Unified Alphabet was legalized in 1987. The choice of which alphabet to use in writing a given Mayan language has become a political controversy related to identity and ownership. Interestingly, the alphabets themselves reflect the insider versus outsider ideological stance of their creators and users. The alphabets are actually quite similar, with only four controversial graphemes (England, 1996, 1998). In the SIL alphabet these graphemes are used in a way that is similar to the Spanish alphabet and which would, presumably, facilitate reading the Spanish alphabet as well. In the Unified Alphabet, the graphemes more closely reflect the pronunciation of the Mayan languages in that there is more one-to-one correspondence between the graphemes and the corresponding Mayan language phonemes. The SIL alphabet has been and continues to be used for publication of (outsider) missionary religious doctrine. The Unified Alphabet is used by Mayan linguistics organizations to publish Mayan linguistic as well as culture-related materials, such as oral tradition and folklore. In particular, the Mayan linguistics organizations Academy of Mayan Languages of Guatemala (ALMG) and the Proyecto Linguistico Francisco Marroquin (PLFM) use the Unified Alphabet in the materials they produce and in the literacy classes they teach. The Unified Alphabet was chosen in 1987 at a meeting in which only Mayas, but no foreigners, were allowed to vote. Although the Unified Alphabet was chosen as the official alphabet for the Mayan languages 14 years prior to the time data were gathered for this study, in 2001 there continued to be a lack of alphabetic consistency in available published materials. While some booklets had been published prior to the officialization of the Unified Alphabet, others were published after officialization but still did not appear to use the Unified Alphabet. These included SLS materials available in a bookstore in the city of Quetzaltenango which were originally published in the 1980s, and were then republished in the late 1990s still using the older SIL alphabet rather than the newer Unified Alphabet. Clearly, SIL seemed reluctant to adopt the Unified Alphabet.

Although the continued use of two different alphabet systems may result in orthographical confusion, the issue is not simply a linguistic one. The alphabet controversy is also about identity. Interviewees lamented that Evangelical Christianity, which is becoming more and more popular in Guatemala, and particularly in San Pedro la Laguna, preaches that the traditional Mayan religion and other ancient traditions such as the Mayan calendar, the Mayan number system, and the Mayan glyphs are unacceptable. One interviewee stated that evangelical Mayas would not send their children to an after-school activity centre where the above-mentioned cultural traditions, as well as Mayan language alphabet literacy, were taught. Later, an interviewee in San Pedro confided that the ALMG-Tz'utujiil (located in San Pedro la Laguna) considered discontinuing the use of the Unified Alphabet and replacing it with the SIL alphabet. Thus, the continued use of the SIL alphabet represents sustained influence from US Protestant-Evangelical missionary doctrine resulting in the suppression of traditional forms of Mayan literacy.

4.2   Mass Media

Another globalizing influence, mass media, presented a form of audiovisual literacy which was threatening Mayan traditions. Telecommunications technology was blamed for introducing outsider culture and values to youth who, already faced with discrimination against them as indigenous people, were abandoning traditional Mayan languages, clothing, and customs. In the words of one interviewee:

> In Guatemala, indigenous people have been very discriminated against, so that now more than before, with the influx of international communications, now the youth don't want to be indigenous anymore. And in order to not be indigenous, youth [find it necessary] to stop speaking their languages and to stop wearing traditional clothing. Those are two very important things that are being lost (Estheiman Amaya, creator of El Regional newspaper).

Another interviewee noted the influence of modern communications, and then singled out television in particular.

> The modernization that is happening in society, before we never even had typewriters, but now there is Internet, telephone by satellite, television. This is the reason I think we are losing (our Mayan language and culture), these changes. And sometimes youth also adopt other ways of thinking. We need to make our youth more aware, more critical. ... Sometimes we should also control what type of TV programs they are watching ... we need to make sure they don't watch too many programs where there are guns, movies, or pornography (Guadalupe*, interviewee from Santa Eulalia).

Most television channels in Guatemala are in Spanish, with much of the programming coming from Mexico, but there are also several English language channels, as well as programming in Italian and German. There are no Mayan language television channels, though a couple of interviewees mentioned that one could occasionally hear Mayan spoken on local cable. For example, the annual Maya Queen pageant or highlights of the annual town festival might be aired on local cable. While a few interviewees mentioned this occasional use of Mayan language on television, most interviewees explained that it would be quite impossible to have a Mayan language television station. According to one interviewee:

> There aren't any [Mayan language television stations]. I think that even if someone pays 500,000 Quetzales [US$60,000] to the television, I don't think they would broadcast a show in Mayan on their channel because then other people won't watch the program. [The reason we have Mayan language radio stations but not TV channels is because] radio is local. There isn't hardly any national radio, few radio stations have national coverage (Luis, interviewee from Santa Eulalia).

Thus, interviewees felt that television could only be used infrequently to promote traditional culture and values. Mainly, television was perceived as an outsider institution.

4.3 Clothing

The declining use of traditional clothing was also a topic frequently mentioned by Mayas during interviews about literacy. This association of clothing with literacy in Mesoamerica harkens back to pre-Hispanic times when "scribes, painters, and weaving women were classified together (on the) ritual calendar" (King, 1994, p. 74) and interviewees associated literacy with patterns of changing language use, and also with the cultural element of clothing. Traditional, colourful, hand-woven, hand-embroidered Mayan clothing was seen as representing a form of literacy because it contained patterns and designs with cosmological significance. Moreover, one can "read" the traditional clothing worn by a Maya person to ascertain the hometown of the wearer, because the different colours, patterns, and styles are specific to different villages. An example mentioned in Son Chanay (1999) describes the interest of illiterate women weavers when they viewed the traditional *huipil* pattern from the town of Patzun, which was printed as a part of a book cover design. This clearly demonstrated how traditional fabric patterns represent a form of literacy which can be read by "illiterate" women. In the words of Otzoy (1996), "Maya dress ... provides the world with a text to be read" (p. 147).

Unfortunately, all over Guatemala, traditional Mayan clothing is being replaced by Western clothing. Used clothing from the United States arrives in Guatemala by the truckload. This clothing is donated by charitable organizations, and then sold by Guatemalan individuals who profit from the sale. The clothing arrives in gigantic bundles or *pacas*. When a new shipment is about to arrive, a store will put up a sign announcing *mañana se abre paca* ("tomorrow a new bundle will be opened"). Thus, the used clothing stores themselves have come to be known in some areas as *pacas*. The clothing is called *ropa americana* (American clothing). Along with English language print and graphic designs from a foreign culture, this clothing also represents a form of outsider environmental print.

This has encouraged the disappearance of traditional clothing in both villages involved in this study. The traditional *huipil* (women's blouse) of Santa Eulalia was not being worn anymore by many adult women. Instead they were wearing *ropa americana* – western blouses, shirts, or sweatshirts – with their *cortes* (traditional women's skirt). The *cortes* worn in Santa Eulalia were rarely those made with the traditional red wool fabric, but instead were from different parts of Guatemala. Older women sometimes wore oversized, colourful beach towels from the United States as shawls. The *capixhay*, a traditional wool poncho worn by men in Santa Eulalia, was now only worn by men in their fifties or older. Similarly, in San Pedro la Laguna women had abandoned the traditional hand-woven *huipil* and had replaced it with a blouse made from machine-made fabric. Only the oldest men in the village still wore the more traditional colourful, hand-woven shirts and knee-length pants of the village. *Ropa americana* was now worn by young and middle-aged men in both villages, as in most of the rest of Guatemala.

Interviewees intensely remarked about the symbolic meaning of wearing non-native clothing. Blaming modern technology, an interviewee explained in detail the losses which were occurring in his Tz'utujiil-Maya language village.

> [In the past we spoke] the real, authentic Tz'utujiil language, but now, its not real, authentic Tz'utujiil. My father's way of speaking was beautiful. … [But] now children speak Spanish, because of technology, because now everyone has a television, the children listen to it, watch cartoons, speak Spanish … so now it is hard for them to understand Tz'utujiil. This is the change that has taken place over the past fifteen or twenty years. Our language, we no longer speak it like we used to. … If we wait long enough, our language will die, like our clothing. … For economic reasons we abandoned our traditional clothing, and now they want to go back … to use the true fabric to make clothing, [but] you can't find it any-more. … It's a struggle, like our Tz'utujiil language. It's not that I don't like it, it's that it's a difficult situation (Marcos*, interviewee from San Pedro la Laguna).

5   Culture-Supporting, Global Forces from the Outside

Critical theory as applied to the fields of education, language planning, and literacy notes the possibility for projects to either empower or to disempower minorities. Tollefson (1991) states that language planning both reflects and transforms rela-tionships of power. Similarly, Street (1999) explains that "literacy practices [can play a role in either] reproducing or challenging structures of power and domina-tion" (p. 7). Finally, Skutnabb-Kangas (2000) notes that formal education can either kill languages or be helpful in reversing language shift.

While some aspects of globalization such as Evangelical religion, television, and the replacement of Mayan traditional clothing with used clothing from the United States were viewed by most Maya interviewees as causing language and culture loss, other global forces were seen as culture-promoting. In particular, education and local media projects funded by international aid organizations, and literacy and library projects influenced by the women's movement were embraced by many Mayas as culture-promoting.

5.1   International Aid Organizations

International organizations and the funds they provide are key elements in many Mayan literacy projects and are working with local organizations to carry out education, pub-lishing, and anti-discrimination projects and campaigns. For example, USAID has helped to fund primary school bilingual education materials in four Mayan languages, kindergarten materials in several other Mayan languages, and adult literacy materials in two Mayan languages. After-school programmes that teach children Mayan language reading and writing, as well as the Mayan number system and the Mayan calendar, have been financed through European government aid programmes. This investigation examined two Mayan language publishing projects, two literacy programmes, and a library project that had received external funding. Unfortunately, while these projects were important for the culture-promoting role they played in Mayan literacy revival, they also suffered from problems of sustainability.

5.2 Publishing Projects

An example of an extremely admirable Mayan language publication project, which closed when external funding stopped, is the newspaper *El Regional*, which was published in four Mayan languages including Jakalteko (also called Popti), K'ichee', Mam, and Q'anjob'al. *El Regional* became the predominant newspaper of the indigenous people of Guatemala and it received the National Communication Prize in 1993 from The United Nations Children's Fund (UNICEF). In 1997 and 1998, it was the newspaper with the largest circulation in the region, and the largest newspaper, by volume, in Guatemala. Estheiman Amaya, foreign national and creator of *El Regional*, proudly told me: "It was the biggest indigenous language newspaper in all the history of Guatemala. … A Mayan newspaper was the biggest in the history of the country!"

But *El Regional* had difficulty becoming commercially viable, especially in the beginning as advertisers thought Mayas would not have enough money to buy their products. Although this changed over time as merchants began to see indigenous consumers as representing a valid market, commercialization became a critical issue after 1995 because international aid organizations were discontinuing their funding of the paper. In 1998, a Danish international organization removed its financial support, and *El Regional* experienced an economic crisis. When another NGO withdrew its support, the newspaper had to be sold. Under different ownership, *El Regional* is currently published in monolingual Spanish rather than in Mayan, and with "mainstream" news rather than indigenous content.

The other Mayan language publishing project investigated was a linguistics and traditional knowledge project in the Tz'utujiil language area of Guatemala. The project had produced several books on Tz'utujiil-Mayan language folktales and oral histories. An indigenous man who had worked for the project explained that his organization was ready to publish more books based on their research, but first needed to identify external funding. He stated:

> What is difficult is obtaining funding. We're working on a document about Mayan medicine and another about jokes, riddles and poems [in Tz'utujiil]. There is no document like this in the Tz'utujiil area. … We already have part of the document but now we're looking for financing in order to publish it. … Our objective is that our children have didactic material in order to do their school assignments, their research papers, but right now there aren't many materials. Some of our books are already published and the students are using them in the schools. Cholsamaj Press published them. That's the organization which publishes [Mayan language and culture] materials. But there has to be an institution which finances

their publication. ... If the institution wants to donate, for example, 15,000 Quetzales [US$2000] or 20,000 Quetzales, our organization can put in a little money, to work together with them (Mateo*, interviewee from San Pedro la Laguna).

When asked why the publishing company did not use the profits from the sale of the book to finance publication, Mateo* explained:

It doesn't work that way, For example, if Cholsamaj Press had funds especially for buying the rights of authorship, then yes, we could sell the book to them. But the problem is that they give us fewer [sample] books [that way]. ... For example, if they were to print one hundred books, they would give us twenty-five and keep seventy-five for themselves, for their publishing rights. But twenty-five books isn't enough for us, for the entire Tz'utujiil speaking area. This could be done, but Cholsamaj doesn't have funds for that [kind of publishing], they simply print the books [and are paid for their work.] (Mateo*, interviewee from San Pedro la Laguna).

The goal is to supply the entire local market with free books, but this is only possible if far more books are sold outside the local area than are given away free inside the local area. However, as this strategy is not viewed as feasible, an alternate strategy would be to finance the majority of the project through donations. Selling books to locals as a way to finance book publishing was not seen as a viable option.

In summary, although they were funded from abroad, these publishing projects played a large role in the creation of Mayan language print materials. Their dependency on foreign funds, however, made the projects unsustainable.

5.3   The Women's Movement

Another culture-supporting global force involved in Mayan literacy revival is the women's movement. Influenced by the international movement in the struggle for women's rights, an official space for women's groups was created through the 1996 Guatemalan Peace Accords. Focusing on ideologies of empowerment, women's groups in Guatemala were playing an active role in Mayan literacy issues. In Guatemala, where Maya women usually keep traditions more so than their male counterparts, they are often found maintaining their native Mayan language and continuing to wear and weave traditional clothing, while the men have often adopted foreign clothing. As with the publishing projects described above, however, the literacy projects being organized and supported by women's groups also faced issues of financial sustainability. Adult literacy classes, such as those in the town of San Pedro la Laguna, Solola, a literacy programme in Santa Eulalia, Huehuetenango, and the town library of Santa Eulalia were all sponsored by local women's associations. In terms of the effect of global forces, not only was the women's movement an international phenomenon, but outsider financial support was solicited in both of these towns. Both had originally received help from Guatemalan agencies, but were later forced to solicit outside aid for their continued existence.

The Foro de la Mujer or Women's Forum which runs the adult bi-literacy programme in the Tz'utujiil Mayan language area of Guatemala is a local branch of the national organization, started under the impetus of the Peace Accords. According to the staff organizer, the local women wanted to focus their project on gender equality and it was decided that funding should be used for literacy instruction. She explained:

> When we did a diagnostic study at the local level we found that the problem was illiteracy, and even though the women wanted to [focus on] gender equality, when there is illiteracy and if men know a little, women will never have equal participation or equality of decision making, so we saw that this was a problem and we made literacy the priority (Juana*, staff organizer, Women's Forum).

Although the majority of the participants are women, because of the Women's Forum intentions to promote gender equality, the literacy classes are open to men as well so that both genders can become aware of women's issues.

Unfortunately, although the local group was part of the larger national organization, no money was ever given by the government to fund the proposals the local women had made. Hence, they decided to look elsewhere for funding and received some from the international organization, Save the Children. The organizer concluded the interview by giving the researcher a brochure and reminding her that they needed assistance from women's organizations in wealthier countries. She stated:

> As women we are all the same, we have the same objectives about wanting equal participation. I think that you women in other countries have already achieved this and we expect you to support us. We still have a long road ahead of us, it's extremely arduous, the means for arriving [at the end of the road] are still lacking (Juana*, staff organizer, Women's Forum).

The adult literacy programme in Santa Eulalia was also influenced by the international women's movement and by a foreign pedagogical approach. Originally funded by a European international organization but housed under the Guatemalan national adult literacy programme known as El Comité Nacional de Alfabetizacion (The National Literacy Training Committee (CONALFA)), the adult literacy programme in Santa Eulalia followed a Freirian pedagogical approach and had a gender awareness orientation in both content and practical set-up. The programme was designed to promote gender awareness and to make both men and women aware of the important role that women play in Mayan culture. Men's classes had male instructors and were separate from women's classes, which had female instructors. The idea was to allow women to have a voice, to not be afraid to speak up, and to allow both men and women to be able to openly discuss the lesson themes without concern about criticism from the opposite sex. The lesson themes focused on topics of traditional Mayan culture, and women sometimes incorporated traditional handicraft sessions into their lessons. As suggested by Freirian pedagogy, themes and generative words which were meaningful to the participants were chosen. The objectives of the programme were to learn to read and write in both Spanish and Q'anjob'al, and to promote critical thinking on the part of the students. Thus, although influenced by outsider philosophy, this adult literacy programme supported Mayan culture by incorporating critical thinking about Mayan traditions.

Lastly, in Santa Eulalia a local women's organization played a role in the creation of a town library, and again outside financial aid was solicited for sustainability.

The idea of a library in Santa Eulalia was originally conceived by the Santa Eulalia Women's Association, which then solicited the help of Decopaz, a Guatemalan organization which provides financial assistance to create social projects requested by community organizations. Decopaz helped with organizing the project and then gave money to purchase books for the library. When the project was taken over by the local municipality, however, it fell apart due to lack of funds. Later, the women's organization regained control of the library and looked to outside funding from a foreign woman. This woman decided to temporarily finance the library, brought books, and set up a bank account to pay the librarian and the rent. Thus, the continuing existence and functioning of the library in Santa Eulalia is a result of the work of the Women's Association of Santa Eulalia and of the monetary assistance of a foreigner. This assistance was intended to be just for a year, until some other solution could be found. Time was passing and the president of the Women's Association, Izabel Francisco Esteban, explained:

> We are asking her now if she is going to continue supporting the library or not. If she is going to continue to support it for another year, then we will continue with the library, if not, then the library will close. That's the sad reality ... and we women are worse off [for it] ... some people think it is not important, but it is important, very important (Izabel Francisco Esteban, President, Women's Association of Santa Eulalia).

Many of the global forces affecting the Mayan literacy movement in Guatemala come from the outside. Some of these, such as religious conversion, mass media, and the adoption of foreign clothing in an effort to avoid discrimination, take a more culture suppressing form. These forces fit with a traditional view of globalization as imperialism. Other outsider global forces, however, such as the international women's rights movement and financial support for Mayan literacy projects on the part of international organizations, are more Mayan culture-supporting.

6   Vice Versa, Sending Mayan Literacy Abroad

Importantly, globalization is not all one-way when it comes to Guatemala. In terms of Mayan literacy revival, global happenings are not simply coming from the outside to affect, positively or negatively, the movement. Instead, globalization has, in some ways, made it possible for Mayan literacy to move from Guatemala to the outside. This last issue of globalization addresses the "vice versa" part of Giddens' (1990) definition, where Mayan language literacy has become available abroad.

6.1   Guatemalan Mayan Clothing

As previously discussed, traditional Mayan clothing can be viewed as a form of literacy in the Mayan worldview. Tourism is an important part of the economy in Guatemala and Mayas have found ways to sell clothing and other accessories made with local fabric to foreign visitors. The clothing is made according to the latest foreign fashion styles, but it uses local machine-made fabric which imitates indigenous hand-woven designs. Sometimes pieces of fabric from old discarded *huipiles*, *cortes*, and Maya men's traditional clothing are also added to the item of apparel. This clothing, and sometimes entire pieces of used, authentic, traditional Mayan clothing as well, then move abroad as tourists return home from their travels. Interestingly, although this clothing is made with the intent of selling it to tourists, some Maya men who are active in the Mayan movement and who are from areas where traditional men's clothing has been lost have begun wearing this clothing as a means of culture revindication.

6.2 Migration and the Exportation of a Q'anjob'al Novel

Although migration has contributed in some ways to culture loss among youth who have left their towns and villages to move to urban areas of Guatemala or to live and work abroad, it has also made possible the export of Mayan language, culture, and literacy. An example of this is the writing of Mayan author Gaspar Pedro Gonzalez. This author has written poetry and two novels in his native language of Q'anjob'al. The migration of large numbers of Q'anjob'ales to the United States, creating especially large expatriate settlements in Indiantown, Florida, and Los Angeles, California, attracted the attention of academic researcher Fernando Peñalosa who created a publishing company called Yax Te' Press. This Los Angeles-based, non-profit organization also facilitated translation and publication of the novels so that there are now bilingual Spanish-Q'anjob'al, and monolingual Spanish and English versions (*A Mayan Life* and *Return of the Maya* are the English language titles). The novels are available for purchase through the Yax Te' website. The first chapter of *A Mayan Life* can also be read online, as can a few Q'anjob'al and Akatekan (a neighbouring Mayan language) folktales. Thus, in this way, Q'anjob'al Mayan culture, language, and literature have been *exported*. Furthermore, the English version of *A Mayan Life* has become popular for use as a textbook in introductory anthropology classes in US universities. The irony of the effect of globalization in this case is that these particular pieces of Mayan literature are available for outsiders to read abroad, but not available for Q'anjob'al language speakers themselves to read in Guatemala. More specifically, the novels and folktales were not in the library of the Q'anjob'al town of Santa Eulalia where some of the data for this study were gathered; nor did the town have Internet access.

6.3 The Internet

Not only can Mayan language publications be purchased through the Internet, and the literature described above be read online, but a number of Internet sites also exist written in Mayan languages. As an example, two websites related to Q'anjob'al are given below. First, as already mentioned, an internet site for Yax Te' Press (www.yaxte.org) sells Mayan language books and links to other websites with folktales and novels in Q'anjob'al and Akateko. Second, an interactive website created by a Q'anjob'al woman who emigrated to Sweden teaches a few Q'anjob'al language expressions, giving translations into English, Spanish, and Swedish (http://hem.fyristorg.com/qanjobal/page16.html). The Internet site provides the written words, and also gives an oral pronunciation. Other Mayan language websites also exist. For example, the websites of many of the Guatemalan Mayan linguistics and culture non-profit organizations also have Mayan language writing, glyphs, and fabric. See, for example, the following websites: www.guate.net/cnem/index.html, www.ameu.org.gt/, and www.laneta.apc.org/rci/defmay. The World Wide Web thus provides a means through which Mayan language culture and print can appear anywhere there is Internet access.

7   Conclusion

Global forces involved in the Mayan literacy revival movement are varied. Many forces come from the outside. An examination of the ideologies behind these forces shows that some could fit the model of globalization as imperialism because their ideology is one of Mayan culture suppression. Specifically, many Mayas lament that Maya youth in particular, and also some Mayas who adopt Evangelical Christianity, are abandoning traditional cultural practices in the face of such global forces as mass media, missionary doctrine, and the importation of used consumer items from the United States. However, other ideologies which originated from the outside, such as the international women's movement and Freirian pedagogy, have been helpful in supporting Mayan culture and literacy revival. Outsider international organizations which support projects aligned with such ideologies are sought by Mayas involved in the revival movement. Unfortunately, financing by some of these organizations has not been completely sustainable.

Auspiciously, Mayas have found ways to appropriate outsider ideas and technologies, sometimes hybridizing them to support their culture, and in some circumstances, exporting Maya culture abroad. In particular, certain forms of Mayan literacy are appearing abroad. For example, patterns on traditional clothing, a form of Mayan literacy, move abroad as tourists bring home Mayan fabric on clothing and accessories purchased in Guatemala. Furthermore, Mayan alphabetic print and Mayan glyphs can be accessed around the world on websites of various Mayan language and culture organizations. Finally, Mayan culture and, to a lesser extent, Mayan alphabetic print in the novels of Q'anjob'al author Gaspar Pedro Gonzalez are available in the United States, with the English language version of this author's first novel used extensively in introductory anthropology classes in US universities. Thus, while the form of globalization as imperialism can be found in the case of Mayan literacy revival, it is also true that in some cases outsider forces are helping to sustain Mayan culture.

Finally, it is noteworthy that Mayan literacy is moving from Guatemala to the outside world, and it is important not to overlook this last form of globalization which includes movement of culture from the "South" to the "North". Although the "South" may or may not directly benefit from the export of their culture (as evidenced in the case of the Q'anjob'al novels), disregarding the existence of this phenomenon and thereby making contributions from the "South" invisible is most definitely disempowering. Future research could examine examples of "vice versa" globalization and the empowering or disempowering effects of this phenomenon on the "South".

Acknowledgements I am grateful to the Centre for Latin American and Caribbean Studies of the University of Illinois-Urbana-Champaign for funding which made this research possible.

References

Baylis, J. & Smith, S. (1995). *The globalization of world politics: An introduction to international relations* (2nd ed.). Oxford: Oxford University Press.

England, N. (1996). The role of language standardization in revitalization. In E. F. Fischer & R. M. Brown (Eds.). *Maya cultural activism in Guatemala* (pp. 156–164).Austin, TX: University of Texas Press.

Ferdman, B. M. (1999). Ethnic and minority issues in literacy. In D. A. Wagner, R. L. Venezky, & B. V. Street (Eds.). *Literacy: An international handbook*. Boulder, CO: Westview Press.

Fischer, E. F. & Brown, R. M. (1996). *Maya cultural activism in Guatemala*. Austin, TX: University of Texas Press.

French, B. M. (1999). Imagining the nation: Language ideology and collective identity in contemporary Guatemala. *Language & Communication, 19*, 277–287.

Garzon, S., Brown, R. M., Richards, J. B., & Simon, A. A. (1998). *The life of our language: Kaqchikel Maya maintenance, shift, and revitalization*. Austin, TX: University of Texas Press.

Giddens, A. (1990). *The consequences of modernity*. Cambridge: Polity Press.

Hinton, L. & Hale, K. (2001). *The green book of language revitalization in practice*. San Diego, CA: Academic Press.

Hornberger, N. H. (1997). Language planning from the bottom up. In N. H. Hornberger (Ed.), *Indigenous literacies in the Americas: Language planning from the bottom up* (pp. 299–320). Berlin: Mouton de Gruyter.

Jiménez Sánchez, A. O. (1998). Mayan languages and the Mayan movement in Guatemala. Paper presented to the Latin American Studies Association, Chicago, IL, September 24–26.

King, L. (1994). *Roots of identity: Language and literacy in Mexico*. Stanford, CA: Stanford University Press.

Otzoy, I. (1996). Women, weaving, and education in Maya revitalization. In E. F. Fischer & R. M. Brown (Eds.). *Maya cultural activism in Guatemala*. Austin, TX: University of Texas Press.

Reyner, J., Cantón, G., St. Clair, R. N., & Parsons Yazzie, E. (1999). *Revitalizing indigenous languages*. Flagstaff, AZ: Northern Arizona University Centre for Excellence in Education. Available from http://jan.ucc.nau.edu/~jar/RIL

Richards, J. B. & Richards, M. (1997). Mayan language literacy in Guatemala: A socio-historical overview. In N. H. Hornberger (Ed.). *Indigenous literacies in the Americas: Language planning from the bottom up* (pp. 189–212). New York: Mouton de Gruyter.

Skutnabb-Kangas, T. (2000). *Linguistic genocide in education-or worldwide diversity and human rights?* London: Lawrence Erlbaum.

Son Chanay, E. (1999). La identidad cultural y la labor editorial. In *Literatura Indigena de America: Primer congreso* (pp. 283–287). Guatemala: Asociacion Cultural B'eyb'al.

Street, B. V. (1999). The meanings of literacy. In D. A. Wagner, R. L. Venezky, & B. V. Street (Eds.). *Literacy: An international handbook*. Boulder, CO: Westview Press.

Tollefson, J. W. (1991). *Planning language, planning in equality*. London: Longman.

Chapter 4
A New Understanding of Globalization: The Case of the Romà

Victòria Miquel-Martí and Tere Sordé-Martí

1 Introduction

Globalization has been portrayed very often as a one-faced phenomenon that should be fought against. If globalization initially was exclusively characterized as the exportation of Western imperialism to the rest of the world, more recently, it has been interpreted through different lenses. While it is true that globalization has represented the spreading of neo-liberal policies around the world, it bears many other faces that often go ignored. From this perspective, we suggest not to oppose or to defend globalization but to face the inequalities that it generates and to find advantages in the possibilities it generates. The idea is to reorient globalization through this phenomenon, trying to extend social and democratic advancements instead of abandoning them. The debate now centres on shifting this phenomenon towards a more social direction.

Globalization not only serves to enlarge markets and impose neo-liberal policies, but it has also served to extend human rights and other democratic achievements. As Sen (2002) highlights:

> Globalisation has contributed to the progress of the world, through travel, trade, migration, spread of cultural influences, and dissemination of knowledge, and understanding (including of science and technology). To have stopped globalisation would have done irreparable harm to the progress of humanity (p. 11).

Analyses that exclusively focus on the negative aspects of globalization have denied the dialogical opportunities opened up by this process that are already creating avenues of participation to globally socially excluded groups like the Romà. As a result of global mobilizations depicted by World Social Forum (WSF), the debate around globalization has moved beyond its exclusively oppositional nature. Instead of opposing it, the challenge now is to ensure that everybody, without exception, can fully participate in this process. Thus, it is necessary to develop a new understanding of globalization.

Universitat de Barcelona and Harvard Graduate School of Education

The notion of dialogic globalization, drawn from dialogical theories and practice, frames this work. Dialogic globalization refers to the extension of democracy, the achievement of freedom and equality, and the creation of social movement networks. Dialogic globalization involves the creation of a public sphere where all people participate through democratic organizations in decision-making processes through an egalitarian dialogue. Dialogic globalization has the potential of promoting new dialogic spaces where multicultural relations are reinforced and improved. In this context, those groups who have always been in the margins can join forces and take advantage of the new possibilities of this global public space. Presenting two cases, the Romí (Romaní women in Romanó) movement and the Learning Communities, we argue that dialogic globalization represents a new space for democratic participation. In this context, the Romà and other minority groups have many more opportunities of inclusion and participation than ever before and are encouraged by the expanding social horizons.

2   The Romà: A History of Globalization

Romà experienced globalization early in their history. As a people without a territory, this ethnic minority originating from India has spread around the globe since their initial exodus beginning in the 9th century. The causes of the different migratory waves are found in the different policies of various regimes where Romà resided, like the Ghaznadian Empire and the Osman Empire. The Romaní Diaspora has been the result of systematic discrimination. The nomadic condition of Romà is not a cultural feature, per se, but rather the result of the fear and the need to flee from persecutions and expulsions (Machiels, 2002). After the original exodus from India, Romà were progressively dispersed throughout Europe, and it was not until the 19th century that considerable groups of Romà began migrating to the American continent. More recently, as a result of the fall of communist regimes and the war in the Balkan area, new waves of Romà have immigrated and sought refuge in Western Europe and North America. Their history illustrates a transnational character, becoming one of the first people to go beyond the boundaries of nation-states. Romà challenge the modern concept of nation-state by proposing a new category: a transnational people unattached to any state or territory. Some have identified this feature as a new way to frame issues raised by the Romà:

> The constitution of a separate state is by no means a natural necessity, especially in modern times of intense movements and contacts. The concept of national State was historically rather a political endeavour for economical influence in a more aggressive world, than a response to a genuine national need. Accordingly, since most nations do have at least a good part of themselves in non-territorial situation, we began to explore the possibilities of affirmation in such a context, rather than to imitate XIX century patterns of 'State'. We consider that this could be a valuable contribution of Romaní thought to universal progress (Cortiade & Duka, 1994, p. 33).

Instead of claiming their own state to defend Romaní interests, the Romà have concentrated their efforts in looking for the recognition of its presence in national territories or the creation of some kind of representative body at the global level. Many initiatives have been undertaken towards creating an international organism that recognizes the legal transnational status of the Romà (Meyer, 2001). It is especially worth noting that the creation of the European Romà Forum resulted from the initiative of Ms. Tarja Halonen, the Finnish president. The Romaní organizations have responded enthusiastically to the initiative, as a series of meetings and seminars have been organized to define it. After consultation with different working groups, the forum has been created as an independent body of the Council of Europe and other institutions with the goal to fight for respect of human rights, fundamental freedoms, and the enforcement of international conventions (Scicluna, 2003; Voulasranta, 2003).

Romà are citizens of different states of the world. Estimates from the International Romaní Union say that there are 12 million spread out among all continents. The European Network Against Racism points out that there are approximately one and a half million Romà in the European Union (Machiels, 2002). Before the enlargement of the Union to the East, Spain used to be the state with the largest population of more than 630,000 (Boletín Oficial de las Cortes Generales, BOCC, 1999). The presence of Romà in many countries of the world is documented in Brazil (Da Costa, 1996), Argentina (Bernal, 2002), and Australia (Morrow, 2000), to mention some.

Despite the geographical dispersion, Romà claim the existence of a common cultural identity. This claim was publicly formulated in the World Conference against Racism celebrated in Durban:

> From the Spanish organization Union Romaní and picking up the majority feeling from the gypsy organizations of the entire world, we want to manifest our absolute unconformity with the denomination used to allude to the gypsy people in the documents that are being elaborated in the diverse Commissions of the World Conference against the Racism. When someone speaks of us he would allude to the *gypsy* people, *Romà*, *romanies*, *gitano*, *sinti* or *nomads* as if they were different people linked by common problems. From our organization, we claim respect for the only name for which the gypsies from all the world want to be known and identified which is the term "ROMÀ" – with tonic accent in the "a" as an acute word. ROMÀ is the plural of the nominative "ROM" and it means simply "GYPSIES." We are the "ROMÀ", that is to say "THE GYPSIES". (...) The gypsies from all over the world are making a great effort so that the society contemplates and accepts us as a single town, integrated for more than twelve million people who live fundamentally in Europe (10 millions) and in America (2 millions and a half). We are bearers of a common history in their origins and of an identical culture in the fundamental thing. The stubbornness of the documents editors in referring to us with multiple denominations contributes to distort still more the image that the majority society has about us, as well as to make more difficult our desire to appear in the presence of the public powers as a town that speaks with a single voice and remains united in the formulation of its fair recoveries (International Romaní Union, 2001, p.1).

The Romà are not only global because of their presence in many different places of the world, but also because of being victims of anti-gypsyism, which relegates them to the margins of all societies. Racism is still prevalent today in many areas of their life, and as Chomsky (1994) notes, "nobody gives a damn about the Gypsies" (p. 58). It is a reality that despite living in wealthy societies, Romà remain excluded everywhere they reside. Racism against them has always marked their journey: many were condemned to slavery, murdered during the Nazi Holocaust, victims of hate crimes, and inevitably trapped within a cycle of poverty.

There are only a few studies that prove the burden of such discrimination on the lives of Romà. A comparative study about the living standards among the Romà in Hungary, Bulgaria, and Romania has been developed at the Centre for Comparative Research at Yale University. The first survey uses family households as the unit of study. The findings demonstrate that there is a positive correlation between ethnicity and living standards, besides educational level and occupation (Revenga et al., 2002). Using the data from the Minorities at Risk project, Fox (2001) identifies patterns of cultural, economic, and political discrimination against the Romà. Fox points out that the Romà are exposed to many more discriminatory barriers, especially in economic spheres, than are non-Romà people. The World Bank study (Ringold et al., 2003) reports that the poverty rate found among the Romaní community is substantially higher than the rest of the population. In some parts of Central and Eastern Europe, Romà poverty rates are ten times higher than the one existing among the non-Romà population. In Spain, a Romaní person is five times more likely to live in poverty than a non-Romaní (Fundación Fomento de Estudios Sociales y de Sociologia Aplicada, FOESSA, 1998).

Education is one of the areas in which the effects of discrimination are more apparent around the globe (Gómez Alonso & Vargas, 2003). As recognized in the Organization for Security and Co-operation report, "the exclusion of Romà extends to every sphere of social life, perhaps nowhere with more far-reaching and harmful effect than in respect of schooling" (Organization for Security and Co-operation in Europe, 2000, p. 6). Throughout Europe, the Romà illiteracy rate approaches 90% of the adult population (Gheorghe & Liegeois, 1995). Research has documented school segregation (Alfageme Chao, 2001) and other forms of discrimination—exclusion from enrolment (European Roma Rights Center, 2002), above average placement in special education (Cahn & Chirico, 1999), compensatory programmes (Centro de Investigación y Documentación Educativa, 2002), below average representation in higher education (Centre of Research in Theories and Practices that overcome Inequalitites (CREA), 2001), and the absolute absence of Romaní culture in schools (Vargas & Flecha, 2000).

2.1   The Multiple Faces of Globalization

Globalization, in all its features, has become one of the most important phenomena shaping society. Globalization is a multidimensional and unavoidable phenomenon. Held and McGrew (2000) define it as follows:

> A process (or set of processes) which embodies a transformation in the spatial organization of social relations and transactions—assessed in terms of their extensity, intensity, velocity

and impact-generating transcontinental or interregional flows and networks of activity, interaction, and the exercise of power (p. 55).

The initial anti-globalization movement has evolved from new understandings of globalization that arose from the World Social Forums. Current analyses go beyond the initial division between anti-globalization and pro-globalization, advocating a new kind of globalization. Within the analysis of global resistance, for example, a wide range of demands from different ideologies can be found. Beck (2000) proposes a cosmopolitan democracy or a plural and world citizenship while others like Held (1995) talk about developing cosmopolitan social democracy.

Without ignoring the increase of inequalities and neo-liberalism, these new understandings of globalization seek alternatives to the pervasive negative effects of this process. It would be misleading to understand dialogic globalization as a Westernization of the world. On the contrary, it actually refers to processes through which each culture will be able to equally participate in the definition of a new interdependent global world. As Sen (1999) maintains, democracy is a value present in many civilizations and not a development that belongs exclusively to the Western world, as it has been very often presented. The Nobel laureate argues that democracy can be considered a universal value not because it has everyone's consent but because "people anywhere may have reason to see it as valuable" (p. 12). According to Sen, anyone will consider democracy as important. Sen argues that to consider globalization as global Westernization is a misreading. Talking about the agents of globalization, he considers that they

> are neither European nor exclusively Western, nor are they necessarily linked to Western dominance. Indeed, Europe would have been a lot poorer – economically, culturally and scientifically – had it resisted the globalisation of mathematics, science and technology at that time. And today, the same principle applies, though in the reverse direction (from West to East). To reject the globalisation of science and technology because it represents Western influence and imperialism would not only amount to overlooking global contributions – drawn from many different parts of the world – that lie solidly behind the so-called Western science and technology, but would also be quite a daft practical decision, given the extent to which the whole world can benefit from the process (2002, p. 2).

George (2003), vice-president of ATTAC (Association pour la Taxation des Transactions pour l'Aide aux Citoyens) and author of the Lugano Report, counters the criticisms formulated about the anti-globalization movement by clarifying its internationalist nature, its commitment to solidarity, and that it is working towards searching for alternatives. This fact underlines the collective dimension of the global action. Through the Internet, these developments have taken very innovative forms, not only in terms of the means of communication but also in terms of coordination, organization, and activities. Globalization can be seen either as a limit to development and to our societies' progress, or as a possibility to intensify a progressive alternative to the status quo. It is precisely our emphasis on the latter understanding that allows us to be able to talk about new opportunities for all social groups in order to participate in the social globalization process.

New challenges have appeared with respect to the participation of socially excluded people. The existence of many more avenues to participate in society does not mean that they are available for everybody. Flecha et al. (2003) point out that while the initial phase of the information society led to a process of social dualism, more recently, a shift has taken place that is characterized by the generalized effort to extend access to new opportunities for everybody. This latter aim is what becomes a key challenge in present-day society. Even though equality and solidarity have been the baseline for the articulation of many social demands, there have been historical instances where different forms of social exclusion have made it impossible for many groups to fully participate in the formulation or even to benefit from the gains obtained. Currently, there are many more opportunities to change this into a reality (Sassen, 2003).

Citizenship is increasingly disconnected from nationality because of the presence of many other non-governmental social actors that are active at a global level. These actions go beyond the boundaries of nation-states, taking new forms and incorporating traditionally excluded voices. These actors are constructing a more inclusive notion of citizenship. In the global context, the concept of presence coined by Sassen (2003) refers to the process through which traditionally invisible actors become political actors, even without having economic or social power. This notion is especially crucial for our analysis of the Romà's participation in the global world. The success of progressive projects depends entirely on their inclusiveness and ability to incorporate the voices of all the social groups without any exception, even the Romaní voice, a people who have remained invisible and silenced throughout their history.

3   Towards Dialogic Globalization

During industrialization, as Weber observed, it seemed that the process of bureaucratization would minimize any kind of human agency. Instrumental rationality dominated many spheres of human life, making any kind of emancipatory action difficult. The original communicative base of modernity was reduced to a rationality based in consciousness that limited the possibility to act upon social structures. Thus, there were two ways to de-colonize the life world from instrumental rationality. We could either eliminate any kind of rationality, or we could reorient it towards a new direction to overcome colonization. While the first one is the option taken by postmodernists that leads to the refusal of any modern related value, the second one consists in bringing agency with its communicative nature back to the centre. It is the second standpoint from which the dialogic turn in social sciences arose (Flecha et al., 2003).

Social science scholars such as Beck (1992) and Touraine (2000) argue that present-day society is moving towards a dialogic tendency in which people have to communicate through dialogue and come to agreements in order to coordinate their actions, solve daily problems, and make decisions about their lives. Giddens (1992) and Beck and Beck-Gernsheim (1995) analysed the new forms that the traditional family and intimate relationships acquire and found that dialogue plays a much more relevant role nowadays than in the industrial era. Along the same lines, Habermas (1984, 1987) explains this shift as recovering the dialogic project of the democratic revolutions, when people decided to manage themselves. Today, the bureaucratized institutions of traditional modernity and the instrumental rationality that colonized our lives are being questioned and people's communicative practices in the lifeworld are arising again. From this perspective, social agents are brought back in and become agents on a global scale. According to Habermas (1984, 1987), besides money and bureaucracy, there is a third source of social integration: solidarity. All the above-mentioned sociological analyses have shown a general trend of the struggle for the creation of many more dialogic spaces that is ongoing in homes, schools, community centres, and workplaces.

Dialogic globalization refers to the processes and initiatives that, within a global framework, are aimed at the extension of democracy and human rights through an egalitarian dialogue. Dialogic globalization opens new possibilities to end the hegemony of the Western world or the postmodern dissolution of any kind of value by offering a procedure where all voices are heard. Dialogic globalization takes into account both structural and systemic barriers that reproduce or even reinforce social inequalities and the difficulties that arise in the construction of another world.

How can dialogic globalization proliferate in a time when wars and oppression are prevalent? In the current global situation, there is a distance between the dialogic globalization that we advocate and the current situation that is experienced by the majority of Romà in the world. It is just the distance between what exists and what we wish to achieve that makes us continue down this path. When we arrive at our goal, this distance will still remain because we will then be aiming at even more egalitarian and democratic goals; the stretch between our aim and what has been used in the past is just an excuse for not fighting at all. As Freire (1997) reminds us:

> The affirmation that "things are the way they are because they cannot be otherwise" is hatefully fatalistic since it decrees that happiness only belongs to those in power … a total denouncement of fatalism is necessary. We are transformative beings and not beings for accommodation (p. 36).

Dialogic globalization has opened up new avenues of participation for many groups. The predominance of dialogic practices, or at least the *preference* for them, has entered the public and the private sphere. The Romà have not remained on the margins of this process as there are many instances in which the Romà are claiming their place in the global context. In the following section, we select two illustrative cases that show how dialogic globalization has affected the Romaní way of life. These cases demonstrate how the sociopolitical mobilization led by Romaní women, arising on a national level, has already acquired an international dimension and how the participation of the Romaní community in local-based projects has widened access to the tools of a global information society. The following cases are just two examples of how the Romà are taking advantage of the opportunities afforded by dialogic globalization in an effort to overcome their social exclusion.

3.1 The Romí Movement

As a *man of respect* (elders who have led an honest life and are considered persons
of reference) recently pointed out in a conference in Granada: "If you women shut
up, the Romà people will become mute." Romí (Romaní women) have always been
the link between the past and the future, as being responsible for carrying forth their
culture and for engaging in constant negotiations towards its transformation. Every
day, through their political and social mobilization, the Romí are disproving stere-
otypes about their gender subordination and disinterest in education. Education is
clearly viewed as being a way both to become present in society and to be able to
participate in the globalised world. The Romí movement has been one of the most
outspoken voices that challenge the idea that studying is incompatible with maintaining their identity as Romaní women (De Botton et al., 2005). Education for
children and themselves has been a central issue in political mobilization and a
clear avenue to being more present on a global scale. These women demand equal
opportunities and outcomes without having to give up their cultural identity (Flecha
& Oliver, 2004). One Romaní activist put it thus: "We try to move forward without
leaving aside our legacy, without giving up our identity. We need the support of our
families and elders … slowly, but all together. In this way, we will reach the same
point but without losing anything" (Centre of Research in Theories and Practices
that Overcome Inequalities (CREA), 2002, p. 25).

The history of the Romí movement shows how dialogic globalization has spread
and has already opened up new spaces for social participation to traditionally
excluded groups, like the Romí. In Spain, the first Romí association, named Romí,
was founded in Granada in 1990 by a group of Romí. The idea was to mobilize all
women to present a powerful front. Education was seen as a tool available to all
women to help their communities move forward. Less than 10 years later, associations have flourished around Spain, and in 1999, Kamira, the first federation of
Romí association, was created in Madrid. Kamira comprises 3,000 women from
around Spain who demand to be heard by society. This pioneer organization aims
at promoting the Romí, the Romaní culture, and a better future for their community.
These women have taken many actions to make these goals a reality: from launch-
ing support programmes in their local communities to presenting demands and
requests to the Spanish Parliament. These women have established an ongoing dialogue among themselves but also with the larger society and their communities.

Among the many demands, they claim the right for their daughters to follow
educational careers and they have started to negotiate for better conditions. The
Romí movement is an example of this potential for action, transformation, and
understanding. To many Romí, active participation in these associations means the
transformation of their private and public lives. De Botton et al. point out that there
is a negotiation process towards a major emancipation of these women. Instead of
taking mainstream feminism as a reference point, many Romí activists have started
to coin the term *Romí Feminism* to refer to the changes these women are incor-
poratingin their lives and their communities. Romí Feminism is characterized by

its emergence from the Romaní culture, and it is from this lens that Romí are contributing to the reformulation of feminism (De Botton et al., 2005). By taking part, these women are also creating changes in their community that result in a more dialogic and egalitarian one.

At an international level, major advancements towards dialogic globalization of Romà have also taken place. At the First European Congress in Seville in 1994, Romí were not included on the agenda. During the Congress, however, a group of European Romí were meeting outside, organizing a European network of Romí. At the end of the congress, these women presented a Manifesto in which among the many demands, education was one of the top priorities as an avenue for social change. In their manifesto, they demanded:

> Reinforce and develop educational measures in order to guarantee equality of opportunities to succeed for our children, sine qua non condition for their social integration as full European Union citizens (Grupo Promotor, 1994, p. 6).

The International Romà Women Network (IRWN) was launched on March 8, 2003 (International Women's Day) with the idea of improving the situation of the Romaní women and lobbying states to comply with the international conventions throughout Europe. There were women representatives from 18 countries. The IRWN serves as a forum to exchange useful information, to network with other associations, and to report human rights violations. An example of advocacy work was when IRWN launched a campaign to denounce forced sterilization of Romà women in Slovakia, or more recently, about the existence of racist statements in the definition of the term gypsy in particular dictionaries. Undoubtedly, IRWN represents a milestone in the Romí movement for the important networking task that it is currently leading, uniting, and connecting activists from all around the world.

These women are not only participants in dialogic globalization, they are making it a reality, spreading dialogic practices throughout the globe by their actions. Romí, from distant parts of the world, have united their voices in claiming their right to decide about their lives and future. In the mean time they are becoming more active, with dialogic practices becoming more common in the global context. The achievements obtained by other groups cannot be denied from them and their families any longer. European society should be accountable in regard to the treatment that Romà have received for centuries, in response to which they have been forced to take action.

3.2 Learning Communities

Dialogic globalization implies an urgent need to extend educational opportunities for all. Education and globalization involves not only access to new technologies but also a deeper transformation that requires a new understanding of the role of education in the global context. Educational systems, for example, should prepare everyone to be able to process information and to adapt to constantly changing situations.

Failure to provide access to educational opportunities represents another way of social exclusion that becomes a source of cyclical inequality. Education has become one of the major aspects that define our social positions. Some analysts have pointed out that education depends less on what happens within the boundaries of the classroom or school and more on lessons learned in the community (Soler-Gallart, 2001, 2003). Schools are not isolated centres but part of communities that, in turn, are part of the new global world. Stromquist (2002), argues that

> the time for protagonistic roles has passed. Their work will be more effective in alliance with other groups of civil society, establishing bridges that go beyond school and community, reflecting and planning with organized groups in other areas of our contemporary world, not only within the confines of the nation-state but also in venues of transnational action (p. 188).

The advocacy of education as a fundamental right and need in a global era has manifested in particular ways in the Romaní community. The Learning Communities project in Spain is shaped by this advocacy. This programme recognizes the communicative and technological needs of Romà and provides an efficient response to them (Elboj, Soler, Puigdellivol, & Valls, 2002; Gomez Alonso, 2002). The Learning Communities project has reduced school failure and dropout among the Romaní community by proving that when Romaní families see education as preparing them to better face the challenges of the current society, they become deeply committed to it. It has not only promoted future access to college of a considerable number of youths, but has also offered a completely alternative school model that allows for inclusion and the equal treatment of different cultures. This experience demonstrates than when Romaní families are part of the reformulation of the school, they become very involved and improve those segregated, low-achieving schools. The Romaní community perceives these schools as an open door to opportunities instead of an obstruction to them. It is necessary to clarify that this project has not been designed exclusively to attend to the needs of the Romaní children but to those groups that have been deprived access to a high-quality education. We offer this example because it is one of the international experiences that are contributing most in opening more educational opportunities to the Romà.

The process of transformation of a regular school into a learning community includes different phases. The first, *sensitization*, consists of engaging in training sessions with the school staff in trying to collectively reflect on the fundamental changes that must be pursued. The second phase consists in reaching a certain level of consensus and commitment to engage in this process, a key step that also defines the nature of the experience. Teachers, staff, students, families, and community members should agree to begin and support this process, otherwise its deliberative character will not be achieved. This process does not include all those who do not care or who are not committed to work for the access to education of marginalized children and families. Once these requirements are met, the community starts to dream about the learning community they want.

The *dream* of the future school, or step three, is reached through consensus by the community, with contributions including, but not limited to, technicians, social workers, leisure time educators, families, students, neighbourhood associations, business people, and city council representatives. The accomplishment of this dream is then considered a shared responsibility, not only by teachers, but by the entire community. Who else will have higher expectative roles in the children's future success than their own families? This action challenges the stereotype that Romaní families are not interested in education. Priorities are established for the upcoming year and work towards those goals commenced. The community may decide to create a public library, chess club, an Internet room, a family literacy plan, or a language centre, for example. A commission composed of teachers, family members, and/or neighbours then mobilizes human and other resources to achieve these shared goals. Schools transformed into Learning Communities have demonstrated the deficit approach systematically attributed to Romà or immigrant families to be false. They are the first to engage in the dreaming process because they are most interested in getting the best education and care for their children, given their marginalization; this is a universal phenomenon.

Deliberative democracy occurs in the community, school, and also in the classroom, which serves the dialogical nature of this work. The project conceptualized and evaluated a new alternative to the ability group, a tracking system that they refer to as *interactive groups*, which consists of grouping students with different ability levels in order to promote horizontal forms of learning (Aubert & Garcia, 2001). The solidarity of the community promoted through these interactive groups overcomes the competitiveness and stigmatization, which are a hallmark of academic tracking, and a superior level of instrumental learning has been documented (Aubert et al., 2004).

Learning Communities, which have operated for 10 years in Spain, have demonstrated how teachers and other professionals who once stigmatized schools that had a high proportion of Romà students now seek admission for their own children in such numbers that they cannot be accommodated. Since it can be inferred that these professionals, as parents themselves, also want the best education for their children, this anecdotally, yet powerfully, illustrates the perceived value of Learning Communities. Without a doubt the dialogue and educational tools provided for these Romaní children better prepare them to face the challenges of the global world which bring us face to face with possible utopias initiated from communities desperately seeking hope in a global context of historic marginalization.

4   Conclusion

The Romí movement and the learning communities' project are only two of many examples that illustrate how the Romà struggle to participate in globalization processes through dialogic encounters. These examples demonstrate the ongoing nature of dialogic globalization that is increasingly available in Spain and elsewhere. Minority groups who have always been at the social margins can join efforts and become main actors in this dialogic process. We have demonstrated how the Romà, through their social participation, are not only reinforcing the dialogic face of globalization but also moving towards overcoming marginalization. In a panel at a conference about Romaní girls' school dropout, where one of the Romaní mothers who participated in the computer laboratory was asked about her dreams, she immediately replied:

> I want to see all my *primas* [cousins] doing whatever you want [referring to those who were sitting in the audience], but those of you who can, to continue your studies in whatever you want. I also want my daughter to go to the university and to work. I want her to have the same opportunities that everybody in this world has.

Such sentiment articulates the hope of the Romà in the global era, and the crystallization of the emerging understanding in this community of the dialogic potential offered by globalization.

5 References

Alfageme Chao, A. (2001, September). Dónde y cómo están los escolares gitanos? [Where and how are Romà students]. *Diálogo Gitano*, 7–8.

Aubert, A., Duque, E., Fisas, M., & Valls, R. (2004). *Dialogar y transformar. Pedagogía Crítica del siglo XXI*. Barcelona: Editorial Graó.

Aubert, A., & Garcia, C. (2001). Interactividad en el aula. [Interactivity in the classroom]. *Cuadernos de Pedagogia*, *301*, 20–24.

Beck, U. (1992). *Risk society*. New York: Sage.

Beck, U. (2000). *Un nuevo mundo feliz. La precariedad del trabajo en la era de la globalización*. [A new happy world. The precariety of work in the globalisation era]. Barcelona: Paidós.

Beck, U., & Beck-Gernsheim, E. (1995). *The Normal chaos of love*. Cambridge: Polity Press.

Bernal, J. F. (2002). ¿Y los gitanos de Argentina? [What about the Romà from Argentina?] *I Tchatchipen*, *37*, 15–17.

Boletín Oficial de las Cortes Generales (BOCC). Diciembre 17, 1999. *Informe de la subcomisión para el estudio de la problemática del pueblo gitano*. VI legislatura. Número 520. Disponible en: http://www.fsgg.org/Informe%20subcomision.htm

Cahn, C., & Chirico, D. (1999). *A special remedy: Roma and schools for the mentally handicapped in the Czech republic country reports series*. Budapest: European Roma Rights Centre.

Chomsky, N. (1994). *Keeping the rabble in line:interviews with David Barsamian*. Edinburgh, Scotland: AK Press.

Centre of Research in Theories and Practices that Overcome Inequalities [CREA]. (2001). *Brudilla Calli: Las Mujeres Gitanas contra la exclusión. Análisis Ex-Post-Facto*. [Brudila Callí: Romaní women against exclusion. Analysis Ex-Post-Facto]. Barcelona: Instituto de la Mujer & CREA (Centre de Recerca Social i Educativa).

Centre of Research in Theories and Practices that Overcome Inequalities [CREA]. (2002). *Informe final etapa 3: La voz de la mujer gitana*. [Final report stage 3: The voice of the Romí]. Barcelona: Instituto de la Mujer, Comisión Interministerial de Ciencia y Tecnología. Ministerio de Trabajo y Asuntos Sociales. Plan Nacional de I+D+I. 2000–2003.

Centro de Investigacion y Desarrollo de la Educación [CIDE]. (2002). *Las Desigualdades de la Educación en España, II*. [The inequalities in education in Spain]. Madrid: Ministerio de Educación y Cultura, Centro de Investigación y Documentación Educativa.

Cortiade, M., & Duka, J. (1994). International Romani Union in action. *Roma*, *41*, 28–41.

Da Costa, C. (1996). Los gitanos en Brasil. [Romà in Brazil]. *I Tchatchipen*, *13*, 47–50.

De Botton, L., Puigvert, L., & Sánchez, M. (2005). *The inclusion of other women: Breaking the silence through dialogic learning*. Dordrecht, The Netherlands: Springer.

Elboj, C. P., I., Soler, M., & Valls, R. (2002). *Comunidades de aprendizaje. Transformar la educación*. [Learning Communities. Transforming education].Barcelona: Editorial Graó.

European Roma Rights Centre [ERRC]. (2002). Barriers to the education of Romà in Europe: A position paper by the European Romà Rights Center. *Romà Rights Quarterly*.

Flecha, R., Gómez, J., & Puigvert, L. (2003). *Contemporary sociological theory*. New York: Peter Lang.

Flecha, A.; Oliver, E. (2004). Romaní women and Popular Education. *Convergence, 37*(2), 7–26.

Fundacion Fomento de Estudios Sociales de Sociologia Aplicada [FOESSA]. (1998). *Las condiciones de vida de la poblacion pobre en Espana*. [The living conditions of the poor population in Spain]. Madrid: Fundación FOESSA.

Fox, J. (2001). Patterns of discrimination, grievances and political activity among Europe's Roma: A cross-sectional analysis, *Journal on Ethnopolitics and Minority issues in Europe*, 2, 2–24.

Freire, P. (1997). *Pedagogy of the heart*. New York: The Continuum Publishing Company.

George, S. (2003). The Lugano Report. London: Pluto Press.

Gheorghe, N., & Liegeois, J.-P. (1995). *Roma/Gypsies: A European minority*. London: Minority Rights Group.

Giddens, A. (1992). *The Transformation of intimacy: Sexuality, love, and eroticism in modern societies*. Cambridge, UK: Polity Press.

Gomez Alonso, J. (2002). Learning communities: When learning in common means school success for all. *Multicultural Teaching, 20*(2), 13–17.

Gómez Alonso, J., & Vargas, J. 2003. Why Romà do not like mainstream school: A voice of a people without a territory. *Harvard Educational Review*, 73(4), 559–590.

Grupo Promotor. (1994). Manifiesto de las Mujeres Gitanas Europeas. [Manifest of European Romaní Women]. *Acobá Caló*, 2(15), 6.

Habermas, J. (1984). *The theory of communicative action: Vol. 1. Reasons and the rationalization of society*. Boston, MA: Beacon Press.

Habermas, J. (1987). *The theory of communicative action: Vol. 2. Lifeworld and system: A critique of functionalist reason*. Boston, MA: Beacon Press.

Held, D. (1995). *Democracy and the global order: from the modern state to cosmopolitan governance*. Cambridge: Polity Press.

Held, D., & McGrew, A. (Eds.). (2000). *The global transformations reader. An introduction to the globalisation debate*. Cambridge: Blackwell.

IRU. (2001). *About denomination of Gypsy people in official documentation of World Conference Against Racism*. Paper presented at the World Conference against the Racism, Durban, South Africa. (accessible at: http://www.unionromani.org/new2001-09-03.htm)

Machiels, T. (2002). *Keeping the distance or taking the chances. Romà and travellers in Western Europe*. Brussels: European Network Against Racism (ENAR).

Meyer, L. H. (2001). Transnational autonomy: Responding to historical injustice in the case of the Saami and Roma peoples. *International Journal on Minority and Group Rights*, 8, 263–301.

Morrow, M. (2000). *Report from Australia*. Paper presented at the V International Romani Union Congress.

Organization for Security and Co-operation in Europe [OSCE]. (2000). *Report on the situation of the Romà and Sinti in the OSCE area*. The Hague: Organization for Security and Co-operation in Europe. High Commissioner on National Minorities.

Revenga, A., Ringold, D., & Martin Tracy, W. (2002). *Poverty and ethnicity. A cross- country study of Romà poverty in Central Europe*. (World Bank Technical Paper no.531). Washington, DC: World Bank.

Ringold, D., Orenstein, M. A., & Wilkens, E. (2003). *Romà in an expanding Europe: Breaking the poverty cycle*. Washington, DC: World Bank.

Sassen, S. (2003). *Contrageografías de la globalización. Género y ciudadanía en los círculos transfronterizos*. [Counter geographies of globalisation. Gender and citizenship in the cross-border circles]. Madrid: Traficantes de Sueños.

Scicluna, H. (2003). *Roma participation in Europe – The way forward.* Strasbourg: Council of Europe.

Soler Gallart, M., & Teberosky, A. (Eds.). (2003). *Contextos de alfabetización inicial* (Vol. 39). [Contexts of initial literacy]. Barcelona: Editorial Horsori.

Soler-Gallart, M. (2001). Lectura dialògica en la primera infància. [Dialogic literacy in early childhood]. *Guix d'Infantil, 3,* 12–14.

Sen, A. K. (1999). Democracy as a universal value. *Journal of Democracy, 10*(3), 3–17.

Sen, A. (2002). Does globalisation equal Westernization? *The Globalist.* (accessible at: http://www.theglobalist.com/DBWeb/StoryId.aspx?StoryId=2353).

Stromquist, N. (2002). *Education in a globalized world. The connectivity of economic power, technology, and knowledge.* Lanham, MA: Rowman & Littlefield.

Touraine, A. (2000). *Can we live together? Equality and Difference.* Cambridge: Polity Press.

Vargas, J., & Flecha, R. (2000). El aprendizaje Dialógico como "experto"en resolución de conflictos. *Contextos Educativos.* [Dialogic learning as expert in conflict resolution]. *Revista de Educación., 3,* 81–88.

Voulasranta, M. (2003). European Forum For Romà and travellers: From Finish initiative to the Franco-Finnish proposal. *Romà Rights, 4.*

Chapter 5
Equity Considerations in the Access to Higher Education in Central and Eastern Europe

Randal J. Zimmermann

1 Introduction

The countries of Central and Eastern Europe (CEE)[1] have emerged from many decades of authoritarian control under the communist party and state system. The educational systems in these countries were closely aligned with a centralized economic planning bureaucracy that determined levels of educational demand according to forecasts about production and services output. During this period, these educational systems were recognized for their remarkable achievements in literacy and gender parity. After the collapse of the communist system in the late 1980s and early 1990s, however, the educational infrastructure faced significant challenges in terms of maintaining quality, relevance, and accessibility in the face of declining financial state support, changing economic demands, and deteriorating physical resources. Opportunities for access to higher education have declined at a time when new economic activities and social expectations require the higher-level skills offered by higher education institutions. Data about trends in the region suggest that levels of educational attainment are decreasing and narrower segments of the population are entering tertiary levels of education. This suggests that policies and practices that once promoted equitable opportunities for access to higher education have been diminished or abandoned. At a time when these CEE countries are trying to engage in new systems of governance and participate in the global marketplace, they are failing to prepare through education increasing numbers of their population with the skills needed to be effective in world, national, and local arenas.

This chapter examines some of the historical and philosophical foundations of equity in the CEE region and explores some of the options available to policy-makers. In this context, equity can be understood to represent the qualitative elements of just, fair, and even-handed treatment that should be considered when assessing policies

University of Minnesota

---

[1] Central and Eastern Europe (CEE), in the context of this discussion, includes the countries of Bulgaria, the Czech Republic, Hungary, Poland, Romania, and Slovakia and the acronym CEE refers to the region in general terms.

J. Zajda et al. (eds.), *Education and Social Inequality in the Global Culture*.
© Springer 2008

that attempt to facilitate non-discriminatory access to opportunities for higher education. The empirical evidence is reviewed along with policy implementation issues that would offer guidance in the selection of some alternatives over other possible choices. The ethical merit and significance of other courses of actions are considered in the framework of the economic, political, and social issues present in the CEE region. Finally, the practical implications of possible policy actions are examined in terms of options that could be implemented in current circumstances by government and education institutions without requiring significant infusions of new financial resources. These options would have the effect of, at a minimum, mitigating some of the current decline in equitable access to higher education opportunities in the CEE region.

2 Background

The education system that developed during the communist period in the CEE countries effectively reached near universal adult literacy in urban and rural populations while achieving gender parity in educational access (Heyneman, 2000; Berryman, 2000). Students from these countries regularly participated in international scholastic competitions and were placed at or near the top of the field in the areas of mathematics and science. Success was inspired by the communist party ideology that for reasons of political legitimacy needed to appear responsive to the interests of the "working and peasant" classes that made up the majority of the populations in these societies (Sadlak, 1996). Under the central-command state system, a monolithic planning bureaucracy set industry and agricultural production schemes that in turn determined labour demands. The educational system was designed to align student enrolments in specialization tracks with forecasted human resource needs. Employment terms and conditions were also stipulated by the state planning apparatus. Party ideology, moreover, did not embrace the economic concepts of unemployment or underemployment. All members of society were engaged in some manner in the regional labour force and, thus, at a minimum were provided essential amenities required for their sustenance.

The perception about the eminence of equity in the educational system has persisted in government policy-making circles and within the educational systems of these countries well after the collapse of the communist system. The social narrative that perpetuates this perception has been challenged by the deep political, economic, and social changes that have occurred over the last decade and more. Data gathered by the Organization for Economic Cooperation and Development (OECD) illustrate some of the fault lines that began to emerge in the educational capacities of the CEE countries. The number of years of full-time education (excluding preschool) that an average 6-year-old child in CEE could expect to achieve in 1989 was 11.21 years. By 1997, this level declined to 10.57 years. Similar comparative data for children in Western European countries were at a level of 15.4 years in 1998 and trending upwards. There was an increase from 13.1% in 1989 to 17.8% in 1997 of participation in tertiary education as a percentage of the relevant age group. In light of the decline in overall years of education, the modest increase in participation in tertiary education can be interpreted as a response to the demand for higher-level knowledge and skills required for employment in the emerging market economies. In comparison to Western European countries where tertiary educational participation levels average 40% of the population, CEE countries lag behind in providing access to higher education and, therefore, in developing a citizenry with higher-level skills.

After the transition, centralized economic planning and control was abandoned in lieu of market liberalization and more democratic forms of government. Strict linkages between the central government and higher education systems were diminished while large state-owned industries and agricultural cooperatives were privatized or closed down. An entirely new commercial sector made up of small and medium-sized enterprises (SMEs) emerged and—similar to larger private industries—they participated in the global trade of goods and services. Success in this arena demands economic efficiency and competitiveness. State governments in CEE have long been accustomed to manipulating national and regional economic dynamics and have been slow to accept their reduced capacities for influencing the global economic markets for the benefit of their countries. Overt meddling by some state governments in the region (e.g., Romania and the Slovak Republic) has resulted in harsh consequences when international financial markets have withheld or withdrawn foreign capital investments.

The social costs to the people of the CEE have also been great. With the collapse of state-owned enterprises and agricultural collectives, millions of people were unemployed. Unemployment reached levels of 40% of the adult population in some countries. Social amenities such as housing, healthcare, and schooling that had been traditionally provided through these state enterprises could no longer be supported. The public services have been transferred to local municipal jurisdiction, privatized, or closed. Given the decline in state power over social services and economic activities, it is reasonable to question the status of equitable access to the higher education.

3   Adapting to Change

All institutions of higher education in the CEE have implemented various strategies to reposition themselves in the new political and economic landscape. These reforms have seldom been carried out under any comprehensive national or regional education system policy framework. In the case of Hungary, where the Ministry of Education developed a comprehensive blueprint for reforming their higher education system, the 1998 national elections brought in a new governing party. The reconstituted government shifted priorities away from the blueprint and, consequently, implementation was never adequately funded or achieved (Darvas, 1999).

National governments have liberalized policies concerning academic structures, governance, programming, curriculum, faculty tenure and compensation, and tuition policies. Most governments have preserved some form of the right-of-education policies that were held over from the socialist past out of fear of negative political consequences. These policies affirm the principle of free tuition for qualified students for university-level, state (public) education. Passage of parliamentary laws in recent years, however, has created loopholes that allow public higher education institutions to impose other cost-recovery fees that belie the original intent of the no-tuition policies. Private educational institutions have also entered the higher education marketplace and provide expanded choices in academic programmes for those students who can afford to pay the generally higher tuition rates. Private institutions also present a form of competition to the public institutions as they compete for the best students and for the best faculty.

National government's direct role in the higher education system has been significantly reduced due to limited financial resources and the devolution of centralized control. One consequence of the reduced state role has been to shift to the institutional level responsibility for policy-making on a range of issues including equity concerns. As higher education systems have become fragmented and have begun operating in quasi-market conditions, there are few inducements or rewards for institutions to aggressively pursue equity policies. To the contrary, the evidence suggests that educational institutions have implemented recruitment and admissions policies that strongly favour meritocracy and ability-to-pay over equity or other socially compensatory approaches (Calero, 1998). This has led to a significant narrowing of population segments, predominantly the higher socio-economic classes, entering the higher education system. From the standpoint of developing human capital at current rates, as noted earlier, the CEE countries are at a disadvantage when compared to western countries as they enter the European Union (EU).

4 Equity Considerations

Equity in access to higher education can be viewed as an issue that reaches to the roots of public higher education's mission by seeking to understand the social function of a university. If the mission is to provide higher-level education to only those students with demonstrated abilities and resources to pay the cost, then, as an institution, it has done little to distinguish itself from private sector enterprises. Some people argue, however, that higher education institutions—especially those receiving public support—have an obligation to not only educate but also serve a societal function of levelling the economic and cultural playing field. All members of society should be given the opportunity to participate in the public or civic domain of higher education that is increasingly viewed as a public entity (Gourley, 1999).

There are two philosophical views that appear to dominate discussions regarding equitable access to higher education. One view can be summarized as an approach based on *meritocratic* or *liberal* principles that offer each individual the opportunity to obtain the highest possible degree in the education system according to his/her aspirations and talent without being constrained by socio-economic background, race, sex, or religion. Equality is proportional to individual initial possibilities. This might be thought of as an equal access to opportunities (de Vuyst, 1999) (P. 94).

The second philosophical view is presented as an *egalitarian* approach that rejects the meritocratic view on the grounds that it fails to deliver the intended results. The egalitarian approach prefers to focus on policies and strategies that will enhance equal access to opportunities. The emphasis is on the equality of outcomes rather than equitable strategies for inputs into the educational system. This philosophy requires a comprehensive and systematic set of considerations in terms of equality of resources and inputs at all levels of education. Implicit to achieving equality of opportunity is the assumption that a given society possesses enough social cohesion and shared values to drive the public policy and political decisions needed to provide adequate levels of inputs and resources across the entire educational system. This approach is reflected in the opportunities-to-learn standards advocated by Darling-Hammond and Ancess (1996) for American schools.

Equity in access to higher education has generally been promoted through three different, but not necessarily separate, tracks: curriculum, selection, and finance. Examples of *curriculum* approaches would include differentiation of subjects (i.e., higher-level skills vs. vocational orientation), use of distance technology, and pedagogical methods. *Selection* encompasses manipulating criteria for admissions through application of entrance examinations, maturity tests, past academic performance, or other criteria related to demographic characteristics. *Financial* strategies would consider policies and programmes that affect tuition rates, or grants and loans made either to the educational institution or student. There is a paucity of published research in international journals about these complex changes in the political, economic, and social arenas in the CEE though over a decade has passed since the fall of communism in the region. There is, however, a modest amount of published research emerging that addresses equity issues in the context of higher education in other developed and developing countries that suggest which policies are most relevant and practical for consideration in the CEE region. In reviewing this literature, the main findings that bear relevance to this discussion are related to socio-economic status of families. As Lewis and Dundar (1999) note:

> One of the best-known findings of educational attainment research is that the student's socioeconomic status (SES) plays an important role. Correlation between socioeconomic background and schooling appears present in both developed and developing countries. It explains an important part in existing inter-generationally transmitted socioeconomic inequality in both types of nations (p. 348).

An additional finding related to SES in extant scholarship is the significance of family resources available for education. As Mora (1997) illustrates:

> From the point of view of the human capital model ... family investment in their children is constrained by family resources—both economic and educational—and they will be able to invest more if they have more resources to spend. A significant fact is that whereas the influence of parental educational levels is strong in the analysis made in the United States, it seems to be even more substantial in other countries with different cultural and/or economic structures (p. 236).

These key findings suggest that the socio-economic background and level of educational attainment in the family of students are the primary factors found to influence and, to a lesser extent, predict the probability of entrance into higher education.

This finding has been shown to be valid across several countries and among differing cultural contexts (Lewis & Dundar, 1999).

Governments eager to demonstrate a commitment to increasing educational opportunity often pursue the quantitative expansion of higher education delivery systems. The decision about where and what type of institutions to establish, however, becomes overwhelmed with political considerations and often leads to many smaller institutions being created that have inadequate staffing and institutional resources to support the programmes they offer. This reinforces perceptions that increasing equity comes at the expense of quality in academic programmes. Increasing access to education through distance technologies is another method that has been implemented and studied. One of the most successful applications of distance technology can be seen in Thailand where they established two 'open' universities during the 1970s. Created to provide access to education in primarily poor rural sections of the country, open universities have shown qualified success in comparison to the highly selective public university system by increasing participation levels from poor, rural students. As Eisemon and Salmi (1995) found, 22% of open university students are from poor rural areas compared to 11% attending public universities. This accomplishment, however, is tempered by the fact that poor, rural dwellers account for 66% of the Thai population while, comparatively, the urban middle class and poor represent 21% of the Thai population, yet account for 55% of student enrolment in higher education. The case of Thailand suggests that while distance education may have the potential to increase access to education *geographically*, it does not necessarily do so in an equitable manner.

Another method to increase equitable access is to allow private sector institutions to establish higher education programmes without central government affiliation. Private institutions are driven by market forces and, as a result, seldom find incentives or rewards for promoting equitable access for students from demographically diverse backgrounds. In Latin America where the partial privatization of higher education strategy was pursued, it has led to what is called the "double injustice" that allowed the most privileged students in countries like Chile, Brazil, and Venezuela to move from top secondary schools to free public universities and left the less privileged students to pay for an inferior education available to them only through substandard private institutions. The final method that can be employed is direct funding from the government to higher education institutions in the form of grants to promote programmes to improve the access of specific groups that are under-represented in the higher education system. While the objectives of this type of funding are laudable, the administration and execution of these programmes both at the government and institution levels are vulnerable to political and bureaucratic manipulations that obscure the final results and, consequently, reduce the overall efficacy of this strategy.

Gender access is one dimension of equity that does not appear to be a significant problem in the CEE. Participation rates for women, as noted previously, were at parity under the communist system and this trend does not appear to have been affected by the economic and governmental transition in the region. Table 5.1 demonstrates that over the 10-year period, 1985–1995, the rates of female participation in tertiary education equaled or exceeded the rates of male participation.

Some policy options for decision makers in this region to consider for promoting more equity in access to higher education opportunities will now be explored along with practical implementation considerations.

5 Policy Considerations

What emerges from the research about which factors influence the probability of student matriculation in higher education is the positive correlation between the socio-economic status and educational attainment of a student's family and his/her entry into higher education. This appears to hold true for developed and developing countries (Lewis & Dundar, 1999). As such, policies that have the objective of increasing access and participation rates of students from disadvantaged circumstances will have to mitigate the influence of lower socio-economic status and educational attainment in families. One traditional method governments have used to promote access to higher education is to subsidize part or all of the tuition costs. This is effective for increasing enrolment rates because it has been shown that demand flexibility to tuition rates is greater than to other private costs of higher education (Calero, 1998). But unless discounts are targeted to specific groups within the population through methods of positive discrimination based on economic or minority status, affluent students will often benefit due to their disproportional representation in higher education.

Educational loans are often viewed as a potentially effective means for facilitating greater participation in higher education from traditionally under-represented groups within a country. The World Bank, among others, has promoted loan schemes in developing countries as a device to facilitate cost recovery for educational institutions while reducing dependence on government support. This policy was further justified as a means of achieving significant equity benefits by targeting loans to qualified students from under-represented groups. In practice, however, loan programmes frequently resulted in a series of negative consequences. In terms of cost recovery, institutions found that once they raised tuition to cover a greater percentage of the instructional costs, they became less attractive to potential students and application rates dropped (Eisemon, 1995). Even increasing the loan amounts to compensate for the higher tuition levels created unacceptable risks for students who feared the burden of repayment would be overwhelming if future income was not adequate for repayment of the loans. This was especially true for students from lower socio-economic strata. In several countries like Kenya and Ghana, the loan default rates reached as high as 81% (Eisemon). The international experience suggests, therefore, that loan schemes have a number of unintended negative consequences. Offering direct grants in the form of scholarships to qualified students of high academic ability from economically and educationally disadvantaged backgrounds have been highly effective in several countries studied by the World Bank (2004).

Higher education policy-making has undergone significant change in the aftermath of political and economic transitions in the CEE. The national governments' relationships to higher education institutions have become more supervisory and rely more heavily on offering incentives for desired actions rather than issuing directives or intervening in the affairs of educational institutions. Higher education institutions, consequently, can no longer depend on the patronage of the state government to provide stable funding and exclusive rights of providing educational services. A very complex network of relationships that each higher education institution must foster with external and internal agents, stakeholders, and actors with influence over policy and funding decisions is now emerging. The increased complexity and pluralistic character of the environment surrounding higher education systems were also recognized by Darvas (1999) who wrote that

> the analysis of change has progressed from discussion of simple functions and coherent structures to the analysis of various, often conflicting, interests, objectives and trade-offs in policy making, all resulting from the multiplicity of actors, stakeholders and other participants in higher education (p. 164).

The policy-making environment in higher education throughout the CEE has become crowded with many agents that have a vested interest in advocating one position or policy over another.

Under previous regimes the actors were primarily from the communist party, with interests external to the educational institution, or factions representing different internal groups (i.e., administrators, faculty, students, and workers). Previously, parents, community representatives, employers of students, not to mention representatives of minorities or disadvantaged groups (who were not officially recognized) had no voice in the policy arena. This has now changed. These groups now exert influence in subtle and direct ways. During the former regimes, claims of educational equity were made but never challenged or verified. The agents and stakeholders that represent the interests of those members of society who felt excluded from access to the higher education system can now exert influence and political pressure to see that their concerns are addressed in the policy-making arena.

Darvis (1999) has also concluded that the notion of "change of higher education institutions as evolutionary is analytically flawed because it assumes the existence of simple causal relationships" (p. 161). He challenges the appropriateness of applying conventional approaches to policy analysis in a manner consistent with Jenkins-Smith and Sabatier (1994) as the stages heuristic. Intrinsic to this approach are the assumptions that policy develops in sequential or linear stages and rationality drives the solution choices. Scholars of political theory and public policy analysis have also challenged these assumptions, maintaining that the policy-making process is more complex and unpredictable (Schlager & Blomquist, 1996). This uncertainty is metaphorically represented by Kingdon's (1985) concept of a "policy primeval soup" (p. 128). The concept of policy primeval soup can be understood by thinking of policy ideas as floating around in communities (i.e., soup) and that these ideas collide and compete with each other until, through a kind of natural selection process, some survive and emerge in confluence with several other factors (e.g., technical feasibility, fit with dominant values, anticipation of future constraints) that position the idea as an acceptable solution for a policy problem.

Another useful way to understand the complexity of the policy development process is analysis through the Advocacy Coalition Framework (ACF) model developed by Jenkins-Smith and Sabatier (1994). This model focuses on the multiple actors and related factors that influence the policy process of change over a span of years, usually a decade or more. The analysis seeks to identify the range of actors that engage in the policy process by forming *coalitions* based on shared beliefs, values, or perceptions of problems that compel the coalition to *advocate* the choice of a policy option (or set of policies) over another (others). Given the broad definition of advocacy coalitions, the ACF reflects the complex and pluralistic nature of the policy-making process.

6   Analysis

Returning to the development of equity policy for higher education in the CEE, one could say that equity is an issue that is floating in the policy community. As a policy issue, equity has not fully emerged because a critical mass of stakeholders has not converged as a coalition to advocate for equity considerations in higher education policy and funding decisions at the institutional and government levels. The CEE region has shared a common experience through the imposition of single-party, communist rule for a significant period of time during the 20th century. The 27 countries that make up the CEE and former Soviet Union have all experienced this period in very different ways, however. The CEE countries only experienced communist rule for a period of approximately 45 years following the end of World War II.

The general trend has been for these countries to experience more rapid reconstruction of their economies and related social systems as compared to the republics of the former Soviet Union, which have struggled more with building institutions in support of market economics and democracy since this is an entirely new undertaking. Moreover, this region contains a bewildering range of ethnic, religious, and cultural diversity. In the Russian Federation, there are currently 9 official languages of instruction and a total of 87 languages are used in other elements of the instructional programmes (Heyneman, 2000). In the diverse histories, cultural and ethnic characteristics have presented formidable obstacles to overcome in the process of building new nations. The pace of development in these countries varies widely, which underscores the importance of appreciating the relative instability of the region when considering the development of educational policies.

In terms of international lending for development assistance, the World Bank has classified the CEE region and its education sector as having higher than average risks due to fiscal, legal, and policy environments that are less predictable than other regions (Berryman, 2000). This assessment severely restricts the level of funding international agencies like the World Bank will make available to assist the higher education sector in strengthening institutional capacities and promoting compensatory

programmes to encourage social equity. The task before the countries of the CEE is
to build nations based on the principles of democracy, open society, and a liberal
market economy. These countries face these challenges in common, however, and
there is a consensus in the scholarly literature that, at a minimum, two attributes of an
open society must be developed to foster economic growth (Heyneman, 2000;
Berryman, 2000). First, civic institutions (government, courts, schools, and community
organizations) must develop strong, effective, and transparent processes to attract
necessary domestic and foreign investment. Second, the creation of shared values and
a commitment across all segments of society to the rules of social participation must
be nurtured. These two attributes build the necessary social cohesion and capital
required to maintain society through self-regulation and, thus, reduce the transition
costs of economic and social interactions.

Schools can play an important role in socializing children to the rights and
responsibilities of citizenship and developing the capacities and perspectives that
support voluntary adherence to shared social rules. It is recognized that higher education systems in CEE have a critical function to ensure that all students leave
school competent in foundation skills and have the ability to apply higher-order
cognitive thinking skills. Failure to achieve this, consequently, will leave entire
generations of young people virtually unemployable (Berryman, 2000). Equity of
access to higher education, as noted by Teichler (1999), "is considered even more
important at a time when higher education is becoming the norm for the majority
of the population because educational disadvantage could lead to social exclusion"
(p. 297). The economic, political, and social consequences from excluding segments of the population will serve to undermine the ethical and moral principles
these countries are striving to foster.

The transition process has left all national governments in the CEE with less
revenue to directly support the higher education systems in their countries. As
a result of the reduced financial connections, governments have modified their
relationships with higher education institutions by becoming more supervisory
and less interventionist (Eisemon, 1995). This has eroded the ability of governments
to sustain their commitment to equity and has left these policies to the discretion
of higher education institutions. There are, however, at least a few policy options
available to governments and education institutions that could preserve some
elements of equitable access to higher education opportunities. On the governmental level, enacting laws to permit the creation of private education
institutions will—at a minimum—increase the quantity of educational supply
and choice for students.

The costs associated with attending private institutions and the quality of the
academic programmes are a cause for concern regarding equitable access. It is
conceivable, though, that absorbing more students into private institutions would
open more places in public institutions that have the ability to provide free tuition
to qualified students from disadvantaged circumstances. Another option that could
mitigate inequity in access to higher education is for state governments to shift
direct subsidies for higher education away from educational institutions and make

these funds available to students through grants-in-aid or scholarships, guaranteed loans, and tuition discounts based on socio-economic considerations, the various effects of which have been considered herein. These options do not necessarily require additional revenues and would be constrained by current levels of government and institutional funding. Some of these policies are, in fact, already in place in some CEE countries and could be adopted by others.

7 Conclusion

All CEE countries have acknowledged the principle of the right to higher education for their citizens and the importance of equity in access to higher education, assenting to the United Nations Educational, Scientific and Cultural Organization (UNESCO) World Declaration on Higher Education for the Twenty-first Century (1998a). The international donor assistance community working in the region, as represented by the World Bank, has also made equity in access to higher education a priority for future loans and technical support (Berryman, 2000). These are indeed encouraging signs. Success in restoring and extending the reputation of the equitable system of higher education in the CEE region will only be achieved through the emergence of committed, persistent, and successful coalitions that will advocate equity policies on behalf of the disenfranchised and disadvantaged groups within and across this region.

The empirical evidence suggests that the socio-economic status and levels of educational attainment in the families of students are the most important characteristics to consider when formulating policies that promote and maintain equitable access to higher education. Policy options for achieving equity in access can be categorized in three general areas that include curriculum, selection, and finance. Of these categories, international experience has shown that the most effective policies for promoting equitable access to higher education are *financial*. Grants-in-aid made directly to students based on merit and consideration of the family financial resources appear to be the most effective way to increase the participation from disadvantaged segments of the population.

The importance of implementing policies that promote equity in access to higher education opportunities in the CEE is to ensure that all segments of the population acquire the cognitive and social skills necessary to participate in the regional and global market economy. Additionally, the countries in the CEE region need the engagement and contributions from all segments of the population in the development of the local and national civic institutions that form the basis of democratic governance. The complexity of reforming the higher education systems in CEE countries has only recently gained the attention of Western academe and international assistance agencies. The dynamics of the public policy-making arena, private sector relationships with academia, programme quality, alignment with labour markets, and promoting equity in levels of participation by disadvantaged populations are all topics for further research and analysis.

Deleeck (as cited in de Vuyst, 1999) introduced the concept of *The Matthew Effect*, a reference to Matthew 25:29 (Revised Standard Version): "For unto every one that hath shall be given, and he shall have abundance: but from him that hath not shall be taken away even that which he hath." Deleeck invokes this ecclesiastical reference to suggest how the benefits of government social programmes proportionally benefit the affluent rather than the poor due to unforeseen social, cultural, and political factors. As the higher education systems in CEE countries have struggled with reforming their institutions, equity concerns have been marginalized to the disadvantage of poor, and typically rural, populations. Only through effective policies that value and promote equity in higher education access will all segments of society benefit from the promise of democracy and the free market system.

8 References

Berryman, S. E. (2000). *Hidden challenges to education systems in transition economies* (1st ed.). Washington, DC: World Bank.

Calero, J. (1998). Quasi-market reforms and equity in the financing of higher education. *European Journal of Education, 33*(1), 11–20.

Darling-Hammond, L., & Ancess, J. (1996). Democracy and access to education. In R. Soder (Ed.), *Democracy, education, and the schools* (pp. 151–181). San Francisco, CA: Jossey-Bass.

Darvas, P. (1999). Higher education development in transitional societies. In J. Brennan , J. Fedrowitz , M. Huber & T. Shah (Eds.), *What kind of university?* (pp. 160–170). Buckingham, UK: SRHE and Open University Press.

de Vuyst, J. (1999). Making the educational system more equal. In J. Brennan , J. Fedrowitz , M. Huber & T. Shah (Eds.), *What kind of university?* (pp. 94–101). Buckingham, UK: SRHE and Open University Press.

Eisemon, T. O., & Salmi, J. (1995). *Increasing equity in higher education: Strategies and lessons from international experience*. Washington, DC: World Bank.

Gourley, B. M. (1999). Against the odds. In J. Brennan, J. Fedrowitz, M. Huber & T. Shah (Eds.), *What kind of university?* (pp. 84–93). Buckingham, UK: SRHE and Open University Press.

Heyneman, S. P. (2000). From the party/state to multiethnic democracy: education and social cohesion in Europe and Central Asia. *Educational Evaluation and Policy Analysis, 22*(2), 173–191.

Jenkins-Smith, H. C., & Sabatier, P. A. (1994). Evaluating the advocacy coalition framework. *Journal of Public Policy, 14*(2), 175–203.

Kingdon, John W. (1985). *Agendas, Alternatives, and Public Policies*. Boston: Little, Brown.

Lewis, D. R., & Dundar, H. (1999). Equity, quality and efficiency effects of reform in Turkish higher education. *Higher Education Policy, 12*, 343–366.

Mora, J.-G. (1997). Equity in Spanish higher education. *Higher Education, 33*, 233–249.

Sadlak, J. (1996). The development of higher education in Eastern and Central Europe in the aftermath of recent changes. In Z. Morsy & P. G. Altbach (Eds.), *Higher education in an international perspective: critical issues* (pp. 157–168). New York & London: Garland .

Schlager, E., & Blomquist, W. (1996). A comparison of three emerging theories of the policy process. *Political Research Quarterly, 49*(3), 651–672.

Teichler, U. (1999). Higher education policy and the world of work: Changing conditions and challenges. *Higher Education Policy, 12*, 285–312.

UNESCO. (1998a). *World declaration on higher education for the twenty-first century: Vision and action* . Paris: UNES CO.

UNESCO. (1998b). *World statistical outlook on higher education: 1980–1995*. Paris: UNESCO.

The World Bank. (2004). World Development Indicators 2004. Washington, DC.

Appendix

Table 5.1 Number of students (in thousands) and percentage female students, 1985–1995 (UNESCO, 1998b)

Region	1985			1990			1995		
	MF	M	F	MF	M	F	MF	M	F
CEE Countries in transition	36.5	33.1	40.0	36.2	33.5	39.0	34.2	30.7	37.7

Chapter 6
The Process of Inclusion/Exclusion in Brazilian Schools: Data from Reality

Marta Luz Sisson De Castro[1] and Janaina Specht Da Silva Menezes[2]

6.1 Introduction and Context

This chapter will argue that certain social policies aimed at the inclusion of pupils within Brazil's educational system can have an effect that is contrary to what was intended. Drawing on data collected in the municipal education system of the state of Rio Grande do Sul, this chapter will focus on policies regarding school meals, pupil transportation, and school violence that can simultaneously be inclusionary and exclusionary by facilitating the inclusion of pupils within municipal schools, while excluding them from a quality education.

To understand how such a social and educational paradox can occur it is important to understand the context within which it evolved, beginning with the structural conditions of municipal education in the state of Rio Grande do Sul, which changed significantly during the period following the 1988 Constitution. At this time, a significant number of municipalities became independent and were free to develop their own educational system. In general, the schools had poor infrastructure and were unable to offer meals to large numbers of pupils due to poorly equipped kitchens, inadequately trained cooks, and unsuitable cafeteria to serve food. This situation created great pressure on school principals to find additional ways to serve good meals to their pupils, and with scarce resources, this new school function served to divert them from their focus on teaching and learning.

Moreover, making school transportation accessible to pupils in rural areas created a new demand on the budgets of the municipal system, often characterized by a large number of small municipalities with less than 10,000 inhabitants. The municipal education system bought buses or vans, hired drivers, and had to pay fuel and maintenance expenses. In some municipalities the services were outsourced to companies paid by the municipalities. But no matter what the solution chosen, all were too costly for municipalities' tight budgets. Thus, the implementation of these policies in association with the work conditions, salary and educational level of elementary

[1] Pontífícia Universidade Católica do Rio Grande do Sul

[2] Universidade Federal do Pará

J. Zajda et al. (eds.), *Education and Social Inequality in the Global Culture.*
© Springer 2008

school teachers led to the inclusion of pupils in the educational system, but to their exclusion from quality education. Issues of school violence that emerged from the data were yet another factor prompting exclusion from quality education, and must be identified as a relevant factor in an environment that encouraged exclusion. Moreover, vandalism and assaults on the school grounds and the formation of gangs and drug dealing within the school environment worked in concert to produce negative effects on the pupils who had to learn to live with fear.

An empirical study carried out in the municipal education system of the state of Rio Grande do Sul between 1997 and 1999 provides evidence for the central argument of this chapter. A survey with all Secretaries of Education at the municipal level (Secretários Municipais de Educação, SMEs[4]), was performed in 1994, and a sample of 22 respondents from the state of Rio Grande do Sul was selected using the criteria of population size and date of foundation of each municipality. Each municipality was visited, and interviews were conducted with the municipality's Secretary of Education and principals. At least one school was visited in each municipality.

The purpose of the qualitative study was to understand the management of municipal education. Data were collected through interviews with the Secretary of Education and principals, visitation of schools, and analysis of education plans and documents about the administration of local education. The study was designed to understand factors affecting the management of municipal education. A major analysis of interviews by educational management category was conducted and a second more in-depth analysis of relevant themes was completed. In all 17 municipalities studied, the question of valuing and educating teachers was mentioned. School transport was a problem for 14 municipalities, and school meals were a concern of 10 municipalities. Moreover, the study identified four levels of interaction affecting the management of municipal education. The first was the personal level, and was associated with the person acting as Secretary of Education, including his education and professional experiences. The second level of interaction was the organizational level, and was related to the development of resources within the municipal system, including the number and size of schools, and the number of teachers and their qualifications. The third level was the interaction of the education municipal systems with other institutions in the community, while the fourth level was related to social systems as a whole, and how they affected the educational management of municipal education. The question of poverty, value crisis, violence, drugs, decreasing role of the state and resources, new education legislation, and the digital divide were salient themes related to educational enactment.

The results indicated a complex, dynamic process giving shape to local education through the interaction of the four levels, as well as the structural conditions of the schools, with the organization of the system being crucial to the educative aim. In the main, municipalities that had more resources were better organized, and had better trained teachers who were more able to offer good education (Castro, 2001). A key point to be emphasized is that greater investments need to be made in Brazilian education in order to break the cycle of low funding, low salaries, and poor student performance. Otherwise Brazilian education will continue to be of low

quality. The chapter begins with the argument that globalisatio᾽   ∞∞
effect on developing countries such as Brazil. Among the cc
most negative is the effect on the role of education for the pɾ
inequality, the schools have assumed a welfare role. The argɩ
oped by analyzing school policies that focus on the provisioη ᴗ.
transportation, the violence of the school environment, and the improνᴗ.
teacher remuneration and working conditions.

6.2   Issues of Globalization

While patterns of globalization have led to new levels of economic and technological development, a significant proportion of the world's population has not
benefited from these processes, and exclusion has resulted. This is a contradiction
to the traditional neoliberal position that links the economy to social development.
According to Assmann and Sung (2000), this neoliberal belief "that modernization
and economic growth is the way to solve social problems is still fashionable"
(p. 87, M. L. S. Castro & J. S. S. Menezes, trans.). Furthermore, these authors suggest that economic development and social development are not directly related
variables, emphasizing that "in a market society like ours, to be unemployed, without the help of the State or family members, means to be excluded from the spaces
and relationships that enable one to live in a dignified manner" (p. 88, M. L. S.
Castro & J. S. S. Menezes, trans.). Developing countries, such as Brazil, are under
strong pressure because this international model of development eliminates people
from the work force and contributes to increasing poverty.

A study performed by the Organization of American States (1998) on education
in Latin America shows that most children (93%) in the 7–12 age group were
enrolled in some level or type of schooling. An analysis of the data indicates that
Latin America is beginning to provide some types of social care which are generally extended to all children at this age level. In spite of these good intentions, this
kind of initiative does not necessarily mean a reduction in social exclusion, which
can be reinforced and expressed in other forms both within and beyond the school
limits. As pointed out by Coraggio (2000):

> All have access to elementary school, but there are elementary schools with wide variations
> in quality, a difference which is hidden under the appearance of a common national school
> certificate. In this case, the appearance of 'for all' dissipates, and the dualism of the model
> becomes evident. A right supposedly universal is exerted in one way by a first class citizen
> (if it is acquired by means of income) and in another way by a second class citizen (if it is
> gained by public action) (p.90, M. L. S. Castro & J. S. S. Menezes, trans.).

In this sense, Assmann (1996) clearly shows three basic functions of schools in the
present-day world that can counteract the exclusion generated by illiteracy:

> There are three types of illiteracy that have to be defeated today: that of reading-writing
> (knowing how to read and write), sociocultural (knowing in what type of society one lives,
> for instance, knowing the market mechanisms), and technological (knowing how to interact

with complex machines). Any school that lacks competence in one of these aspects is socially backward (p. 22, M. L. S. Castro & J. S. S. Menezes, trans.).

The broadening of the education system in Brazil and Latin America does not ensure that the school will offer an education that will overcome these three types of illiteracy. Furthermore, in the specific case of Brazil, despite the continuous growth of educational care for groups entitled to compulsory education, there are still many who do not even manage to get a place in a school. According to data presented in the National Plan of Education (Plano Nacional de Educação, PNE), 2.7 million children aged 7–14 were not enrolled in any type of school in 1996. On the basis of statistical results, the following questions emerge: Is it possible for youngsters, mostly from the lower-income classes, to reflect, react, and change their reality? What function, if any, will they be able to perform in the internationalized market? These questions set the scene for the reflection that follows:

> The exclusion of children from school at the appropriate age, either by government neglect or by omission of the family and society, is the most perverse and irreversible form of social exclusion. It denies a basic right of citizenship and reproduces the circle of poverty and lawlessness by taking away from millions of Brazilians any prospect for the future. In most situations, the fact that there are children out of school does not have as its determining cause the deficit of places at school. It is actually related to the precariousness of teaching and the conditions of exclusion and social lawlessness within which large segments of the Brazilian population live (Programa Nacional de Educación (PNE), 2001, p. 6, M. L. S. Castro & J. S. S. Menezes, trans.).

Superimposed on these issues is the fact that Brazil is no longer considered a poor country, although it has one of the worst income distributions in the world. "International comparison using per capita income places Brazil among the richest developing countries, and, therefore, does not allow it to be classified as a poor country" (Barros, Henriques, & Mendonca (2000), p. 126, M. L. S. Castro & J. S. S. Menezes, trans.). In this context, social exclusion appears as one of the new and perverse faces of globalization.

It is generally perceived that two exclusionary processes occur concurrently. One originates in the sociopolitical and economic context within extra-school conditions that render access to, and retention in, the educational system either difficult or impossible. The other is related to intra-school conditions, represented by quality indicators expressed in public and private schools by high failure rates, and by the difficulty in accepting cultural differences related to language, gender, or race.

It is nothing new to state that Brazilian education policies are based on the conditions set by the World Bank, resulting in discursive homogeneity between their agents and Brazil's. Since 1990, the Bank has declared that its major objective is "the attack on poverty" and, consequently, the attack on social exclusion. What one notices, however, is that its investments in the social sector aim to prevent situations from becoming politically volatile, which would put at risk political support for structural adjustments. These social policies, characterized by the expression "for all"—health, water, sanitation and education for all—actually do not include jobs, and therefore do not include income for all (Coraggio, 2000). These are basic conditions to fight inequalities and achieve citizenship. Policies to fight exclusion must be based on a serious project that seeks to "deconcentrate" income, a basic factor for reducing social inequalities. One should recall Cervantes who wrote "where there are inequalities there is no freedom", especially when we want to emancipate people from their social exclusion.

The acknowledgement of the problems of poverty and exclusion in a given context can support the search for feasible solutions and the reorganization of forms of resistance and struggle. Thus, this study constitutes an initial attempt to construct a vision of the social exclusion process related to the school environment. It begins by discussing perspectives of various SMEs in the state of Rio Grande do Sul. The data used in the analyses were collected in two surveys carried out previously by one of the authors.

While it is beyond the scope of this chapter to comment on all topics related to social exclusion, it will focus on school welfare programs as related to meeting the nutritional and transportation needs of elementary school students. While transportation and school meals were originally conceived as policies to fight students dropping out of school or failing to pass, surveys carried out with the Secretaries of Education (SMEDs) revealed that spending time and resources in welfare activities often took educational managers away from their main responsibilities, the political-pedagogical process. The contradiction of these policies is that while facilitating the inclusion of youngsters in schools, it excludes them from an educational process of equal quality for all.

This chapter will also discuss the issue of drugs and violence within the schools because these factors reflect a broad process of social exclusion. Thus, exclusion is not simply a problem identified among pupils from less privileged social classes, but is also problematic for professional educators, affecting both teacher training and remuneration. The discussion which follows will posit that social issues are shaping educational processes, and will suggest the need to salvage the important inclusive role that can be played by education for pupils from lower income classes.

6.3   School as a Venue for Welfare

For several reasons the Brazilian public school has gradually become the worker's school, marked by its welfare character that makes the work of an educator more complex, and very often more difficult. The fight for better salaries and working conditions led the teachers in the state to several strikes during the 1980s, and a significant number of middle class pupils left the public schools whenever the parents could afford the payments to private institutions. Moreover, the remuneration of teachers in the state public system in the last 15 years has drastically declined leading to a deterioration of the quality of human resources in the educational system. The area where the school is located determines who will attend that school, and public schools located in the outskirts of the cities tend to have very poor pupils. These factors help to explain the social welfare character of public education in the Brazilian context:

Besides its pedagogical purposes, the school has social responsibilities that extrapolate teaching and learning, especially when the pupils come from poor families. In order to ensure that learning takes place it becomes necessary to broaden the provision of welfare, above all in the low income municipalities. Certain procedures such as financial support for paying school meals, school books and school transport are often adopted (PNE, 2001, p. 6, M. L. S. Castro & J. S. S. Menezes, trans.).

The perspective of most local governments is to fight poverty with economic approaches to achieve economic results. Attention to issues of citizenship and social welfare has received less support. A previous study done by Castro (1995) showed that the explosion of social problems in the school context led to higher levels of student exclusion. If the public school seeks to fulfil its social role by providing the right to education for those who are marginalized in a capitalist society, it must take on additional roles and responsibilities beyond those traditionally expected within an academic setting. While this chapter will discuss the school's welfare role with regard to school meals and school transportation, it needs to be emphasized that the authors are not opposed to the use of the school, a public social space, as an instrument to promote welfare measures and to fight exclusion. The purpose here is to show the complexity of the role of the school when it takes up responsibilities associated with the well-being of pupils, and how imbricate are inclusion and exclusion, two apparently dichotomous variables.

6.4   School Meals

The offer of social services is a recent development within Brazilian public schools and it is an important factor that draws children to school and guarantees attendance. For some children, school meals are the only regular meals they receive in a given day. Within this setting, this discussion will focus on the legal basis for this policy and it will analyze selected data from an empirical study that posits that offering school meals is a factor that fosters inclusion because students come to school to eat. The administrative effort to offer meals at school reduces the time and resources that would otherwise be invested in educational services. Moreover, funding of school meals and other social programs within Brazil's schools are generally insufficient and create new dilemmas for the schools.

In an attempt to reduce the high rates of school failure and contribute to the improvement of teaching quality, the Federal Constitution of 1988 determined that it was the duty of the State to "provide care to the student, at the elementary level, by means of supplementary programs of teaching/learning material, transportation, meals and health care" (Art.208, Clause VII). Considering that the provision of school meals might reduce the school dropout rate, the Ministry of Education and Sports, by means of the National Fund for Development of Education (Fundo Nacional de Desenvolvimento Escolar, FNDE[6]), established the National Program of School Meals (Programa Nacional de Alimentação Escolar, PNAE), which provides for "the largest food supplementation program of the world"(Federation of

Municipalities, Rio Grande do Sul, FAMURS, 1997, p. 39). The objective of this program is to provide 15% of the daily requirements of calories and proteins for public pre-school and elementary school pupils.

The PNAE also aims to "use the offer of at least one adequate daily meal, to improve the learning conditions, establish good eating habits—educate people for nutrition and reduce dropout rates and school failure" (Ministry of Education and Culture (MEC) 2001, p.1).

Currently, the per capita value of school meals correspond to Brazilian Real (R$)0.13/pupil/day at the elementary level, and R$0.06/pupil/day at the pre-school level and in programs sponsored by philanthropic organizations. As these amounts have been frozen since 1995, they have a long way to go to ensure higher standards of quality for school meals. The PNAE meal program is only a supplemental program, however, and it requires that states and municipalities will complement the program with funding. Such expectations, which appear logical and just, may be very unfair for the poorer states and municipalities which have very low tax revenues and very little possibility of complementing scanty federal funding. Moreover, this policy ignores the different social and economic differences throughout the nation, and as such contributes to the maintenance of inequalities throughout Brazil.

In a letter with the title "*A educação municipal quer ser ouvida*"(Municipal Education wants to be heard), the Eighth Forum of the National Union of Municipal Leaders of Education in 2001 (União Nacional de Dirigentes Municipais de Educação, UNDIME) expressed its indignation at the amount of funds transferred by the federal government to PNAE:

> [W]e will continue at the crossroads of having to offer school meals, receiving, from the Federal government, extremely low values, which causes us to provide meals without the minimum amount of nutrients for our children who come mainly from the most excluded strata of our society (p.2, M. L. S. Castro & J. S. S. Menezes, trans.).

As long as the Federal Government assumes that small resources per capita are sufficient for school meals, which are viewed as a policy move to prevent hunger and diseases, it will continue to fail to address the real issues of nutritional education and pupil health.

Information indicates that despite the fact that federal funds made available for school meals were well below the amount needed to provide high standards of quality, these resources were very important in the budgetary context of the city administrations studied. Article 3, of Law 10.697/96 (by State Law n°.11,602/2001) determined that "the States, Federal District and municipalities will no longer depend on proving that they have not defaulted on their obligations to the federal government in order to receive funds related to the maintenance of school meal programs and school textbooks". This was designed to fight against social injustice, which penalized children belonging to the less privileged classes of our society. Problems experienced by municipalities before the enactment of this law were explained by one SME who said:

> Our situation is still serious, so much so that our mayor went to Brasilia. We have historical debts to the INSS (National Social Security System), and to the FGTS (Fund of Guarantee

of Time Worked), which made the city administration default; the city administration was written into the Registry of Defaulters (Cadin- Cadastro de Inadimplentes), in the SPC (Credit Protection Services) of the city administrations, and we have not even received the transfers of money for the meals, the city schools are not in an appropriate condition to receive money to buy the meals. So we bought for the two first weeks, thinking that channels would then open, but it is a very long bureaucratic route. We paid this, and afterwards in fact, I bitterly regretted it, because I should have purchased desks, chairs, textbooks (SME Interview Transcript, p. 29).

Despite the fact that the children's nutritional needs were not being fully taken care of by the school meal programs, it was possible to determine how indispensable they were in the context of the study, as reflected in the following interview by another SME:

There are pupils who arrive in the morning and the teacher and school lunch lady cannot wait to give them a meal at the normal times. Something has to be offered to these students in order them to be able to work (SME Interview Transcript, p. 29).

The awareness of the importance of these meals for the children made some SMEDs seek advice in order to create, within a limited budget, a balanced menu, or at least one as nutritious as possible. In many schools, there was an entire infrastructure that had to be managed and maintained (canteen, industrial kitchen, freezers, refrigerators, etc.), which required time and the availability of human resources in order to provide students with meals.

The main point here is the deviation from an academic focus where educational issues were often less important than administrative goals. This dilemma is illustrated by the following comment from an SME:

[T]he administrative issue is much greater than the pedagogical one; I have not yet managed to become involved in the pedagogical one, although I have a very good pedagogical group. Administrative work really takes up much of one's time. (SME Interview Transcript, p. 1).

In many cases, the school is aware that this should not be its first priority. However, due to the social appeal of school meal programs, and the exclusionary nature of Brazilian education, the role of the school must take on several dimensions.

Moreover, there is such an involvement in these programs that we often find the principals or teachers taking on the role of lunch ladies or janitors. It should be pointed out that the welfare character of school care for some of the SMEDs investigated does not necessarily obscure a greater challenge:

[O]ur objective is not the meal, our goal is a political-pedagogical project for the schools, to work with the people along the lines. Meals are something necessary that we do as we go. Other factors must be developed, because otherwise the children don't learn, and they lose by it (SME Interview Transcript, p. 8).

The previous discussion suggests that there are a myriad of ways to analyze school meal programs. While it is clear that schools must retain an educational agenda as their main responsibility, they still remained deeply involved in the issue of school nutrition and meal programs. The variety of roles taken on by the school does produce anxieties that must be addressed, however. Having become the school of the working classes, the public school has taken on a welfare role as it mediates between pupils and public service agencies (Castro, 1995), and these new responsibilities often divert schools from their main function of educating youth.

Clearly, the school meal policy has attracted students, and has a great social and nutritional value for the lower class children because it has helped to include them in Brazil's educational system. However, it simultaneously takes away resources that should be invested in books, teacher training, and educational material that would enrich the pedagogical experience for these same children, and thus it excludes lower class children from quality education. Like the school meal program, school transport is another policy that includes children in the educational system, while excluding them from a high-quality experience due to the expenses and administrative effort expended on these non-pedagogical programs.

6.5   School Transportation

School transportation is another policy related to the process of inclusion/exclusion of Brazilian children from education, particularly from good education. Rural education is a cause for concern in most Brazilian municipalities because the physical condition of rural schools is precarious and creates serious obstacles to quality education. Moreover, rural schools are often taught by a single teacher who lacks training and qualifications, yet is responsible for teaching pupils of different grades in the same classroom. The combination of these factors contributes to the high percentage of school failures within rural schools. It should also be noted that the municipalities surveyed in the state of Rio Grande do Sul are not significantly different from the conditions in other regions of Brazil.

As an attempt to improve the conditions of education in rural areas, a large number of SMEs have started a process of merging schools, which, from 1997 to 1999, reduced by 16.5% the number of schools located in the rural areas of Brazil (Statistical Synopsis of Basic Education, 1999). In order to provide better teaching conditions and, in some cases, reduce the high cost of education in the rural area, the SMEDs have transferred a number of students to larger and/or better equipped schools. Bussing the school children was the alternative found to enable the merger to be put into effect. It should be noted that the bussing of school children is taking place not only in the rural areas, but throughout Brazil, and that in the case of Rio Grande do Sul, the studies that provide an overview of the school merger process have not yet been disseminated. The school merger generally follows the national trend.

The federal government has been contributing to these dynamics by means of the National Program of School Transport (Programa Nacional de Transporte Escolar, PNTE), whose purpose it is "to offer school transportation pupils living in rural areas, in order to ensure their access to and permanence in school, for eradicating school evasion" (MEC, 2001b, p.1, M. L. S. Castro & J. S. S. Menezes, trans.). The program consists of financial aid[8] to the municipalities to purchase buses, microbuses, vans, and boats, with the latter being used in areas such as in the Amazon Region.

Considering that the PNTE is aimed exclusively at the municipal sphere, and that Article 211 of the Brazilian Federal Constitution (1988) determined that the Union, States, and Municipalities should cooperate to organize their educational systems, and that they should also define "forms of collaboration in order to ensure the universalization of elementary school", the involved municipalities have signed an agreement in which they guarantee transportation of pupils attending state schools as well as their own schools, free of charges. "One has to carry this student who is not ours. He belongs to the State system, but one has a counterpart ... one has to support him to continue studying, otherwise he will not come" (SME Interview Transcript, p. 2).

The attempt to facilitate the student's access to school and reduce the rate of school dropouts has encountered serious obstacles including (a) the heavy expense of school transportation consuming a significant share of the education budget; (b) the state's financial transfers that only cover part of the expenses of their own pupils; (c) the high cost of maintenance; and (d) the insufficient number of vehicles to transport a large number of pupils. These factors have often contributed to negative social phenomena, such as, "the first to leave home to be the last to get home. There are children who arrive as late as almost 2 pm. This makes it very tiring!" (SME Interview Transcript, p. 8).

The conviction that transporting school children is one of the instruments that may help promote greater success at school, led the Eighth Forum of UNDIME to make the following proposition:

> Let the states really pay for the pupils who are transported by the municipalities, establishing quick, flexible ways of making the decision feasible, beyond what is established, via FNDE. One priority should be the lines of financing, with an end result being the acquisition of school transportation for the municipalities (2001, p. 3, M. L. S. Castro & J. S. S. Menezes, trans.).

Empirical data have indicated that, in most cases, the cost of transportation is too high for municipal budgets. Actual school transportation costs are almost higher than the expenditures for personnel, and it quickly becomes one of the largest expenses for some Municipal Departments of Education. "School transportation, this is the highest expenditure for education in the municipality. Obviously, this does not take the payroll into account, but school transport significantly raises the budget" (SME Interview Transcript, p. 11). There are many reasons for the high cost of transportation which depends on the size of municipalities, costs of maintenance of buses, conditions of the roads, and whether or not there is an outsourcing of services.

Some situations caused a certain amount of anxiety because the cost of transporting pupils exceeded the established limits, forcing the SMEs to follow and inspect the involved transportation companies. What was revealed from their study was several attempts to form a cartel, which was indicated by the fact that the cost per passenger did not vary significantly between various competitors. In one of the municipalities with a rather widespread rural population, it was suggested that there should be an alternative school calendar as a way to overcome problems associated with high transportation expenditures and challenging road conditions:

> So we have to transfer the pupils to the central schools and we have approximately two thousand pupils... there are children, then, who leave their homes at seven or eight o'clock in the morning and return around two o'clock in the afternoon; they stay at school for three or four hours. They spend more time on the muddy roads. So we thought up another type of care, which was to have the students stay at school the whole day, so he goes there in the morning, stays the whole morning, has lunch, stays there in the afternoon, and goes home in the afternoon. We divided the pupils into A and B. Those in Group A come to school on Monday, Wednesday and Friday, and group B on Tuesdays and Thursdays, and reverse this the next week (SME Interview Transcript, pp. 3–4).

With this alternative calendar, transportation costs were reduced, and so also was the problem of availability of classrooms and physical space, since only 50% of the pupils would be present on any given day. This program was still in the initial phase of implementation when the interviews were conducted, so the pedagogical outcomes of this program are currently unknown. The SME of that municipality was himself aware of the need to discuss education systematically. "Sometimes I ask the people here, when are we going to sit down to discuss education? Because we have a serious problem here, such as school transportation" (SME Interview Transcript, p. 3).

In some cases, the delineation of the areas covered by the municipalities can in itself become a problem for the bordering Municipal Departments of Education. The difficulty in establishing clear territorial limits between rural municipalities sometimes makes it hard for these departments to distinguish which of them is responsible (including financially) for the transportation of the schoolchildren who live in these places. Due to differences between, and the conditions within, each municipality, transportation has become one of the most serious problems in the administration of municipal education. In this context, there is the question of what the role of education should be, or, more broadly, what is, the role of school and what are the possibilities that school programs might modify the impact of economic and social factors.

While the transportation of students is necessary to guarantee access to education in rural areas, the implementation of this policy has led to the use of a large proportion of educational resources, which, in turn, has put strong demands on administrative personnel and their ability to deliver a sound academic program. In this sense the policy of providing school transport has had a negative effect on the quality of education offered in these municipalities.

6.6 Violence

While school meals and school transport are policies developed to meet the needs of lower socioeconomic class pupils in the Brazilian context, the previous analysis has demonstrated how these two policies had the effect of including children in the educational system, while excluding them from a quality education. Another factor affecting the quality of education is the existence of violence within the school environment. Violence is a problem which is not acknowledged by the government, and therefore has no public policy in place to prevent it. Nonetheless, it is a constant concern for poor children living in slum areas. Moreover, the absence of a public policy to stop violence within the school context is yet another factor which excludes lower socioeconomic class children from a quality education in Brazil.

Violence is an issue reported by the principals of the municipal schools investigated. The types of violence range from situations occurring within the school grounds—sometimes discipline-related and involving families—to problems with different forms of external violence that occur in the neighborhood where the institution is located. Moreover, many of the interviewees were concerned about thefts and robberies at the institutions under their responsibility. TVs and VCRs locked away behind bars were a common sight at the schools visited.

The SME of one municipality researched reported on a school that was considered the worst in the municipality, located in a very problematic neighborhood, which experienced a violence-death confluence:

> The worst school in the municipality (…), I worked there. When I arrived at that school I had a 3rd grade, with eighteen pupils. I was very happy, eighteen pupils, very few pupils, that I want. Eleven were outlaws, eleven carried a gun in their belt. Of the eleven children, last year, when I did a study (I taught religion), seven have already died (SME Interview Transcript, p. 13).

Despite these imbrications, society at large has denied the antagonism and precariousness of the human condition, rendering death invisible to daily life. Death, in general, has become a camouflaged subject, avoided and forbidden, even at the schools. Violence and death, transmitted on television, have become characterized as shows and, as such, fictitious and distant from reality:

> As they become shows, these unique human experiences begin to lose their qualitative dimension and their non-interchangeable character and are reduced to a point experience, without any memory and dialogue about the social foundations of society. (Assmann & Sung, 2000, p. 101, M. L. S. Castro & J. S. S. Menezes, trans.)

In denying death, man forgets his human condition and no longer recognizes himself or the human condition of people who suffer the processes of "exclusion and social insensitivity" (Assmann & Sung, 2000).

The pupils previously mentioned in the report who repeated grades sequentially were immersed in a society that cried at the TV drama, but closed to the reality of life surrounding them. They came from marginalized families in which violence was a constant presence. This daily life was reflected in the classroom by their play activities:

> It came from a family culture in which everyone was an outlaw … when they were to act in a play, it was always scenes of death, fights, knifings. This was always present, I even despaired, but I continued to go there. … I have some people from that class who are now working (SME Interview Transcript, p. 15).

Though a teacher made several attempts to bring them back to a path that would critique and overcome their reality of violence, few managed to reconfigure their future, as demonstrated from the following teacher's experience:

> They passed, they had been 5 or 6 years in the third grade, and they entered the 4th grade. I follow them all the way to the 5th grade in mathematics, because they bothered everyone. Nobody wanted them, and I didn't want them to be expelled from school, so I followed them on to the 5th grade. I was head teacher of class 53, which was always a smaller group of pupils. They accompanied me, they were always with me, and they managed to pass properly; they went to exhibitions, to museums ... they didn't touch anything. Only, of course, there were days when they ... at night, I knew that they had done this or that, there were shoot-outs even. ... The first one who died, we all went to the funeral. When I returned from the funeral, I discussed all this with them. Two of them were real outlaws, and they no longer are. They work, they have jobs (SME Interview Transcript, p. 14).

At the time of this interview, the teacher was the Secretary of Education in that municipality. That initial experience, along with 20 years of follow-up on those youngsters, drove her to develop programs and partnerships related to education in the street. This included the implementation of cultural workshops that would enable forms of paid activity for young people from the lower classes, who often lacked adequate family guidance, and were neglected by the government.

The reports generally confirm the idea that school is no longer able to deal with the many social problems it encounters, though the reward is significant for those who manage to remove even a single pupil from the path leading to trouble. One of the principals interviewed, for example, shared the case of a student who was significantly influenced by a limited amount of attention and understanding to help change his future:

> It is not emotional. ... It is much easier not to bother to be concerned with people, because then they do not take up so much of your time. Doing the right thing takes more time, wears one out more, but there is something, when you come home at night and say: "Well, I can sleep because I'm sowing something good. Something good will come of this sooner or later." We have the example of a student who was rebellious from the first grade: he was beaten up a lot by his father and mother and they called him stupid. One day he was going home angry, the teacher had expelled him from the classroom. He was leaving furious, crying. ... I called him for a chat, and I spent the rest of the morning with him. You must have seen him: he wears a little goatee, and works here at City Hall. ... He is studying and working, he is a completely different person. When he sees me, he says: "Oh Beth, that was a great time in that school. How I used to enjoy chatting with you." In those days it would have been easier to say: "I'm not going to waste time, go away, let him fend for himself. Let the parents do what they can do. It is none of my business." Now, he is helping his sick mother (SME Interview Transcript, p. 13).

The idea imparted is that we should not be discouraged by challenging goals. Rather, we need to value the positive effects achieved with some pupils. Despite the fact that the reports showed a reality characterized by violence, they ultimately indicated that an alternate direction was possible and made us reflect on the need to rely on hope:

> When I look around, I see only lack of hope in the world. And, despite everything, I and everyone has to try and find a source of hope. We have to believe in man, despite man (Assmann & Sung, 2000, p. 105, M. L. S. Castro & J. S. S. Menezes, trans.).

Hope implies an a priori internalization of the human condition of those who are included in the system society, and those who are excluded share similar circumstances. Hope makes people glimpse alternatives and begin to bet on the possibility of change. Assmann and Sung (2000) define "human hope" as a "horizon woven with desire", emphasizing the need "for us to build a world into which many, many worlds fit", and that hope is built by solidary actions among all people (p. 103, M. L. S. Castro & J. S. S. Menezes, trans.). Hope is a strategy to deal with violence, even if only small victories are possible. Hope is essential for keeping the educational spirit alive in schools, and is a means for teachers to express their care and concern for their pupils.

6.7   Remuneration, Training, and Working Conditions of the Teachers

The study found that, in general, the municipalities surveyed struggled to assign a fair value to their education professionals. This problem becomes greater when the analysis takes into account the new Law of Guidelines and Fundamentals of National Education (Lei de Diretrizes e Bases da Educação Nacional, LDB) which is based on the concept that every school system must enhance the value of education professionals in terms of the Rules and Regulations and Career Plans of Public School Teachers (Estatutos e Planos de Carreira do Magistério Público, Art. 67). These regulations stipulate, for example, that teachers can only be selected through competitive examinations, that professional training must be continued, and that there must be appropriate working conditions. If these requirements are not followed, the quality of teaching may be in jeopardy, leading to the exclusion of students from quality education.

During the process of data collection, the researcher recalled that the hands of one of the teachers at a rural school showed signs that she did heavy work daily. The teachers who participated in the study generally did all of their own housework, besides working 40 hours a week at the school. The accumulation of tasks performed by these teachers, who sometimes did not have the minimum level of training required to work at their assigned school level, usually made it difficult for them to provide an appropriate learning experience for their students. In many municipalities untrained teachers were still a reality to be overcome by the SMEDs included in this study.

Concomitant with this scenario of underprepared teachers was the issue of inadequate remuneration. Within this context, some of the people who worked at the SMEDs remarked that the salaries were low, but that they are better than those paid by the State, and that at least they are paid on time.It was also observed that the low salaries limited or prevented teachers from updating their knowledge, and sometimes from even completing initial training. Teacher education depends on many factors such as the availability of local appropriate education. In some municipalities where this is available, up to 93% of their teachers have higher education (SME Interview Transcripts). This has been possible, in part, due to the integration of the municipal systems with the local universities which provide special programs for teachers, ranging from transport to the closest universities to on-the-job training courses. Unfortunately, in-service training for teachers is limited, due to the fact that many do not have enough time to study, and the municipal systems are not able to pay for substitute teachers. Weekend courses, if not superficial, are a feasible option and, in many cases, are the only available source for professionals who must improve their teaching, but cannot take time away from the classroom.

When considering conditions necessary for the improvement of the situation for professional educators, it is important to emphasize the need for salary improvement, which is currently quite low. In interviews there were often complaints about low salaries, though this was not surprising as it is quite common to relate teaching with low salaries. This situation, when taken together with the minimal chance for financial incentives from the State and municipalities, works against the implementation of courses for teacher training and continuing education.

The municipalities that began to receive funds under the Law of the Fund of Maintenance and Valuing of Teachers (Fundo de Manutenção e Valorização do Magistério, FUNDEF) generally had their salaries increased through a bonus, since 60% of those funds were to pay professional teachers (Art. 67 of Law 9324/96). On the other hand, the municipalities who had part of their educational resources transferred by FUNDEF to other municipalities because of lower pupil enrolment, were in a more problematic situation, and will continue to undergo difficulties with regard to raising their teachers' salaries and ensuring better conditions for their further education.

Several factors related to social exclusion could be examined in this context. As Codo (1999) writes, insofar as teachers earn a very low salary, they are most likely unable to update and carry out work that will lead to higher competence and professional autonomy. These adverse conditions limit teachers' actions and involvement and may lead to teachers leaving the profession.[10] This factor has significant implications for the issue of social exclusion, since, depending on the conditions, the educator may become the socially excluded person. These conditions also promote a self-perpetuating cycle where the teacher earns such a low salary that it is impossible for him/her to progress any further, and without any progress will continue to be badly paid and further weaken the status of this group of professionals. Moreover, these conditions can reduce the chances that schools will be able to improve difficult social situations previously discussed. This cycle of low expectations, performance and results must be broken in order to offer quality education to all Brazilians. The results of the interviews also indicated the need for the SMEDs to work on the issue of enhancing teachers' worth, including better working conditions. They also need to receive a salary that will allow them to live with dignity and to obtain the minimum requirements for personal and professional survival. Career plans that are being developed in the different municipalities provide the possibility for enhancing teachers' professional training, experience, and updating, which will encourage them to seek new levels of achievement within their schools.

Achieving these new working conditions will, however, depend on a greater societal effort to overcome current social inequalities by demanding that educational authorities assign greater value to the task of education.

6.8 Evaluation

The perception that all citizens are responsible for national policies of education, and that the school constitutes both an instrument of social inclusion and exclusion, prompted this study. Within this chapter we have analyzed the process of social exclusion in the municipal welfare programs with regard to school meals and school transport. We have also discussed issues related to violence within schools and municipalities, and the remuneration, training, and working conditions of elementary school teachers.

We observed that, although school meal and transport programs were designed to deal with student failures at school, they also became a contributing factor that perpetuated social inequalities/exclusion within the context investigated. When the National Program of School Meals (Programa Nacional de Alimentação Escolar, PNAE) ignored the existence of significant budget differences between city administrations, while expecting financial contributions to the funds provided by MEC, it contributed to maintaining social inequalities within Brazil. Children in poorer municipalities ultimately received meals that were of lower quality than those offered to children of wealthier municipalities. Based on analyses of the interviews, it was concluded that the food and school transportation program, among other activities, absorbed a large amount of SMED time and resources, and encouraged the social exclusion of young people.

The above discussion suggests that violence as a social problem prevented the development of a quality education for all. It was observed that remuneration and training were seen by the interviewees as necessary and directly related to the enhancement of professional educators. Low teacher salaries prevented progress in the training/qualification of teachers and contributed to teachers, as a group, becoming both socially and professionally marginalized.

6.9 Conclusion

The policies of providing school meals and transport for children made access to education possible to a large number of poor children, but offering these services had a negative effect on the quality of education offered by the system. These two underfunded policies functioned as a palliative to the real problem of poverty and exclusion. When we consider that they were identified within an environment charged with violence, uncertified teachers, and very challenging working conditions and low salaries, we have a deeper understanding of the inclusion/exclusion process.The awareness of the interconnection among all people may be one of the motives surpassing the barriers of individuality—a characteristic of globalization—in order to seek greater human understanding. In this sense, the excluded/different would become part of the whole and would share equally in the human condition.

Acknowledgments This study was connected to the Graduate Program in Education at the Pontifical Catholic University of Rio Grande do Sul and is part of the Integrated Project Management of Basic School, funded by FINEP (Funds for Studies and Projects) and by Fapergs (Foundation of Support for Research of the state of Rio Grande do Sul), performed during the period 1996–1999.

6.10   References

Assmann, H. (1996). *Novas metáforas para reencantar a educação.* [New metaphors to re-enchant education]. Piracicaba, Editora da UNIMEP.

Assmann, H. & Sung, J. M. (2000). *Competência e sensibilidade solidária. Educar para a esperança* [Competence and solitary sensibility: Educating for hope]. Petropólis, Rio de Janeiro: Vozes.

Barros, R. P. de., Henriques, R. Mendonca, R. (2000) Desigualdade e pobreza no Brasil: Retrato de uma estabilidade inaceitável. [Inequality and poverty in Brazil: Portrait of an unacceptable estability]. *Revista Brasileira de Ciências Sociais, Associação Nacional de Pós-Graduação e Pesquisa em Ciências Sociais* [National Association of Graduate Study and Research in Social Sciences] , *São Paulo, 15*(42), 123–142.

Castro, M. L. S. de (1995). A Gestão da Escola Básica: Autonomia e Identidade [The management of elementary school: Autopnomy and identity]. In Estudos Leopoldenses, São Leopoldo, *31*(143), 61–64.

Castro, M. L. S. de (2001, Month). The management of municipal education: The role of the superintendent a Brazilian perspective. Paper presented at the Annual Meeting of American Educational Research Association, Seattle, WA.

Codo, W. (Coord.) (1999). *Educação, carinho e trabalho. Burnout, a síndrome da desistência do educador, que pode levar a falência da educação.* [Education, care and work: Burnout, the syndrome of the giving up of the educator that can lead to school failure] Petrópolis, Editora Vozes, Confederação Nacional dos Trabalhadores em Educação, Universidade de Brasília, Laboratório de Psicologia do Trabalho.

Coraggio, J. L. (2000). Propostas do banco mundial para a educação: sentido oculto ou problemas de concepção. [Proposal of the World Bank for education: veiled meaning or a conceptual problem]. In: Tommasi, Lívia De; WARDE, Mírian Jorge e HADDAD, Sérgio (Orgs.]. *O Banco Mundial e as Políticas Educacionais.* (The World Bank and educational policies) 3 ed. São Paulo: Cortez.

Federation of the Association of Municipalities of the state of Rio Grande do Sul [FAMURS] (1997). O Município e a Educação [Municipality and education] Rio Grande do Sul: Federação das Associações dos Municípios do Rio Grande do Sul.

Ministerio da Educacao e do Desporto. (2000). *Sinopse Estatistica da Educacao Basica: censo escolar 99* [Statistical synopsis of basic education: 99 school census] Instituto Nacional de Estudos e Pesquisa EducacionaL: Brasília.

Ministério da Educação e do Desporto (2001). *Programa nacional de transporte escolar Brasília.* [National Program of School Transport] Retrieved July 5, 2001, from http://www.fnde.gov.br/programas/pnte.htm

Organization of American States (1998). *Education in the Americas. Quality and equity in the globalisation process.*

Plano Nacional de Educação. (2001, January 10). *Diário Oficial [da República Federativa do Brasil], Brasília.* [English translation].

Chapter 7
Private Resources in Educational Finance and Equality Implications: Evidence from Peru

Mariana Alfonso

7.1 Introduction

Governments of most developing countries face tight fiscal budgets that do not allow them to expand access to education, increase equality of educational opportunities, and improve the quality of the education delivered as they would like. The international lending community has taken sides on this issue. Torres (2003), in a critical review of the World Bank's involvement in education, summarizes the international credit agency's position as follows:

> The current systems of finance and management are frequently not well suited to meeting these challenges. Public spending on education is too often inefficient and inequitable. In view of the competition for and pressure on public funds, new sources of financing are needed (p. 301).

Given the fiscal constraints, and following the guidance of the international lending community, developing countries have been trying to find alternative methods for financing the provision and expansion of education. These alternative sources of educational finance can include the reallocation of public spending from other publicly funded activities to education, the generation of new tax revenues to be destined to education, and the reliance on private funds to supplement public spending on education (World Bank, 1995). This chapter focuses on the last source of financing education: The reliance on private funds to finance the provision of education.

There are two main forms in which a government can rely on private funds to supplement public spending on education. One of these methods is the use of tuition fees in public schools to recover part of the costs of the provision of education. The other is the establishment of to allow for an expansion of the educational system (Glewwe & Patrinos, 1999; World Bank, 1995). Both alternatives depend mostly on household contributions, implying that private spending on education may become an even more important part of the total cost of education. Even at present, however, household spending on education can represent a substantial portion of both household income and household spending, particularly among poor and rural ones. Moreover, "differences in private resources to education among social groups

Inter-American Development Bank. The views expressed here are those of the author and do not represent the official position of the IDB.

may exacerbate educational inequalities among social groups" (Tsang & Kidchanapanish, 1992, p. 180). Thus, a movement toward the use of fees and private schools could increase existing inequalities and inequities in the educational system—a negative side-effect that even the World Bank has acknowledged.

Among the developing countries that have followed this prescription and increased the reliance on private funds to finance educational expenditures, Peru, a low- to middle-income Latin American country, offers an interesting case to analyze. This country has made notable progress in increasing educational opportunities, with total enrolment growing from 14% of the country's population in 1950 to 33% in 1994. The high participation rates observed in the Peruvian educational system are accompanied, however, by relatively low levels of public spending on education and high levels of household contributions (World Bank, 2001; Wu et al., 2000). For example, in 1994 the level of public spending on education as a percentage of the Gross Domestic Product (GDP) was only 2.8%, while households' contributions to education added to approximately 2% of the GDP (author's estimates based on Peru's 1994 Living Standards Measurement Survey [PLSS], Banco Central de Reserva del Peru, 2001, and World Bank, 2001). These figures indicate that in Peru, two fifths of the educational costs seem to be borne by families. As Wu et al. state:

> Peruvian households contribute relatively more to education than their counterparts in many countries, so that total expenditures on education in Peru (public and household) are more in line with the international comparators (p. 386).

Peru's reliance on private resources to help finance education raises questions of equity across households and of constraints on the educational attainment of children from poorer families. Therefore, it is imperative to have an understanding of the factors that determine household spending on education in this country. Thus, this chapter tries to answer the following research questions: (1) How does private spending on education vary by household characteristics? (2) Is relying on private contributions to finance education an equitable alternative? (3) What are the determinants of private expenditures on education in Peru?

Utilizing the 1994PLSS, this chapter argues that Peruvian households consider education to be a necessity. The willingness to pay for it, however, is relatively low. The Peruvian government therefore cannot solely rely on increments in household income to increase the levels of household expenditures on education in such a way to finance access to, and quality improvements of, schools. In addition, results suggest that relying heavily on private expenditures to finance education has a negative impact on equality of educational opportunities, affecting particularly children of indigenous descent living in rural areas.

7.2 Conceptual Framework: Private Resources in Educational Finance

Although official statistics of educational costs are usually limited to the public component, and though government allocations usually constitute the most important source of education financing (Wu et al., 2000), in many countries a substantial portion of educational costs is borne by private households. Since this chapter analyzes the determinants of educational spending incurred by Peruvian families, as well as issues of equality from relying on such financial sources, it is important to first define what one means by *private resources devoted to education* and characterize the diverse forms that these resources can take.

There are basically three categories of private resources for education: direct private costs of education, household contributions to school, and indirect private costs of education (Tsang, 1994, 2002). Direct private costs of education are expenditures that parents make on their children's schooling, such as expenditures on school fees (tuition), textbooks, uniforms, and additional expenses for transportation and food as a result of schooling. Household contributions to schools are donations that families and school personnel make to the school either in cash or in kind. Finally, the indirect private costs of education represent the economic value of forgone opportunities of schooling. Indirect private costs represent the opportunity cost—in terms of lost income—of sending a child to school instead of, for example, involving the child with income-generating activities.

In any study of the role of private resources in the financing of education one would ideally include three categories of private resources. Data limitations which will be discussed shortly, however, prevent an empirical analysis that incorporates the concepts of household contributions and indirect private costs of schooling within the calculation of total private resources devoted to education. This is a problem that affects the present study as well as previous research. As Tsang (2002) indicates, most studies that attempt to estimate the amount of private resources destined to education fail to compute household contributions and indirect costs of schooling because information on these costs are not readily available. Although opportunity costs of schooling are sometimes considered negligible at the primary level, they tend to be substantial at the secondary level. But even at the primary level these indirect costs can be considerable for low income and rural families. Rural households in low-income countries need the help of their children with agricultural production, household chores, and with the care of younger siblings (Tsang). As a result, the present study might underestimate the financial sacrifices that families, particularly low-income and rural ones, have to make in order to send their children to school.

What are the consequences in terms of educational equality that arise from policies that increase the public sector's dependency on private resources for financing expanded access to education and improved educational quality? The literature on private contributions to education suggests that relying on private sources tends to increase the existing educational inequalities in developing countries. A study using Thai data found an inverse relationship between the economic burden of schooling and household income, meaning that the percentage of total household resources devoted to education decreases with increases in household income (Tsang & Kidchanapanish, 1992). Another study conducted in Vietnam also found that the willingness to spend on education increases as household incomes rise. This indicates that wealthy Vietnamese families could contribute more to their children's schooling if it were needed (Glewwe & Patrinos, 1999). In addition, two studies on rural Peru find that increasing schools' user fees reduces enrolments less among the wealthiest group as compared to the rest of the rural population (Gertler & Glewwe, 1990, 1992). The studies cited also indicate that family income is positively related to the demand for children's education, as higher income families devote or are willing to devote more resources to the education of their children. Lastly, a study on urban and rural Peru indicates that low-income families spend less, in absolute terms, on their children's education but that they spend a considerably higher percentage of their income on public primary schools than high-income families (Grupo de Análisis para El Desarrollo [GRADE], 2001).

In summary, private resources are very important for financing schooling, particularly in developing countries, but relying heavily on them can contribute to the reproduction of educational inequalities. Thus, it is extremely important to understand what determines these expenditures if one were interested in reducing inequalities in schooling access and increasing retention rates among the poorest. This chapter explores in detail the experience of Peru, a country that relies intensively on private resources to supplement the public financing of education. But before analyzing the factors that contribute to the amount of resources that families dedicate to schooling and discussing the equality implications, one needs to contextualize the environment under which the policies that entail a higher reliance on private funds for financing education were introduced.

7.3   Peru's Education Policies in the Early 1990s: An Overview

When evaluating the equality implications of changes in a country's educational policy, it is important to contextualize such policy changes by providing a characterization of how the country's educational system functions. This characterization not only works as a framework of reference for the empirical analysis to come, therefore supporting restrictions that are made in this analysis, but it also provides the context under which the increased reliance on private resources has taken place.

The Peruvian education system—as of 1994, the year for which data are available for the empirical analysis that follows—is structured into four levels: initial, primary, secondary, and tertiary. Since only the primary and secondary levels of schooling are compulsory according to Peruvian law (World Bank, 2001), the empirical analysis as well as the current description focus only on these two levels. Primary education comprises six grades and is intended for children in the age group between 6 and 11 years. Secondary education is offered to the age group between 12 and 16 years and is organized in two cycles: the first having a common curriculum for all students in grades 7 and 8 and the second having a diversified curriculum that lasts 3 years and is divided into science and humanities. There were approximately 8 million students enrolled in all levels of formal and nonformal education in Peru in 1994, of which 51.9% were enrolled in primary schools and 26.1% in secondary institutions (World Bank).

When evaluating the impact of policy changes on educational inequalities, it is also important to understand the larger macroeconomic and political environment under which the policy changes are being introduced, as well as the short-term effects that these policies have in changing the educational landscape. Peru is a country that has experienced severe structural adjustments in the early 1990s, affecting all government sectors. The first years of Fujimori's government were characterized by policies aimed at restoring fiscal discipline. As a result, a series of measures were implemented to contain public expenditure, to mobilize private resources, and to delegate the financing and operation of social services to the regions.

How did these fiscal measures affect the education system? The rationalization of the public sector between 1991 and 1993 resulted in a 72% reduction in employment in the central administration of the Ministry of Education. A new Constitution sanctioned in 1993 extended compulsory and free education from primary to secondary education. But in order to meet this new constitutional mandate in a scenario of containment of public spending, the government passed a law that encouraged the establishment of private schools (World Bank, 2001). As a consequence, the number of private schools increased significantly. As illustrated in Fig. 7.1, private institutions of higher education have grown steadily to represent close to 50% of all institutions of this level, and the share of private schools shows the largest increases at the secondary level. In addition, enrolments in private institutions grew at higher rates than in public ones, particularly at the secondary level (World Bank).

Given the increasing relevance of private schooling in Peru during the 1990s, one can expect household spending on education to have increased. Thus, it has become extremely important within this context to study the determinants of private

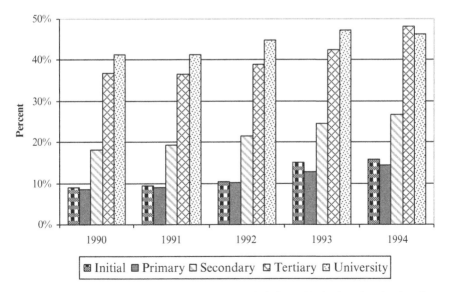

Fig. 7.1 Private schools as percentage of total schools in Peru (Author's estimation based on World Bank, 2001)

spending on education in Peru. By using data collected in 1994, this chapter allows for an estimation of the short-run effects that these educational policy changes have had on equality of educational opportunities.

7.4   Description of the Data and Sample

In order to estimate the short-term equality consequences of an increased reliance on private resources to finance educational expenditures in Peru, this chapter employs data from the 1994 PLSS. This household survey was developed by the World Bank, and designed and conducted by Cuánto S.A., a Peruvian research group. The 1994 PLSS provides data for 6,623 households from a nationally representative sample, and collects information covering diverse aspects of household welfare, such as health, education, employment, consumption, and income (Steele et al., 1998). The survey contains detailed information on the education of all household members, including expenditures on education and information on the school attended for all household members currently attending school. Data were collected for private expenditures on tuition and matriculation fees, books, uniforms, and transportation and food expenses related to schooling.

The household sample was designed to be representative of the population in Peru based on census data from 1993. The sample was stratified into seven geographic areas: Urban Costa (coast), Rural Costa, Urban Sierra (highlands), Rural Sierra, Urban Selva (jungle), Rural Selva, and Metropolitan Lima. Furthermore, a three-stage sampling process was conducted. First, the country was divided into primary sampling units (the geographic areas mentioned above), then into secondary sampling units (segments containing an average of 100 households), and finally into tertiary sampling units (individual dwellings). This complex sampling design is taken into account in the statistical analysis that follows. If one does not correct for this survey design, the standard errors will be incorrectly estimated and therefore the significance of the coefficients overestimated.

The sub-sample used in this chapter consists of children between 6 and 18 years of age who were in school at any point in time during the 1994 academic year, enrolled in either primary or secondary educational institutions. Any individual who was 18 years old and already enrolled in a tertiary institution was excluded. The selection of only those enrolled in primary and secondary schools is a consequence of the relatively low numbers of sampled individuals who were enrolled in higher education institutions as well as the fact that Peruvian education is compulsory up to the secondary level, as previously discussed. This restricted sub-sample has 5,126 observations. Among these 5,126 students, 67.3% were in primary schools and the remaining 32.7% were at the secondary level. Finally, out of the 4,480 observations for which the type of school is known, 12.1% were enrolled in a private school.

Descriptive statistics for the demographic and background characteristics of students in different types of schools, weighted to be representative of the overall Peruvian population in primary and secondary schools, are shown in Table 7.1.

The table clearly indicates that primary students differ considerably from secondary students. On average, Peruvians students enrolled in secondary schools come from wealthier households than those enrolled in primary schools, and they also spend more on education than primary students—indirectly suggesting that secondary schooling is more costly than primary schooling in Peru. Secondary students are more likely to live in urban areas, speak Spanish, and enrol in a private school than their primary counterparts. Finally, they come from households where the head has more years of schooling and is less likely to be an agricultural worker. These differences between primary and secondary students indicate that, in spite of the impressive increases in enrolments that this country has experienced in the past decades, secondary schooling is still somewhat unattainable for the most disenfranchised households, given the high costs involved. The differences are also indicative of the poorer performance and preparation for secondary schooling of low-income students, because they generally attend lower-quality public schools (Somers et al., 2004) and have fewer family advantages that could help them succeed academically.

Table 7.1 also suggests that there are significant differences between public and private schools with respect to the demographic and household backgrounds of the students. Compared to public schools, private schools have a proportionally lower enrolment of students from language minorities (1.5% compared to 16.3% in public schools). Moreover, students in private schools come from households with higher levels of income, of smaller size, and where the household head has significantly more years of schooling (on average, 13.1 years of schooling compared to only 6.9 in public schools). The students' parents are also more likely to have white-collar occupations. In addition Somers et al. (2004) found that in Peru 4th-grade students who attend private schools have considerably higher test scores (by more than half of a standard deviation) in both mathematics and Spanish than those who attend public schools. These descriptive statistics suggest that public schools are, on average, of lower quality than private schools, although these data do not indicate whether this difference in performance is because private schools do a better job in educating primary students or simply because they enrol the best students in terms of ability and socioeconomic background. These large differences between public and private schools provide evidence that, in Peru, the current policy of encouraging the establishment of private schools to expand enrolment in a context of contained public spending could be highly inequitable. Sending a child to a private school implies an average direct expenditure of 940.7 soles per year, an amount that could be particularly burdensome to households with relatively low incomes. For example, the average household income for the lowest quintile is 2590.4 soles. Then, for a student from a household in this quintile, going to a private school implies that a family will spend, on average, 36% of its total income on the education of only one child.

The large disparities in background found for students in secondary and in private schools suggest that (a) enrolments in secondary education in Peru are still low for children with low levels of socioeconomic background, and that (b) private schools enrol students from better-off families and involve large per-child expenditures, being therefore "out of reach" for low-income households. The heavy reliance on private spending for financing the educational system and on the expansion of private schools for increasing enrolments, which are two of the policies that have been put in place in Peru in the 1990s, is expected, thus, to have negative consequences in terms of equality of educational opportunities.

7.5 How Are Private Expenditures in Education Distributed in Peru?

One of the research questions of this chapter asks how private expenditures on education vary by household characteristics. As previously stated, this chapter measures only direct private expenditures on education. Since the opportunity costs of sending a child to school could be very high, particularly in rural areas of a developing country like Peru, this chapter provides a lower bound estimate of the private contributions to schooling.

In Table 7.2, the descriptive statistics for quintiles of total per-child private spending on education result in the following observations:

(1) The percentage of minority language students decreases significantly when one moves away from the lowest to the highest quintile. Students who speak Quechua are highly over-represented among the low and middle-low quintiles of private expenditures on schooling.
(2) High levels of expenditures on education correspond to high levels of household income. Total household income is almost three times higher for the highest quintile group in comparison to the lowest quintile. However, as the GRADE (2001) study points out, low-income families spend a considerably higher percentage of their income on education than high-income families.
(3) Seventy per cent of students in the lowest quintile reside in a rural area, while this is the case for only 10.4% of those in the highest quintile.
(4) Households that spend more on their children's schooling have heads with higher levels of education and are more likely to have white-collar occupations. In the highest quintile, household heads have on average 11.2 years of schooling. In contrast, in the lowest quintile the household head has on average only 4.6 years of schooling.
(5) Even when their child is enrolled in a public school, Peruvian families spend considerable amounts on education. This conclusion is derived from the observation that 93% of the children for whom spending on education is in the high-middle quintile (quintile 4) are enrolled in public schools.

The second research question addresses the issue of whether relying on private contributions for the finance of education is an equitable alternative. This question can be answered by using a Lorenz curve to illustrate the proportion of total private expenditures on education by income quintile. The Lorenz curve for total private expenditures on education, shown in Fig. 7.2, indicates that private expenditures (in

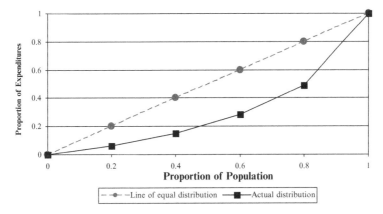

Fig. 7.2 Lorenz curve for incidence of private expenditures on education (Author's estimation based on PLSS, 1994)

public and private schools as well as in primary and secondary instruction) are quite inequitable in Peru, with the lowest income quintile accounting for only about 6% of the total private expenditures on education, and the upper quintile as much as 50.9%.

Thus, it can be concluded from Table 7.2 that private spending on education varies substantially by household and student characteristics. Households from lower socioeconomic backgrounds and those of indigenous descent in particular spend considerably less on their children's education. Moreover, the Lorenz curve shows that private expenditures on education are unequally distributed. In addition, the two analyses emphasize previous statements that Peruvians spend significant amounts on their children's education even when they send their children to public schools, and these expenditures are also unequally distributed. Thus, in a context of fiscal constraints, a policy that increases the reliance on family resources for financing part of the costs of delivering education and encourages the establishment of private schools for expanding enrolments is likely to reinforce the inequalities in educational opportunities that already exist in Peru.

7.6 Determinants of Private Spending on Primary and Secondary Education in Peru

7.6.1 Empirical Strategy

To determine the key factors that affect the amount of private resources devoted to primary and secondary schooling in Peru, this study employed an ordinary least squares (OLS) regression model. The unit of analysis was the child in school, and the dependent variable was the logarithm of total private expenditures on education, per child, in soles.

The explanatory variables consisted of three groups. The first group included three student characteristic variables. They were a dummy indicating whether the child was female, and two dummies for the child's first language (with Spanish as the reference category). These three variables were expected to show a negative coefficient. Since Gertler and Glewwe (1992) find that parents in rural Peru are more willing to pay for secondary education for boys, one expects a negative sign for the female dummy. It has been shown in the previous section that language minorities are over-represented among the lowest quintiles of private expenditures on education, so it is reasonable to assume that this relation would hold in the context of an OLS regression.

The second group of explanatory variables comprised schooling characteristics, with dummy variables for private schools and for enrolment at the secondary level (public schools and primary level were, respectively, the reference categories). These two variables were expected to show a positive sign, since it has been found in previous sections that private expenditures on education are significantly higher for private schools and for the secondary level. It is important to indicate that in this exercise the private school indicator is taken as exogenous. One needs to recognize, however, that enrolment in a private school, instead of a public one, might be the consequence of a decision made based on unobserved individual and household characteristics that could also affect the level of spending on education. That is, one would expect this dummy to be correlated with the error term of the private spending equation. This limitation should be considered when interpreting results.

The last group comprised household characteristics. Total household income was measured in soles in its logarithm and was expected to have a positive sign consistent with the previous analysis on the distribution of private expenditures on education. The second household characteristic was the number of children under 18. This variable was expected to have a negative sign, assuming that households with more children of school age would necessitate lower per-child expenditures on education for a given level of income. Two variables controlled for area of residence: one was a dummy for living in a rural area, and the other was a dummy indicating residence in metropolitan Lima. The first was expected to have a negative sign and the second a positive one, based on findings from previous sections. A dummy indicating whether the household head was female has also been included. Haddad and Hoddinott (1994), in a study of intra-household allocation in Côte D'Ivore, conclude that when females have bargaining power, they tend to spend a larger share of the household income on food and goods related to the schooling of their children. The inclusion of the dummy for female household heads as a proxy for the bargaining power of females can test whether this finding holds true for Peru. Finally, a set of four variables describing the household head was included. The first measured the household head's years of schooling, with an expectation of a positive coefficient, and the others the head's occupation (the reference categories are executive, professional, and management occupations).

Five models have been estimated using these covariates. The first model used the complete sample of students in primary and secondary education, independently of the type of school they were enrolled in. The second model was restricted only to students enrolled in the primary level, and the third to students in the secondary level. The fourth and fifth models estimated the determinants of private expenditures on education for public and private schools, respectively. The results of these estimations are shown in Table 7.3.

7.6.2 *Findings*

The results presented in Table 7.3 indicate that total household income is a significant determinant of private expenditures on education, a result that holds across all models. The coefficient is less than one, indicating that education is not a luxury good in Peru. It is relatively low for primary and public schools, grows larger for secondary schools, and is quite high for private schools. In addition, the coefficient suggests that every doubling of household income increases overall expenditures on education by 29%, but only by 25% if the student is enrolled in a public school and by a high 66% if the student attends a private school.

A second result that holds across all models is the one regarding the number of children in the household. An additional child in the household decreases the amount spent on education, per child, by levels between 7.7% (for children enrolled in public schools) and 17% (for children in the primary level). Years of schooling of the household head is consistently significant in the five models estimated. An additional year of schooling of the household head increases the amount spent on education by levels between 3.3% and 5.6% (the first for children in secondary schools and the latter for children in primary schools).

Other variables that have significant coefficients in at least one of the models are (a) parents of Quechua children spend on schooling approximately 56% less than parents of Spanish-speaking children, (b) parents of children who speak a language that is neither Spanish or Quechua spend larger amounts on their children's schooling in comparison to their Spanish- and Quechua-speaking counterparts, (c) living in a rural area reduces the amount spent by families on schooling, and (d) households that send their child to a private school spend the incredible magnitude of 337 times more than households who send their child to a public institution.

It is interesting to note that the dummy for gender of the student is statistically insignificant, a result that implies that female students are not discriminated against, within their household, at least in terms of amounts of monetary resources that the household devotes to their education. Last, households headed by females do not spend more on education than households headed by males, ceteris paribus, implying that the Peruvian data does not provide support for Haddad-Hoddinott's (1994) hypothesis.

7.6.3   Interpretation of Findings

What do the findings presented above suggest? There are several conclusions that can be drawn from the estimation results presented in Table 7.3. First, wealthier families spend more on their children's schooling. Although the coefficient on household income suggests that education is a necessary good in Peru, the overall income elasticity is low at 0.29. In contrast, Glewwe and Patrinos (1999) find for Vietnam that the elasticity of private expenditures on education with respect to income is around 0.55, or 55%. This suggests that the Peruvian government cannot rely heavily on increases in income to bring greater expenditures on education to either recover costs or improve educational quality.

Second, parents sending children to private schools spend considerably more on education than parents who send their children to public schools. This result, thus, suggests that expanding the private sector to increase access to education might have detrimental equity effects, particularly because low-income families might have to make a tremendous financial effort to send, or simply be excluded from sending, their children to private schools.

Third, households with highly educated heads spend significant amounts on education. This implies that highly educated parents are not only financially able to contribute to their children's schooling but they might also be more willing to pay for their children's education. That is, highly educated parents, more than less educated parents, might place a higher value on education independent of their ability to pay for it, since ability to pay is controlled for by including the household income as an independent variable, suggesting an intergenerational transmission of human and cultural capital. In other words, more educated parents value education highly and either send their children to private schools, where student achievement is, on average, higher (Somers et al., 2004), or supplement their children's public schooling by providing books and private tutoring.

Fourth, the insignificant coefficient on the female household head variable suggests that, in Peru, households in which females have total bargaining power do not spend more on education than households headed by males. This suggests that Haddad-Hoddinott's (1994) finding for Côte D'Ivore, indicating that when females have bargaining power they tend to spend a larger share of the household income on children's schooling, does not replicate with Peruvian data.

Lastly, rural and Quechua households, groups traditionally marginalized in Peru, spend significantly less on their children's schooling. These results suggest that relying on policies that increase the government's dependence on private funds to finance education by, for example, establishing user fees in public schools would have a negative impact not only on the enrolment levels but also on the educational attainment of these, already marginalized, groups.

7.7   Summary and Policy Implications

Following the debt crisis and hyperinflation of the 1980s, the Peruvian government implemented in the early 1990s structural adjustments that affected the education system. These structural adjustments reduced considerably Peru's public spending on education as a percentage of its GDP. In spite of these reductions, enrolments increased substantially. The large expansion in enrolments observed in Peru can be partially explained by an increased dependence on family's expenditures to finance part of the costs for the provision of education, and on the encouragement for establishing private schools. Both policies, sometimes promoted by international lending agencies like the World Bank (1995), have had negative short-term consequences in terms of equality of opportunities in the educational system.

The 1993 law that encourages the establishment of private schools to allow for increased enrolments while simultaneously containing public spending is expected to have a negative impact on equality. In 1994, the largest proportion of students attending private schools came from high-income, highly educated, urban and Spanish-speaking households. Moreover, sending a child to a private school in Peru is a very expensive enterprise for a poor household, who could spend about 36% of its total income by sending only one child to a private institution. Therefore, the Peruvian government should use fiscal incentives to encourage the establishment of private schools in rural areas, and it should introduce scholarships and/or vouchers targeted at low-income children from households where the head has low levels of education. This would equalize participation in the private sector by poor families, if indeed increased participation of the private sector in the provision of education is desired.

The analysis of the variations in private spending on education by household characteristics, and the analysis of the distribution of such expenditures by quintiles of household income, has illustrated that the amounts spent privately on education are highly unequally distributed in Peru. Private expenditures on education vary considerably by household characteristics. High levels of expenditures correspond to high levels of household income even when the child is enrolled in a public school. Relying on family resources to finance part of the education costs therefore is a policy that has proved to reinforce existing inequalities in the Peruvian educational system. To mitigate the negative effects of depending on private financing, the government could try to redistribute public spending from the more affluent metropolitan Lima to the poor rural areas, particularly in the Sierra where large numbers of Quechua students reside.

Finally, the analysis of the determinants of private expenditures on education has shown that education is a necessity in Peru but the willingness to pay for it is relatively low; as household income doubles, expenditures on education increase only by 29%. Thus, the Peruvian government cannot solely rely on increments of household income to increase private levels of expenditures on education as a mechanism for financing educational quality and access to secondary schools. The elasticity of income indicates that such an increase will not be high enough. Most importantly, it is a very inequitable alternative as Peruvian families are already contributing significant amounts to their children's schooling. The resources needed for improving educational quality and access to secondary schools should come from redirecting public spending to rural and impoverished areas, in particular to Quechua domains, and from targeting scholarships to these segments of the population instead of from additional family contributions. Peru is an example of a country that, due to globalization trends and structural adjustments, has capped the level of public spending on education and encouraged the establishments of private schools. This chapter has demonstrated how unequal these types of policies that force families to increase their financial contribution to education can be.

7.8 Conclusion

This chapter has shown that, despite the improvements made by Peru in terms of total enrolments and its mandate from the 1993 Constitution to make education compulsory, secondary education still largely excludes children from the most disadvantaged households. The direct private costs involved in sending a child to secondary school are relatively high for the poorest households (and one could assume that the indirect costs are the highest for this group). The Peruvian government should try to minimize such costs through, for example, scholarships targeted at low-income, rural, and, in particular, Quechua children between 12 and 18 years.

Acknowledgments Earlier versions of this study have been delivered at the 2002 Annual Meeting of the Comparative and International Education Society in Orlando, Florida, and at the 2003 Congress of the Latin American Studies Association in Dallas, Texas. The author would like to thank Henry M. Levin, Mun C. Tsang, the attendants at the Economics and Education Seminar at Teachers College, Columbia University, and anonymous reviewers for their helpful comments and suggestions, and Tia Dole for her editing assistance. All errors remaining are solely mine.

References

Banco Central de Reserva del Perú [Central Reserve Bank of Peru]. (2001). *Series estadísticas* [Statistical Series]. Retrieved December 12, 2001 from http://www.bcrp.gob.pe

Gertler, P., & Glewwe, P. W. (1990). The willingness to pay for education in developing countries: Evidence from rural Peru. *Journal of Public Economics, 42*(3), 251–275.

Gertler, P., & Glewwe, P. W. (1992). The willingness to pay for education for daughters in contrast to sons: Evidence from rural Peru. *The World Bank Economic Review, 6*(1), 171–188.

Glewwe, P. W., & Patrinos, H. (1999). The role of the private sector in education in Vietnam: Evidence from the Vietnam Living Standards Survey. *World Development, 27*(4), 887–902.

Grupo de Análisis para el Desarrollo [GRADE]. (2001). Las familias y el financiamiento de la educación pública en el Perú [The families and the financing of public education in Peru]. Retrieved December 12, 2001 from http://www.grade.org.pe/boletin/04/art01.htm

Haddad, L., & Hoddinott, J. (1994). Women's income and boy-girl anthropometric status in the Côte D'Ivore. *World Development, 22*(4), 543–553.

Somers, M-A., McEwan, P. J., & Williams, J. D. (2004). How effective are private schools in Latin America? *Comparative Education Review, 48*(1), 48–69.

Steele, D., Hall, G., & McIsaac, D. (1998). Peru: Living standards measurement survey 1994. Retrieved December 15, 2001 from http://www.worldbank.org/html/prdph/lsms/country/pe94/docs/pe94sid1.pdf

Torres, R. M. (2003). Improving the quality of basic education? The strategies of the World Bank. In E. R. Beauchamp (Ed.), *Comparative education reader* (pp. 299–328). New York: RoutledgeFalmer.

Tsang, M. C. (1994). Private and public costs of schooling in developing nations. In T. Husen, & N. Postlethwaite (Eds.), *International encyclopedia of education*. New York: Pergamon Press.

Tsang, M. C. (2002). Comparing the costs of public and private schools in developing countries. In H. M. Levin, & P. J. McEwan (Eds.), *Cost-effectiveness and education policy* (pp. 111–136). Larchmont: Eye on Education Publishers.

Tsang, M. C., & Kidchanapanish, S. (1992). Private resources and the quality of primary education in Thailand. *International Journal of Educational Research*, *17*(20), 179–198.

World Bank. (1995). *Priorities and strategies for education.* Washington, DC: The World Bank.

Table 7.1 Descriptive statistics of Peruvian students by level and type of enrolment (Author's estimations based on PLSS 1994)

Demographic and background characteristics	All samples	Primary			Secondary			All levels	
		Public	Private	All	Public	Private	All	Public	Private
Student characteristics									
Age of student	11.986	10.278	9.2386	10.188	15.211	14.954	15.169	11.962	12.177
Student is female	0.4992	0.5005	0.5491	0.5048	0.4890	0.4924	0.4896	0.4966	0.5200
First language									
Spanish	0.8538	0.8114	0.9835	0.8264	0.8866	0.9869	0.9029	0.8371	0.9852
Quechua	0.1143	0.1488	0.0047	0.1362	0.0869	0.0131	0.0749	0.1276	0.0090
Other language	0.0319	0.0398	0.0118	0.0374	0.0265	0.0000	0.0222	0.0353	0.0057
Schooling characteristics									
Total expenditures on education (annual in soles)	214.12	92.918	873.14	160.82	172.96	1004.5	308.47	120.23	940.67
Public school	0.8856	–	–	0.9130	–	–	0.8370	–	–
Private school	0.1144	–	–	0.0870	–	–	0.1630	–	–
Primary school	0.6391	–	–	–	–	–	–	0.6588	0.4859
Secondary school	0.3609	–	–	–	–	–	–	0.3412	0.5141
Household characteristics									
Total household income (annual in soles)	11145.5	8453.2	22072.7	9638.5	11625.5	25074.7	13817.1	9535.7	23615.9
Household size	6.7629	6.9599	5.9163	6.8690	6.7473	5.6896	6.5749	6.8873	5.7998
Number of children in household	3.9170	4.2312	3.1166	4.1342	3.6738	2.8020	3.5317	4.0410	2.9549
Rural residency	0.3378	0.4366	0.0683	0.4046	0.2563	0.0276	0.2191	0.3751	0.0474
Residency in Metropolitan Lima	0.2380	0.1841	0.3474	0.1983	0.2861	0.4231	0.3084	0.2189	0.3863
Household head is female	0.1088	0.1006	0.0846	0.0992	0.1338	0.0849	0.1258	0.1119	0.0848
Years of schooling of household head	7.6201	6.5186	13.056	7.0875	7.6637	13.193	8.5648	6.9093	13.127

Occupation of household head									
Executive, managers, professionals	0.1031	0.0670	0.2888	0.0863	0.0946	0.3296	0.1329	0.0764	0.3098
Public service, clerical, and trade	0.2146	0.1737	0.3275	0.1871	0.2556	0.3038	0.2634	0.2016	0.3153
Service	0.0612	0.0638	0.0528	0.0628	0.0644	0.0274	0.0583	0.0640	0.0397
Agricultural worker	0.3360	0.4199	0.1198	0.3938	0.2652	0.0734	0.2340	0.3671	0.0959
Manual worker, laborer	0.2851	0.2756	0.2111	0.2700	0.3203	0.2659	0.3114	0.2908	0.2393
Number of cases (unweighted)	3,817	2,344	176	2,520	1,110	187	1,297	3,501	367

Table 7.2 Student, schooling and household characteristics for quintiles of private expenditures on education (Author's estimations based on PLSS 1994)

Demographic and background characteristics	Lowest	Middle-low	Middle	Middle-high	Highest
Student characteristics					
Student is female	0.5366	0.4731	0.4912	0.5006	0.4991
First language					
Spanish	0.6657	0.8058	0.8732	0.9119	0.9770
Quechua	0.2952	0.1597	0.0783	0.0553	0.0158
Other language	0.0369	0.0345	0.0485	0.0328	0.0072
Schooling characteristics					
Public school	0.9914	0.9760	0.9733	0.9295	0.5945
Private school	0.0086	0.0240	0.0267	0.0705	0.4055
Primary school	0.8595	0.7334	0.6277	0.5753	0.4466
Secondary school	0.1405	0.2666	0.3723	0.4247	0.5534
Household characteristics					
Total household income (annual, in soles)	6941.5	7726.4	9210.9	11407.4	19207.1
Household size	7.4640	7.0879	6.8799	6.4409	6.0955
Number of children in household	4.8146	4.3278	3.9628	3.5518	3.1207
Rural residency	0.7041	0.4435	0.3086	0.1992	0.1037
Residency in Metropolitan Lima	0.0707	0.1559	0.2439	0.3080	0.3759
Household head is female	0.1017	0.1115	0.1207	0.1122	0.0976
Years of schooling of household head	4.5521	6.2888	7.0847	8.2141	11.2478
Occupation of household head					
Executive, managers, professionals	0.0395	0.0551	0.0573	0.1139	0.2308
Public service, clerical and trade	0.0867	0.1837	0.2265	0.2580	0.2940
Service	0.0462	0.0701	0.0633	0.0706	0.0545
Agricultural worker	0.6269	0.4312	0.3353	0.2409	0.1058
Manual worker, laborer	0.2007	0.2599	0.3176	0.3165	0.3148

Table 7.3 Determinants of private spending on education, Peru 1994 (Author's estimations based on PLSS 1994)

Explanatory variable	All levels and schools	All schools		All levels	
		Primary	Secondary	Public	Private
Student characteristics					
Student is female	−0.0609	−0.0419	−0.0904	−0.0617	−0.0788
	(0.0342)	(0.0443)	(0.0565)	(0.0354)	(0.1009)
First language					
Quechua	−0.4125*	−0.4765*	−0.1565	−0.4287*	−0.3041
	(0.0788)	(0.0968)	(0.1280)	(0.0779)	(0.3009)
Other language	0.2820*	0.1999	0.4335*	0.2557*	−0.4668
	(0.1090)	(0.1084)	(0.2111)	(0.1113)	(0.3604)
Schooling characteristics					
Private school	1.2169*	1.3415*	1.1410*	–	–
	(0.0696)	(0.0967)	(0.0788)	–	–
Secondary school	0.3750*	–	–	0.4448*	−0.0411
	(0.0364)	–	–	(0.0414)	(0.0845)
Household characteristics					
Ln total household income (annual, in soles)	0.2895*	0.2677*	0.3416*	0.2309*	0.6642*
	(0.0345)	(0.0379)	(0.0548)	(0.0365)	(0.0856)
Number of children in household	−0.1319*	−0.1573*	−0.0751*	−0.1326*	−0.1287*
	(0.0187)	(0.0214)	(0.0219)	(0.0188)	(0.0488)
Rural residency	−0.3906*	−0.5185*	−0.0932	−0.4415*	0.3508
	(0.0752)	(0.0884)	(0.1120)	(0.0770)	(0.3421)
Residency in metropolitan Lima	0.0562	0.0620	0.0769	−0.0102	0.3634*
	(0.0637)	(0.0710)	(0.0780)	(0.0664)	(0.1170)
Household head is female	−0.0752	0.0198	−0.1605	−0.0791	0.2440
	(0.0774)	(0.0960)	(0.1033)	(0.0828)	(0.2249)
Years of schooling of household head	0.0478*	0.0542*	0.0357*	0.0469*	0.0412*
	(0.0061)	(0.0072)	(0.0084)	(0.0061)	(0.0164)
Occupation of household head					
Public service, clerical, and trade	0.1288	0.1597	0.0541	0.2150	−0.0675
	(0.1173)	(0.1658)	(0.1197)	(0.1348)	(0.1615)
Service	−0.0113	−0.0187	−0.0465	0.0566	−0.1210
	(0.1633)	(0.2392)	(0.1425)	(0.1769)	(0.2980)
Agricultural worker	0.0356	0.1291	−0.1027	0.1206	−0.3668
	(0.1316)	(0.1818)	(0.1519)	(0.1403)	(0.3571)
Manual worker, laborer	0.1094	0.1639	0.0046	0.2209	−0.1650
	(0.1129)	(0.1652)	(0.1271)	(0.1345)	(0.1433)
Constant	1.8040*	2.0314*	1.6320*	2.2613*	−0.3471
	(0.3455)	(0.4273)	(0.5325)	(0.3555)	(0.8052)
R-squared	0.4935	0.4960	0.3868	0.3336	0.4505
Number of cases (unweighted)	3,817	2,520	1,297	3,454	363

Standard errors in parentheses; * indicates significance at the 0.05 level.

Chapter 8
Defying the Odds: A Study of Grade 11 Female Students in Eritrea

Kara Janigan

8.1 Introduction

Issues of gender inequality in schools within developing countries have been gaining increased attention globally over the last three decades, especially since the 1990 World Conference on Education for All in Jomtien, Thailand. As a result, a plethora of educational data exists detailing the marginalized position of girls and young women in sub-Saharan Africa. However, very little is known about the life experiences of female students who have succeeded within harsh educational systems despite highly unfavourable odds. As noted by the United Nations Development Fund for Women (UNIFEM), "a complete picture requires both narratives and numbers" (UNIFEM, 2000, p. 62). In exploring that picture, this chapter presents research findings that provide insights about previously unheard voices of some successful female students. While this study is "a close-up look at one aspect of one segment of a larger world" (Bogdan & Bicklin, 1998, p. 198), the focus will be pulled back to consider broader contextual factors that favourably affect the academic success of these students.

A brief review of literature on girls' education in sub-Saharan Africa, followed by background information on Eritrea, will set the context for this study which focused on 19 female students in their final year of secondary school in Debarwa, a rural village in Eritrea. The study examined from an ideographic perspective factors enabling these students to succeed and those serving as obstacles to their success. A summary of student profiles will shed light on the background of the participating students whose experiences and perceptions are presented. Finally, conclusions of the study will lead to implications for actions in the hope of enabling more female students to succeed in school, in both Eritrea and other sub-Saharan African countries.

Ontario Institute for Studies in Education at the University of Toronto (OISE/UT)

8.2 Girls' Education in Sub-Saharan Africa

Issues related to girls' education in sub-Saharan Africa have been examined and well-documented in recent years (Leach, 1998; Samoff, 1999; Stromquist, 1999). Statistics reveal the severity of challenges, particularly in terms of access, equity, and quality within educational systems in many countries (UNICEF, 2000; United Nations, 2000; World Bank, 2001). Sex-disaggregated statistics detailing who is going to school and how they are performing expose significant gender gaps. Research conducted to determine the reasons for these gaps has revealed many common economic, social, and cultural factors serving to severely limit girls' educational opportunities in countries throughout sub-Saharan Africa, including Eritrea.

Despite efforts to reach gender parity in enrolment, the United Nations Educational, Scientific and Cultural Organization (UNESCO, 2000) reports that, between 1990 and 1998, the gender gap reflected by gross enrolment ratio has increased in sub-Saharan African countries. Furthermore, as students move up the educational ladder the gender gap between the number of girls and boys increases. When this gap is examined in terms of rural and urban disparity, it is found that girls living in rural communities face a "double disadvantage", according to the United Nations Children's Fund (UNICEF, 2000). Brock and Cammish (1991, as cited in Leach, 1998) note how

> the lowest enrolments of girls—and the largest gender gaps—are inevitably in the poorest and least economically developed areas, especially in the rural communities where educational provision is poor, among children of the poorest families, and among children of ethnic minorities (p.13).

Turning attention to the performance of girls who are attending school, statistics and studies also reveal significant gender gaps in repetition, dropout, and failure rates at all levels of the educational system (Heneveld & Odaga, 1995; see also Dorsey, 1989; Hyde, 1994; Mbilinyi & Mbughuni, 1991 as cited in Heneveld & Odaga, 1995).

In an effort to better understand the reasons for these realities, factors related to why girls account for less than half the school population have been well researched, are well known, and many are interrelated. They are socio-economic, sociocultural, political, institutional, and school factors (Samoff, 1999). Poverty plays the most significant role, however, in determining a girl's chance of being educated. Even when free schooling reduces or eliminates direct costs of sending a child to school, opportunity costs, such as the loss of time that could otherwise be used for labour, must also be incurred. Intertwined with issues related to poverty are the social and cultural factors that further serve as barriers for parents to send their daughters to school. Samoff summarizes these factors as:

> parental attitudes, gender-differentiated expectations for future income (based at least in part on gender-differentiated salary scales), the labour and household responsibilities of women, the absence of role models at home and in school, explicit and implicit discouragement for pursuing particular courses of study, parents' educational achievement, family religious and moral precepts (p. 409).

Social and cultural factors regarding traditional views of a girl's role in society p
a particularly dominant role. Leach (1998) reveals the depth of these factors:

> [A]s girls reach puberty and marriageable age, parents are reluctant to let them travel long distances to school, especially in insecure rural areas. Fear of the shame of pregnancy outside marriage is a strong reason for parents to keep daughters at home (p. 14).

In terms of religion serving as a barrier, Kelly (1984) points out that it is widely assumed that education for Muslim girls is limited as a result of the religion's view of women's place in society. She states that "whether religion, particularly Islam, depresses women's access to education is not at all clear independent of other factors" (p. 85). Kelly cites the example of Islamic countries where women's enrolment ratios are higher than in non-Islamic countries, particularly in higher education (Howard-Merriam, 1979; Meleis et al., 1979; Mustaffa-Kedah, 1975–1976; O'Shaughnessey, 1978; Smock, 1981, as cited in Kelly).

School factors also act as barriers to girls' education. As Kelly (1984) states, "making schools available to women needs to be distinguished from making them accessible to women" (p. 87). Barriers within school range from curricular issues such as gender stereotyping in textbooks, and the effects of the "hidden curriculum" in the form of teachers' negative attitudes towards female students, to issues of personal security and comfort in the classroom and on the journey to and from school. Girls and young women in sub-Saharan African countries face challenges in terms of educational access and achievement at many different levels. This is particularly true for female students in Eritrea. The following section details Eritrea's economic context, the challenges to traditional roles of women which make the Eritrean case unique, and the harshness of its education system, particularly for female students.

8.3 Eritrea's Economic, Societal, and Educational Context

Eritrea is a small country bordered by Ethiopia and Djibouti to the south, Sudan to the north and west, and the Red Sea to the east. With an economy and infrastructure devastated by the 30-year struggle for independence, Eritrea has some of the lowest social and economic indicators in sub-Saharan Africa. In 1999, Eritrea's Gross National Product (GNP) per capita was US$200 (World Bank, 2001). Its population, estimated at just over 4 million in 2000 (Central Intelligence Agency, 2001), consists of nine ethnic groups, the largest being Tigrinya. Roughly half the people are Muslim and the other half Christian, with 82% of the population living in rural areas (United Nations, 2000).

Since, as Sweetman (1998) points out, "schools and education systems reflect the social context from which they come" (p. 3), it is important to mention the unique challenges to the traditional status of women that have taken place within Eritrean society over the last 30 years. Eritrea's struggle for liberation from Ethiopia began in 1961 when 'fighters' were exclusively male (Stefanos, 1997, p. 668).

ın People's Liberation Front (EPLF) was formed. Describing
ist (Firebrace & Holland, 1984, p. 131), the EPLF believed all
formerly marginalized, especially women, needed to actively
ırs of society (Firebrace & Holland, p. 30). As a result, women
ɔme 'fighters' (Stefanos, p. 668). By the mid-1980s, 30% of
 ̣women. More than 15% of these were active combatants (Firebrace
& Holland, p. 41).

Furthermore, the EPLF envisioned very non-traditional roles for both men and women 'fighters' at the front where traditional divisions of labour for men and women were abandoned. Cowan (1984) describes how women at the front "crew tanks, take part in guerrilla units and generally suffer the same hardships and take the same responsibilities as their male comrades" (p. 148). As 'fighters', these women were highly visible, respected members of society making extremely valuable contributions within the public sphere.

After gaining independence in 1991, the leaders of the EPLF formed the government and developed policies addressing issues of equality within the educational system. In 1995 the Eritrean Government adopted the goal of making basic education available for all citizens ("Macro Policy Document", 1995, as cited in Ministry of Education (MOE) and UNICEF, 1996). Its education policy included the "provision of a seven year basic education to all citizens with a special emphasis on girls' education" (MOE, 1996, as cited in MOE and UNICEF, 1996, p. 8).

In terms of the education system, the Eritrean case exemplifies many of the challenges to girls' education detailed earlier in a subcontinental context. After a 30-year fight for independence, Eritrea's school system was severely disadvantaged with only approximately one third of the school age population, aged 7–11, having access to primary schooling in 1998/99 (MOE, 1999). Furthermore, it was projected that only 4 out of 100 children starting grade 1 would complete grade 11 (UNICEF, 1997, p. 21).

Eritrean educational statistics reveal many disparities between girls and boys. There are fewer girls than boys at all levels in the education system. Data regarding student flow rates reveal discrepancies between girls and boys in promotion, repetition, dropout and failure rates, with boys performing better than girls in all areas and at all grade levels. In all cases these gender gaps became wider as students moved up the educational ladder.

Especially evident is the inefficiency of the educational system at the elementary level. A hypothetical cohort reconstruction based on actual flow rates from 1998/99 indicates that of 1,000 students who began grade 1 in 1998/99, only 177 would graduate from grade 5 without repeating a grade (MOE, 1999). Furthermore, it would take 8.8 years for the average elementary student to pass through the 5-year elementary cycle (MOE, 1999). Based on this information, many girls beginning school at 7 years of age would be 16 by the time they completed grade 5, if they had not already dropped out. Given the traditional practice of early marriage for girls, this inefficiency has a much greater impact on the lives of female students when compared to their male peers.

When considering the intersection of gender and rural/urban disparities in education, the situation in Eritrea is most extreme. According to UNICEF (2000), when compared to other developing countries, Eritrea has the greatest urban/rural divide, with 79% of children in urban areas attending school while only 24% of rural children attend school. While disparities exist for girls in all parts of Eritrea, they are most extreme in the lowland areas where the average net enrolment for girls was estimated to be 11% in 1994/95 (MOE, 1995, as cited in MOE and UNICEF, 1996, p. 15). Few girls attending school in these areas complete primary school as repetition and dropout rates for girls are significantly high.

In a study focusing on obstacles to girls' education in Eritrea, poverty was found to be the most serious barrier to parents sending their daughters to school. Since girls are responsible for performing essential household tasks, the loss of labour coupled with the direct cost of school supplies results in an opportunity cost that families living in poverty cannot afford (MOE and UNICEF, 1996, p. 22). When a family is poor the parents tend to give preference to sending their sons rather than daughters to school (MOE and UNICEF, 1996, p. 23).

Such parental decisions cannot be separated from societal and cultural factors serving to support them. As stated in the same report (MOE and UNICEF, 1996), "in the context where girls are 'born to marry' (and therefore lost from the family), parents see little economic value in educating girls" (p. 22). Furthermore, "socio-cultural factors and socialization processes which constantly present a subservient wife and mother role for girls affect their self-image, performance and attainment in school and their career aspirations" (MOE and UNICEF, 1996, p. 24).

Research conducted on girls' education in predominantly Muslim lowland areas reveals that cultural and religious factors were far greater obstacles to girls' education than the need for girls' labour at home, costs, and distance from school. These factors related to "fears about the loss of the girls' traditional values (respect, obedience, virtue) and thus, about their reduced marriageability" (MOE and UNICEF, 1997, p. 7–8). These factors were by far of greatest concern because it is believed that "a girl's livelihood is marriage" (MOE and UNICEF, 1997, p. 9). As a result, "education may prevent her from marrying—and at best, it is irrelevant. How will she live if she doesn't marry?" (MOE and UNICEF, 1997, p. 8).

Barriers to girls' education exist even before the girls get to their classroom since the average distance students walk to school ranges from 2.2 km in the capital to 8 km in rural areas. This means that some children spend four to five hours walking to and from school each day (MOE, 1995, as cited in MOE, 1997, p. 9). Again this has a great impact on the lives of female students whose personal safety may be at risk when walking long distances to and from school.

Once at school, several other barriers exist. One report (MOE and UNICEF, 1996) notes how "teachers' attitudes, behaviour and teaching practices have perhaps been the most significant determinants for female persistence and academic achievement and attainment" (p. 21). The report also describes how teachers, reflecting widely held societal attitudes, "treat girls in class in a derogatory and diminishing manner" (p. 21). This is compounded by a lack of role models as less than 30% of teachers in Eritrea are women (p. 20). Parents are also unlikely to send their daughters to school when the education system is perceived to be of poor quality and not relevant to the needs and aspirations of the parents (MOE and UNICEF, 1996, p. 24). This, coupled with low parental expectations of their daughters' achievement in school and her career prospects, further reduces a girl's chance of receiving formal education.

Despite all the barriers and challenges to girls' education in Eritrea, however, there are young women who defy staggering odds and survive the harsh educational system. The following section details a study that allows these success stories to be understood on an individual level. These stories breathe life into all the statistics and reports on girls' education as they reflect lives lived.

8.4   Methodology

The purpose of this research was to investigate the life experiences of successful female students within a harsh educational system where female students are marginalized. The intention of this study was not to generalize the experiences of these students or to represent them, as Mohanty (1988) warns against, as "a singular monolithic subject" (p. 61) but rather to better understand their perceptions and experiences. Through this study their voices can be heard. A deeper understanding of the factors and forces that empowered these particular young women to succeed against very unfavourable odds will provide valuable insight as to how effective actions can be taken to enable more girls to succeed academically, in Eritrea and other sub-Saharan African countries.

The study was conducted in Debarwa, a small village south of the capital of Asmara that serves as a market centre for neighbouring villages. Typical of a rural highland community, farming of grains and vegetables is the dominant form of economic activity and the vast majority of the population is Christian from the Tigrinya ethnic group. A few families are Muslim Tigrinya. The research was conducted at this location because the community knew the researcher who had been a teacher at the Junior Secondary School from 1994 to 1996. Debarwa is representative of a highland rural community, and thus research done in this location primarily reflects social and educational practices within the dominant Christian Tigrinya rural population in Eritrea. Insight is also gained into some aspects of these practices within the Muslim Tigrinya population, however, due to the study's sample group.

Female students in their last year of secondary education were asked about the difficulties they face and the factors that have enabled them to complete their schooling while the vast majority of young women their age have married and left school. The questions explored were as follows: Why are these particular students still in school? What difficulties do they face? How have they overcome obstacles in the past? What support do they receive? What enables them to succeed in the formal school system? Why had they attained a level of education that so few females do?

Qualitative data, gathered through semi-structured interviews with 19 students, revealed obstacles these students faced as well as support they received which enabled them to achieve academic success. Using available sampling, just under half of all the grade 11 female students beginning their final year of senior secondary school at the Debarwa Senior Secondary School were interviewed. Relevant educational statistical data and reports were also examined.

Interviews were conducted in September 2001, with each participant interviewed once. The time and place of the interviews were arranged in accordance with the desires and needs of the students. The average length of an interview was one hour and the vast majority of the interviews were conducted in English without a translator. The odd time when a student was struggling to express herself in English, she was encouraged to speak Tigrinya. These comments were later translated. The quotes in this article reflect the exact words of the participants.

8.5 Summary of Student Profiles

The 19 students who participated in this study were largely representative of the grade 11 female school population in Debarwa, both in terms of their individual characteristics and their family background, although there were a few exceptions. Since Debarwa is predominately inhabited by Christians of Tigrinya ethnicity, all but one of the students came from such a background, the exception being of Muslim Tigrinya origin. Three quarters of the students came from farming backgrounds. More than half the students had fathers who were farmers and all but two had mothers whom they described as taking care of the home. The mothers of two students took over the family farming when their husbands died and the non-farming fathers worked either for the government or in the private sector. One student's mother and father were 'fighters'. While some 'fighters' have been de-mobilized, many people continue to be 'fighters' and work as civil servants as this student's parents did.

Four students came from families where neither parent has received formal schooling. Nine of the students' mothers had received some schooling while 10 had not. Of the mothers who had received schooling, the highest level was grade 7. Four students had fathers who received primary schooling, three students' fathers had some junior secondary level education, one student's father had completed grade 8, while three of the students' fathers were quite educated, having completed secondary school or university.

Given the economic impoverishment of Eritrea, there is a relatively narrow variation of economic circumstances for families living in the rural areas. However, families from small villages, such as those surrounding Debarwa, generally have a lower standard of living than those living in larger centres. Roughly half the students in this study came from Debarwa while the others came from smaller neighbouring or distant villages. Three families living in distant villages made economic sacrifices so that their daughters could rent a room in Debarwa and continue their education

under more favourable conditions. Considering family size as an indicator of socio-
economic status, 10 of the 19 students came from families with 5 or fewer children.
These families were smaller than the average family in Eritrea. This would result
in lower direct costs related to sending their children to school since all school-age
children in all the families of the participants attend school. The one exception was
the brother of a student whom she described as "sick" and thus unable to attend
school.

As for the students themselves, almost all had moved efficiently through the
harsh education system having completed 11 grades of schooling in 11 or 12 years,
since the average age of these students was 19. This shows their strong academic
performance. Only one was married, as it is extremely uncommon in Eritrea for a
married woman to continue her schooling. The student of Muslim faith had been
engaged since she was 14. Truly exceptional was the one married student who had
just given birth to her first child. She lived very close to the school and had a great
deal of family support allowing her to attend school. Only two of the students had
to walk to and from a neighbouring village each day to attend school. Half of the
remaining students came from Debarwa, while the others either rented a room,
lived with a relative in Debarwa, or lived in the local convent. Also of significance
is the fact that two thirds of the students had a relative who was either studying at,
or who had graduated from, the University of Asmara, which is the only university
in Eritrea.

8.6   Findings

When attempting to understand the factors and circumstances allowing these
female students to succeed in the Eritrean school system, it is difficult, if not impossible, to completely separate the different factors as many are interrelated.
Furthermore, the diversity of the students' life experiences also makes generalizations impossible. That said, students spoke predominately of issues that have been
categorized in three groups of key factors affecting their academic success. These
key factors are: family, self, and school. Through data analysis it became evident
that these factors could serve either as obstacles, posing difficulties for the students
as they strive for academic success, or as enablers, helping them to achieve success,
depending on the circumstances. The following sections present these obstacles and
enablers.

8.6.1   Family

Family-related factors are central to the success of the students. These factors provide the foundation which enabled the students in this study to succeed, as it was the
parents who opened the door to education for their children. The effect of parents'

decision-making regarding schooling for their children is especially critical in Eritrea since only a third of primary school-age children had access to school in 1998/99 (MOE, 1999). It is also, ultimately, the parents who determine whether their children continue in school. This is particularly true given the traditional practice of early marriage for girls.

Within these parameters, it is clear that the parents of the students in this study greatly value education for their daughters. This is true regardless of whether or not the students' parents have received any formal education. Many students spoke of their father's and/or mother's support and encouragement and how highly they valued education. One emphasized that she was still in school because "my father like education because he cannot learn. Because at that time he don't learn because of colonization, war". Another student described her father as being "very intelligent and interested in learning". She said he is very "angry" that he received only a few years of education because he was needed to do family farming while his brother was educated further, eventually becoming a doctor.

It appears that, for at least one student, parental support, her hard work, and academic success has allowed her a certain degree of control over her life. This sense of empowerment is evident in the following statement:

> My family, they are not educated but they tell me I am studying hard. I am worrying of education, my lessons. I study so that they think about me 'she must educate. She is wanting to educate. So that we have to help her.' They think like this so that they don't tell me to married me.

Speaking about her own and another student's father, she also said: "[W]hen I speak out about education they don't interrupt me." She was referring to how she studies late into the evening at her friend's house. Understanding that the conditions must be favourable enough to allow these students to be in school in the first place, their hard work and academic achievement seem to give them a certain sense of power and control over an aspect of their life.

8.6.2 Self

While it is the parents who opened the educational door, it is ultimately the students' personal beliefs, attitudes, and perceptions that lie at the core of their success. Within the key factor of self, motivation and determination are critical in determining academic performance and are influenced by all other factors. Although it is impossible to determine the precise reasons for a student's level of motivation, the following comments provide insight into several factors that appear to be significant.

Several students made reference to their self-imposed obligation to work in their home, even when urged by their mothers to spend time studying. As one student explained, there is a strong sense that it is wrong not to help. When describing the work her family was doing at harvest time, she said: "[A]lways we are working all the day because we should help our parents because we are their children.

Even when they say don't work, how can we as they are working?" Another said: "She [my mother] said 'study hard'. If I said 'I help you', [she would say] 'no. Study, only study'. But I help sometimes."

In terms of enablers, some students are motivated by the desire to take advantage of the opportunities they have. One spoke of being "lucky" to receive a high level of schooling. Another said, "chance is good" when comparing her experience to that of her parents, neither of whom attended school. Similarly, one student compared her experience to that of her older sister who left school after grade 8 to marry.

Students' determination and motivation were also demonstrated through strategies they used to help them succeed in school. Roughly one quarter of the students in this study spoke about how they choose to sit with male students at the front of the class, as the brightest and best students tend to sit there. One student described how "[I] sit with boys. The boys is very, very clever". Another student explained:

> I like sit with boys because when you sit with girls you are talk, not listen the teacher. If sit with the boy you cannot talk with the boy. Only you are ashamed and you listen the teacher. And then you ask to the boy about the school about the learning how to it to learn you ask the boy you cannot ask to her. Why? Because if she talk and I talk with other things. Yeah, not about the school.

In this way, students use restrictive cultural norms, which discourage female students from chatting with male students, to their advantage. Where they chose to sit in class is used by some of the students as a means of self-regulation as several said it reduced the likelihood of their being distracted during class. As one student noted: "[I]f I sit with girls, I start joking but with boys, I don't joke."

All the students spoke of the great deal of effort they put into their studies, even when facing various obstacles such as time constraints. Most students spoke of studying after completing their housework. A few spoke of waking up in the middle of the night for an hour or two of quiet uninterrupted study time. One student described how, after going to sleep at 9 p.m., she sets her alarm clock to wake her at 1 a.m. so that she can study for a couple hours before going back to sleep. "Yeah, I like to study in night. There is no … nothing noise." She explained that, while she sets her alarm to wake her up each night, if she is too tired to study she will go back to sleep. Similarly, another student described how, at 2 a.m., "that time is very nice, not noisy". She studies for about an hour and a half before going back to sleep. "If I tired, I sleep but always I wake up."

Students also spoke of strategies they used when they had questions about their school work. One relied heavily on her cousin who was attending university, as she explained, "most [questions] I will ask to my cousin". Another student asked other students, especially the "clever" ones, for help. One student explained how, when studying, she writes down questions to ask her teachers. She said: "When I go to school on the break time I met the teacher that I want. I ask them. They help me at that time."

When speaking of their experiences, students often mentioned issues related to three predominant and highly interrelated societal beliefs: the academic capabilities of female students, the suitable age for females to marry, and the appropriate aspirations for girls and young women. Implicitly serving as an obstacle for girls and young women in the education system in Eritrea is the widely held belief that 'girls are not as clever as boys'. Students in this study disassociated themselves from this belief since they themselves were proof that female students were capable of achieving academic success. When speaking to this issue, some students shrugged and smiled, implying a 'what can you do about it' attitude. One said: "[Y]ou can [say that 'girls are not as clever as boys'] but you don't know that." Several students strongly and clearly rejected this belief. "I don't accept it", stated one student. Another simply replied, "wrong".

The practice of early marriage can also be a major obstacle to girls' education as female students rarely continue schooling once married. In terms of this practice, many students stressed the importance of how the female students themselves think about early marriage. Students understood this to be as important as the attitude of the students' parents, since they believed acceptance of this tradition would diminish a student's determination to overcome the various challenges they faced in order to succeed in school. One student noted that a female student who faces difficult circumstances might consider early marriage as an easier option than struggling with school. She noted: "[T]he problem is first, specially for girls in the village, the school is very far. They are tired and they want to married." Another linked parental views of early marriage to that of the daughter by noting that

> 10% girls are finished in grade 11 in school because for girls the culture is not good in Eritrea. When our parents only knows when a girl grows she must married. School is not necessary for her. They said like this so that ... they are not weak. The girls are not weak but their mind is interrupted. Their parents say to them you have to married. She is thinking about school and about the marriage. So that makes ... can make her weak.

This type of thinking would clearly reduce a student's motivation to put energy into her studies and to continue in school.

Almost all students in this study were adamant about not wanting to marry until they had completed their schooling and had obtained a job. The exceptions were the students living at the convent who intended to become Sisters once they finished school. In a typical statement, one student said: "I'm thinking I do not like to get married at this age but after I finished my school and I get a special job. And especially my husband he have to get a job. After that, it is life." Stressing the importance of her thoughts, one student commented: "[M]y aim is to get marriage when I go to university and I finish it. When I got job, I will get married. But as I am a student, I should be a student. I never think about marriage."

Twelve of the students spoke explicitly of their hope to score high enough in their matriculation exams to allow them to gain admittance to either the University of Asmara or the Asmara Teacher Training Institute. A few mentioned the desire to become a doctor, a teacher or an engineer. One student's determination is clearly evident when she said:

> I hope to get ... to enter university. It's the only thing I hope with my thinking. I always think when I sleep to go to university only. After I get to university nothing ... any work I can take from the university I can work.

It is important to understand that, in the past, only a very small percentage of students in Debarwa were admitted to a post-secondary institution because the competition for the small number of places is fierce. The students in this study were well aware of this. However, despite such highly unfavourable odds, they remain focused on their goal. None spoke of what they would do if they were not accepted to a post-secondary institution. It appears that it is precisely this type of positive thinking and focused energy that enables these students to maintain their high level of motivation and determination to succeed academically.

The desire to give back to their family was also commonly expressed, serving to motivate these students to succeed. In Eritrea, it is customary for wage earners to give money to their family. As one student said: "I don't want marriage. I finish school. I get a job. Then I helping country and family." Another student expressed her appreciation for all the help she has received from her family and how she hoped to help them in the future. She stated: "[W]e are lucky to be where we are. We have the education and we hope we are going to support them [our parents] and they will get relief."

Some students were motivated by their desire to remain in the public sphere. These students understood that early marriage and a lack of education for girls would likely result in a life restricted primarily to their home. As one student noted: "[I]f finishing school, I can get job, I can working. I can get money by myself. If I not finishing school only my husband is get job, only staying in the house. That's not good." Thus, the exposure of a high level of schooling appears to result in female students aspiring to non-traditional lifestyles.

Many students mentioned their enjoyment of learning. Their statements revealed how strongly they valued education. When asked why she was not yet married, one student replied: "[I am] happy I learn. After I finished, [I will become a] Sister." Another remarked: "I am interested to know anything about education." This was echoed by another student who said: "I want to learn. I want to know many things."

8.6.3 School

Students' comments on school factors also provided valuable insight into their challenges and successes. With regard to teachers' support, just under half either said they did not have any "special teachers" or did not mention the support of teachers at all. A "special teacher" was defined as one who was particularly supportive and helpful to them personally. In contrast, seven students mentioned a particular "special teacher". It appears that teachers' words and actions have contributed significantly to the students' perceptions of their academic capability and potential. One student explained how a teacher's concern for her progress had an immediate and significant impact on her academic performance when she recalled:

> [F]irst semester is very, very bad results when teacher ask me. 'Why? You are clever student.' 'I know' [I said]. [He then said,] 'When I learned [teach], when I explain, always

listen to me. Why are you get less marks? Ask me. Please improve your results.' First semester for chemistry 78 [out of 100]. Oh, very bad results. 'I am very angry' [the teacher] says to me. 'You are clever student. Always, when I explain, listen to me.' 'Oh, I improve. Teacher please, I improve my results' [I said]. And I get for second semester 93 [out of 100].

Another student stated: "[S]o many teachers have helped me." She went on to describe the support she has received from three teachers in particular. She stressed how they said: "[Y]ou are a good student. You can get the highest level." Along with words of encouragement, approachability was often mentioned as being one of the attributes of a "special teacher". Many of these students valued teachers who made it clear they would answer any question. One student recalled the help she received from her teachers. "I go to her for help, about biology. She is helping me always. In a week, two or three days. And I come to her house and in the school. Also like that, she help me."

One challenge related to the school environment is the sexual harassment experienced by some female students. One student described a male student hitting a female student when she rejected his advances. Another student, when offering advice to female students, admonished girls saying "don't [be] shameful for other things like that. When boys asking for bad words [say] 'please, I am a student. Don't ask like that. If finished my school, okay. But don't say like that at this time. I'm studying'".

In summary, the findings revealed three significant factors affecting the academic success of the participants in this study. These key factors, family, self, and school, can have either positive or negative implications depending on the circumstances. Family support is key. Students' determination, motivation, and academic ability are other key contributors to success. Teachers support and school culture also heavily influence success levels. These factors combine, whether positively or negatively, to create an environment where girls and young women in Debarwa can achieve success in school.

8.7 Implications for Action

The purpose of this research was to provide insight into the perceptions and experiences of female students, in a rural environment in Eritrea, who are defying highly unfavourable odds by completing their senior secondary education. It is evident that certain commonalities exist despite the varied experiences and family circumstances of the 19 students who participated in this study. The students' academic achievement can be greatly attributed to strong parental support, their high degree of motivation and determination, and their ability to block out, ignore, or reject negative societal beliefs which form implicit obstacles to their success.

When considering enabling factors, attention must be given to the students' immediate family as the centre of their circle of support. The education level of parents, particularly the father's, influenced the academic success of the participants in this study. A high percentage of parents had received some level of formal education, which is surprising considering the educational, political, and economic conditions which existed during the time they would have attended school in rural Eritrea. Even more exceptional, however, was the number of the students' mothers who received at least a few years of primary education. Eight (42%) of the 19 mothers received some level of formal education. It is likely that many of the students' parents, especially their mothers, have overcome even greater obstacles in order to attend school than those faced by their daughters. Thus, parents with some level of education are more likely to understand the importance and benefits of educating their daughters and, as a result, send them to school. The provision of non-formal adult education then could result in a multiplier effect since parents with some level of education are more likely to educate their daughters. This could ultimately result in more girls and young women attending school.

It is important to note that all of the families are from the dominant ethnic group, Tigrinya. Furthermore, with the exception of one Muslim family, all are Christian. Historically, those amongst the Christian Tigrinya highland population were far more likely to be in a position of privilege, such as having access to educational opportunities, than any other ethnic group in Eritrea. If this study were conducted in rural areas in the predominately Muslim lowlands, where girls are most marginalized in terms of education, it is highly likely that those who succeed would be fewer in number and have faced even more obstacles, particularly in terms of societal and cultural factors, than the young women in this study.

An examination of families also revealed that these students' parents sent all their school-age children to school regardless of gender, with the exception of one child who was described as "sick". While this may be partially attributed to their relatively favourable economic circumstances, of far greater importance was the parents' attitude regarding the value of education for *both* their sons and daughters. Students in this study came from families who encouraged their children to go to school for as long as they could and the families were willing to make sacrifices to enable this to happen.

The importance of family support was not limited to parents. Many of the students had a relative who was attending or had graduated from a post-secondary institution. They considered these relatives, the vast majority of whom were male, to be an important source of encouragement and support. The female students in this study, then, represented a kind of "next generation" of family members to achieve a high level of educational achievement. This is extremely significant. Whereas most of their older female family members received only a few years of schooling, if any, these young women were able to reach the end of their secondary school education with the possibility of continuing further. By defying the odds, these determined young women proved that girls *are* as clever and as capable as boys when given sufficient support and encouragement.

The findings of this study provide clear evidence that female students struggling against highly unfavourable odds need to be supported individually as well as at family and school levels in order to succeed academically. This study shows that, despite pervasive negative dominant societal beliefs, some female students who receive support and encouragement are able to block out, ignore, or reject these pernicious beliefs. The overriding importance of a students' self-concept requires that proactive measures be taken to enable more girls and young women to see themselves as capable of academic success. Despite the severe shortage of time mentioned by the students in this study, efforts should be undertaken at the school level to provide a regular place and time for female students to come together to study and share their experiences. This would go far in alleviating feelings of isolation implicit in being one of a limited number of female students.

In terms of efforts at the family level, initiatives should be undertaken to capitalize on parents demonstrating their belief in the value of education for their daughters by sending them to school. Eritrean educational statistics show, however, that most of these girls are unlikely to receive more than a primary education. These parents need to be encouraged not only to allow, but also to enable, their daughters to continue their schooling. They need to understand that their daughters are as capable of academic success as their sons. Since some parents view time spent walking to and from school as time wasted and/or as presenting a safety risk for their daughters, junior and secondary schools need to be built in the more remote areas. Easy access to levels of education beyond primary would reduce some obstacles for parents sending their daughters to school, and for the female students themselves. A reduction or elimination of direct costs, such as buying school supplies and uniforms, would also reduce obstacles for female students.

Another key element in the education of girls and young women is the number of years it takes for a female student to move through the education system. It commonly takes a student up to 9 years to complete 5 years of elementary school, if the student has not already dropped out. As shown in this study, the inefficiency of the education system has far greater repercussions for female students than for male students due to the practice of early marriage for girls. Parents may see the repetition of grades by students as indicative of the poor quality of the education system. Thus, parents might consider early marriage for their daughter as a better option than a time-consuming and inadequate education.

8.8 Evaluation

It is crucial to recognize that efforts to improve the education system for female students cannot be framed solely in academic terms, as if all things were equal for male and female students in the classroom. Unless this is earnestly acknowledged and addressed, it is unlikely that efforts to improve the quality of education will be as successful. Female students need to feel more comfortable and accepted in the classroom. If they are, they are more likely to participate without reservation, which is crucial if they are to get the most out of their educational opportunities.

Since teachers are responsible for setting the tone of the classroom, it is important that initiatives be directed towards the teachers. One important initiative would be to increase the number of female teachers at higher grade levels. These teachers would demonstrate that women are as capable of participating in academic endeavours as men, thus serving as role models. In addition, it is highly likely that female students may feel more comfortable asking female teachers than male teachers for help.

Furthermore, interventions such as the conducting of gender sensitivity workshops need to be encouraged. This type of awareness-raising is vital despite its controversial nature within a highly patriarchal society. It is critical that efforts to increase gender sensitivity be supported and seriously undertaken. Ensuring that *all* those involved in the field of education, including directors and supervisors, are exposed to gender sensitivity initiatives is also crucial.

Finally, it is very important to educate parents who do not value education for their daughters as to its benefits and importance. Of all the challenges facing girls' education, this is the most difficult. Interventions aimed at lessening or eliminating obstacles for female students, as discussed above, could certainly remove some of the reasons why some parents do not see the value of education for their daughters.

There is a Tigrinya saying that "little by little the egg will walk". While things may improve and circumstances change "little by little", there are many possible proactive measures that could and should be undertaken to enable more girls and young women to succeed in school in Eritrea.

8.9   Conclusion

From the findings of the study, it was found that the students' parents first opened the doors for their daughters' success by allowing and encouraging them to go to school. Their parents continued to allow the educational door to remain open by rejecting the common traditional practice of marrying their daughters off at an early age, thus ending their schooling. With the educational door firmly open, it is the individual students' high degree of motivation, determination, and academic ability that allows them to succeed. Their determination enables them to block out, ignore, or reject negative societal beliefs about girls' academic capabilities. It enables them to maintain non-traditional aspirations for their future. Students even mentioned using restrictive cultural norms to their own advantage. By doing well in school and receiving parental support, they have been able to delay getting married. This is important because married women rarely continue going to school in Eritrea. Thus, through their academic success, these young women are able to have a degree of control over their lives that most of their peers do not. This study shows that strong, determined young women are working towards fulfilling their hopes and dreams of a better life for themselves and their families. As with many other young women in sub-Saharan Africa, they are the future. Supporting and encouraging their academic efforts will certainly go a long way in enabling them to fully contribute to the national development of Eritrea. Through their empowerment, the country is empowered.

References

Bogdan, R. C., & Bicklin, S. K. (1998). *Qualitative research for education: An introduction to theory and methods.* Needham Heights, MA: Allyn & Bacon.

CIA Factbook (2001). Retrieved February 17, from http://www.odci.gov/gov/cia/publications/factbook

Cowan, N. A. (1984). Women in Eritrea: An eye-witness account. *Review of African political economy*, 27/28, 143–152. Baltimore, MA: Alternative Press Index.

Firebrace, J., & Holland, S. (1984). *Never kneel down: Drought, development and liberation in Eritrea.* Nottingham, England: Russell Press.

Heneveld, W., & Odaga, A. (1995). *Girls and schools in Sub-Saharan Africa: From analysis to action.* Washington, DC: World Bank.

Kelly, G. (1984). Women's access to education in the Third World: Myths and realities. In S. Acker, J. Megarry, S. Nisbet, & E. Hoyle (Eds.), *World Yearbook of Education 1984: Women and education* (pp. 81–89). New York: Nicholas.

Leach, F. (1998). Gender, education and training: an international perspective. *Gender and Development*, 6(2), 9–18.

Ministry of Education. (1999). *Eritrea: Essential education indicators 1998/99.* Asmara, Eritrea: Ministry of Education.

Ministry of Education & UNICEF. (1996). *Girls' education in Eritrea: A state of the art review.* Asmara, Eritrea: UNICEF.

Ministry of Education & UNICEF. (1997). *Girls' education in Eritrea.* Asmara, Eritrea: Ministry of Education.

Mohanty, C. (1988). Under western eyes: Feminist scholarship and colonial discourses. *Feminist Review*, 30, 61–88.

Samoff, J. (1999). No teacher guide, no textbooks, no chairs: Contending with crisis in African education. In R. F. Arnove, & C. A. Torres (Eds.), *Comparative education: The dialectic of the global and the local* (pp. 393–431). Lanham, MA: Roman & Littlefield.

Stefanos, A. (1997). Women and education in Eritrea: A historical and contemporary Analysis. *Harvard Educational Review*, 67(4), 658–688.

Stromquist, N. (1997). State policies and gender equity: Comparative perspective. In B. Bank, & P. Hall (Eds.), *Gender, Equity, and Schooling: Policy and Practice* (pp. 31–62). New York: Garland.

Sweetman, C. (1998). Editorial. *Gender and Development*, 6(2), 2–8.

UNESCO. (2000). *World education forum final report.* Paris: UNESCO.

UNICEF. (1997). *Children and women in Eritrea: 1996, An update.* Namibia: UNICEF.

UNICEF. (2000). *The progress of nations.* New York: UNICEF.

UNIFEM. (2000). *The progress of the world's women.* New York: UNIFEM.

United Nations. (2000). *Statistical yearbook* (45th ed.). New York: United Nations.

World Bank. (2001). Retrieved February 16, 2001 from *http://devdata.worldbank.org*

Chapter 9
Voices of Teachers in Academic and Vocational Secondary Schools in Egypt: Perceived Consequences of Educational Reform for Quality and Equality

Nagwa M. Megahed

9.1 Introduction

Teachers as "key actors" in the educational processes may promote, modify, or challenge educational reforms drawing upon their own meanings and perceptions of the reforms. This chapter examines teachers' perceptions of a 1997 secondary education reform in Egypt, which was implemented during its first phase (1999–2006) as the Secondary Education Enhancement Project. The reform was planned to convert hundreds of commercial schools into academic schools and sought to reduce the need for extra-school, private tutoring. Focus group interviews were conducted with 12 teachers working in academic and commercial secondary schools in Cairo, Egypt. Attention is given to these teachers' perception of the reform's likely impact on the quality of secondary education and the post-secondary educational and occupational opportunities for students from different socio-economic backgrounds. In addition, the chapter clarifies how teachers' views of the 1997 reform differ depending upon whether they conceive of schooling as promoting social mobility or as reproducing social inequalities.

With the globalization of the economy and moves toward promoting free trade, many countries have embarked on comprehensive economic reform and structural adjustment programmes. This economic transition has increased the demand for skilled workers, which was viewed as a pressure to reform the secondary education sector, the largest supplier of skilled labourers. During the 1980s and 1990s, in Egypt, as in other countries, secondary education reform focused on improving educational quality and equality (Acedo, 2002). Nonetheless, unequal secondary and post-secondary educational and occupational opportunities among students from different socio-economic background has continued and, in some cases, increased.

Existing literature offers varying explanations of the causes and effects of educational reforms in different societies, and the relationship between schooling and social inequality (Acedo, 2002; Martin, 1991; Sedere, 2000). In their analysis, functionalists argue that educational reforms are initiated when there is a need to realign the system to better match the requirements of the changing economy, since

Ain Shams University

changes in the economy and in education are viewed as benefiting the society generally (Ginsburg, 1991; Sedere). In Egypt, for example, some scholars emphasize the importance of stratifying secondary schools to differentiate curricular programme tracks. They believe that admission to secondary schools should be based on students' abilities and capacities and that the division between academic and vocational schools is necessary in order to meet the requirements of the economy specifically, and the society more generally (Shaban, 1981).

For functionalists, educational stratification is required because different occupational positions need to be filled with persons with varying levels of native ability or relevant training (Arum & Beattie, 2000). Schools among other social institutions and organizations in any given society select and allocate individuals. "The essential purpose of this [kind of] control is to distribute the individuals so that each is placed according to his[/her] talents and able to perform successfully his[/her] social function" (Sorokin, 2000, p. 19). From this view, schooling provides a meritocratic mechanism for allocating individuals to different occupations, which, for example, allows for the upward social mobility of capable, motivated children of parents with lower occupational status (Collins, 2000).

In contrast, from a conflict perspective, educational reform is undertaken in order to protect or increase the educational, political, and economic benefits that certain groups enjoy at the expense of other groups (Ginsburg, 1991). Some Egyptian scholars strongly criticize the tracking system of secondary schools and consider that the stratification within public schools contradicts the ideal of equal educational opportunities, which the government has adopted, at least rhetorically, since the 1952 revolution (Ali, 1989). From the conflict perspective, unequal power and wealth among social class, gender, and/or ethnic groups are reproduced through schooling (e.g., tracking, curriculum differentiation, and testing). Bourdieu (2000), for instance, argues that there is a relationship between the academic success of children and the social position of their family, and between the position filled by the children and their parent. Within stratified society, each social class has its level and type of "cultural capital". These "differences in 'cultural capital' lead to inequality in educational achievement and related occupational attainment. … Privileged members of society … [are] rewarded by both school personnel and employers, who coded these [members] as being more worthy and deserving" (Arum & Beattie, 2000, p. 4). As Hallinan (2000) observes: "Academic achievement is related to students' background, minority and low-income students are disproportionately assigned to lower tracks" (p. 220). In this way the hierarchical structure of society is reproduced through education. From the conflict perspective, the meritocratic ideology embodied and disseminated through schools helps to legitimate inequalities in education as well as in society (Bowles & Gintis, 1976; Morrow & Torres, 1995).

Those subscribing to conflict and functionalist perspectives, thus, would interpret differently the findings reported by El-Shikhaby (1983), based on his survey research study of 517 students in vocational and academic public secondary schools in Egypt. The study indicates that there is a very strong, significant relationship between father's occupation, parents' education, and family income, on the one hand, and student placement in vocational versus academic secondary schools, on the other. The study, furthermore, points out that there is a strong positive significant relationship between students' socio-economic background and their academic achievement.

It is not only scholars who differ in their analysis of schooling and educational reform. Teachers' views on educational reforms may be framed by ideologies of social mobility and reproduction that are associated with functionalist or conflict theoretical perspectives. Teachers also vary in their view of schooling as promoting social mobility or as reproducing social inequalities, with their perspectives shaped by personal experiences as students and family members, and by their professional observations of, and interactions with, the students in their classrooms. In his examination of how a group of pre-service teachers conceive of the nature and legitimacy of extant class, race, and gender relations in schools and societies, Ginsburg (1988) categorizes the perspectives of pre-service teachers interviewed into three general orientations: (1) teachers emphasizing schooling's role in reproducing inequalities; (2) teachers highlighting social mobility as opposed to social reproduction; and (3) teachers showing concern about individual attitudes and prejudice, and not with social structural features of society. This chapter examines how academic and commercial school teachers perceive the consequences of a 1997 educational reform for quality and equality in Egypt, clarifying how teachers' perceptions of the reform differ depending upon whether they conceive of schooling as promoting social mobility or as reproducing social inequality.

9.2   Educational Reform and Social (In)Equality in Egypt

In 1997 the Government of Egypt developed a 20-year secondary education reform programme for improving educational quality and equality. The first stage of this reform consists of a 7-year project (1999–2006), known as the Secondary Education Enhancement Project [SEEP] (Ministry of Education [MOE], Arab Republic of Egypt,1999; World Bank, 1999b; Megahed, 2002). The 1997 reform aims at expanded and more equitable access to higher education by converting 315 vocational/commercial secondary schools into academic secondary schools, from which students are most likely to enter universities. It also includes developing common core courses (Arabic, English, mathematics, science, and social science) and incorporating the use of technology into the classroom practices and student assessment methods in both types of secondary schools – an action that may reduce students' reliance on out-of-school private tutoring. In addition, the reform focuses on enhancing teacher performance through in-service training programmes in the use of technology.

The reform was motivated at least in part because of an economic and unemployment crisis. Sixty per cent of the country's unemployed population in 1998 were secondary school graduates, with the large majority (76%) of these being graduates of vocational secondary schools (MOE, 1999; World Bank, 1991, 1999a).

Among the reasons identified for the unemployment was the poor quality of vocational school programmes, the low level of knowledge and skills of its graduates, and a mismatch between the education system and the labour market, especially with the changes in employment opportunities that occurred after the implementation of a comprehensive Economic Reform and Structural Adjustment Program (ERSAP) beginning in 1991 (World Bank, 1999b; Program Planning & Monitoring Unit, Arab Republic of Egypt, 1998; MOE, 1999).

In contrast to the 1997 reform, the Egyptian government's previous educational reforms during the 1980s and 1990s were aimed at increasing the proportion of students attending vocational versus academic schools (Megahed, 2002). The earlier reforms were designed as responses to the economic transition toward privatization and the increased demand for skilled workers. Under the pre-1997 reform system, approximately 65% of students at the end of the preparatory level (grades 7–9) were streamed into vocational secondary schools, with little chance of accessing university education, while less than 35% were streamed into academic secondary schools, which virtually guaranteed a place in a university or another type of higher education institution (MOE, 2000). The 1997 reform's objective was to reach 50% of the students attending each type of secondary school by converting 315 commercial/vocational schools into academic schools.

The reform may extend educational and socio-economic opportunities for at least some of the predominantly lower class population of students who were previously enrolled in vocational secondary schools, because they will likely attend academic secondary schools under the reform. Traditionally, students admitted to vocational secondary schools tend to be those whose scores on the Basic Education Certificate Examination do not qualify them for admission to academic secondary schools. Students, parents, and the society perceive vocational education to be "second-class" (Richards, 1992, p. 4) and vocational education and manual work in Egypt are seen as attributes of "losers" (Sayed & Diehl, 2000; Heeti & Brock, 1997). Moreover, most of the graduates from vocational secondary schools neither enrol in the university nor are they likely to be employed in the formal economy. In contrast, a majority of academic secondary school graduates have guaranteed access to higher education and have a better chance to find a good job after completing their education.

The reform was also designed to reduce students' reliance on private, out-of-school tutoring by emphasizing the use of technology in teaching the common core courses, curriculum-based assessment, and student report profiles. In academic secondary schools, the instruction has been organized around textbooks and an examination syllabus, lecturing as a teaching technique, detailed reviews of content before each set of memorization-based assessment exams and final high-stakes national exams. Such an "exam-driven system" (United States Agency for International Development (USAID), 2003)) made out-of-school private tutoring essential for students' achievement.

The "need" for private tutoring in secondary education in Egypt—and other societies (Bray, 1999; Bray & Kwok, 2003; Chew & Leong, 1995; Popa & Acedo, 2003)—introduces a strong source of socio-economic bias in education, since families are not in equal positions to pay the tutoring fees. The Egyptian Ministry of Education has stated that the widespread practice of out-of-school "private tutoring partly defeats the democratic purpose embedded in the constitutional provision of 'free' public education" (Program Planning & Monitoring Unit, 1998, p. 5). However, historically, in Egypt "schooling was never entirely free [even during] the best of times: a parent had to pay a tiny entry fee, buy a school uniform, provide a bite of food. ... Moreover, what is disastrous is the need for private tutoring" *(Life at the bottom,*1999, p. 11). For students attending academic secondary schools in 1992/93, for example, rural and urban family expenditure on tutoring and additional books comprised, respectively, "14.3% and 10.6% of family annual income" (Fawzey, 1994, p. 36). Because of tutoring, the per-child cost of education is higher for the family than for the state/government, especially in grades 11 and 12 in the academic secondary school.

Low-income families are less likely to be able to pay for private lessons than is the case for middle- and upper-income families. An indication of the effect of bias created by the need for private tutoring is that 80% of students of lower class origin got poor grades on the Academic Secondary Certificate Examination, upon which access to university education is based (World Bank, 1991). Thus, if the reform is successful in reducing the need for private tutoring to succeed in the examinations, it may reduce a source of inequality of educational opportunity.

Teachers' support for, or resistance to, the 1997 reform may depend on how they view the reform as benefiting or harming certain groups of students. Academic school teachers and commercial school teachers might vary in their perceptions of the reform and its implications for quality and equality for different groups of students in different types of secondary schools. And their perceptions could be informed by whether they perceive of schooling as promoting social mobility or social reproduction for students. Some teachers may view the stratification within the education system (i.e., the hierarchical arrangement of academic and vocational/commercial schools) as necessary because not all students have the same (genetically or culturally determined) academic abilities. From this perspective students can be upwardly or downwardly mobile depending on their ability and effort, and students in the two types of schools differ with respect to such ability and efforts. Thus, these teachers may view the 1997 reform and the 1999 SEEP as unnecessary or, worse, giving access to academic secondary schools to students who do not deserve to be there.

In contrast, other teachers may consider that the educational system—with its stratified programmes and private wealth requirements for tutoring to promote exam success—insures that inequalities in social background are reproduced by educational and occupational attainment. For them, the reform may be perceived as a step in the right direction or at least a rhetorical move that calls attention to structured inequalities in education and society.

Transferring educational reform from policy to practice is not simply a technical process but rather personal and social processes that involve teachers' (as well as other practitioners') thoughts, perspectives, and actions. Thus, it is likely that teachers' ideologies of schooling as promoting social mobility or as reproducing social inequalities will frame how these teachers perceive, evaluate, and respond to the 1997 educational reform in Egypt. Given this, two major questions are addressed in this study of teachers' perceptions and ideologies:

1. What are the similarities and differences between academic and vocational (commercial) school teachers' perspectives on secondary education system, during both the pre- and post-1997 reform and the 1999 SEEP, with respect to:

   (a) Their assessment of the secondary and post-secondary educational opportunities provided to students enrolled in different types of secondary schools?
   (b) Their evaluation of the quality of secondary education provided to students from different socio-economic backgrounds attending different types of secondary schools?

2. In what ways are teachers' ideological perspectives on schooling as promoting social mobility or as reproducing social inequalities related to their perceptions of the impact of the 1997 reform and the 1999 SEEP on educational quality and equality for students?

To answer these questions, a convenience sample of 12 teachers was interviewed in Cairo, Egypt. The interviewees include male and female core/academic subject teachers working in both types of secondary schools as well as commercial/vocational subject teachers employed in commercial schools with teaching experience ranging from 5 to more than 20 years. This sample provides insights into the differences and similarities among and within different groups of teachers and their perceptions of educational reform and social (in)equality in Egypt, although it does not represent the perceptions of all academic and commercial school teachers. The interviews included three groups of teachers: (a) five academic subject teachers who were working in an academic secondary school; (b) three academic subject teachers who previously taught in commercial secondary schools for two years before they obtained posts in the academic secondary school; and (c) four vocational subject teachers who were working in a commercial secondary school (see Table 9.1).

The interviews were conducted in August 2001 just before the first 100 commercial schools (out of 315) were converted into, and began operating as, academic schools. A standardized open-ended interview (Martella et al., 1999) was designed and used to conduct the tape-recorded group interviews of two to five participants each. Two group interviews were conducted in a public academic secondary school *Madrassa Thanawayia Aama*. The first group included five participants (A1–A5) and the second included three participants (AC1–AC3). In addition, two group interviews were conducted in a public commercial secondary school *Madrassa Thanawyia Tijaryia*; each group included two participants (C1, C2 and C3, C4). Both academic and commercial schools are located in north Cairo in the "al-Sahel" district and surrounded by urban, suburban, and rural areas, from which their students are drawn.

Table 9.1 Interviewees by gender, teaching subject, years of experience, and types of schools

Teacher	Gender	Subject	Years of experience	Types of schools
A1	Female	Arabic (Head teacher)	27+	1975–1982: preparatory school
				1982–present: Academic secondary school
A2	Female	Chemistry	15+	1987–1992: Preparatory school
				1992–present: Academic secondary school
A3	Female	Philosophy + Sociology (Head teacher)	21+	1981–present: Four different academic secondary schools
A4	Male	Social Sciences (School-Undersecretary)	29+	1972–1980: Preparatory school
				1980–present: Two different academic secondary school
A5	Female	Biology	16+	1986–1989: Preparatory school
				1989–present: Academic secondary school
AC1	Male	English	17+	1985–1988: commercial secondary school
				1988–1992: Academic secondary school
				1992–present: Academic secondary school
AC2	Male	Mathematics	18+	1984–1989: Commercial secondary school
				1989–present: Academic secondary school
AC3	Male	Arabic	17+	1985–1989: Commercial secondary school
				1989–present: Academic secondary school
C1	Male	Commercial Studies (Head teacher)	27+	1975–present: Two different commercial secondary schools
C2	Female	Commercial Studies	7+	1994–present: Commercial secondary school
C3	Male	Computer Sciences (Head teacher)	22+	1980–present: Commercial secondary school
C4	Male	Computer Sciences	5+	1997–present: Commercial school

Interviewees were asked about their views on the secondary and post-secondary educational and occupational opportunities for their students and the quality of secondary education provided to students from different socio-economic backgrounds, during both the pre-reform and post-reform periods. Data were analysed following a qualitative approach through which the transcribed interviews were read carefully and coded systematically (Bogdan & Biklen, 1998).

9.3   Teachers' Perceptions of the Reform's Impact on Eduational Quality and Equality for Students

With any proposed educational reform and under the notion of free public education, the government of Egypt repeatedly announces its commitment to promote equal educational opportunities at all levels or across programs at a certain level. Two academic subject teachers agree with their colleague in viewing this announcement "as an old song, which doesn't interest teachers or their students any more" (Teacher AC1). Overall, the academic and commercial school teachers interviewed considered the 1997 reform, especially the 1999 SEEP, as not being sufficient to achieve educational equity and quality for their students.

Four academic school teachers considered that increasing the proportion of students enrolled in academic schools will negatively affect the quality of academic schools because it means decreasing the current score of the final preparatory level examination that is required for entering the academic schools. For these teachers, decreasing the required score for entering academic schools will consequently increase the percentage of students in these schools who are "unqualified" for academic education. For example:

Increasing the enrolment in academic school means accepting students of poor learning skills and abilities. These students will not be able to obtain high grade or compete for a place at the university. This definitely will reduce the quality of academic school (Teacher A1).

The majority of students from lower class usually obtained poor grades, dropped out, or transferred to one of the vocational schools. Increasing their proportion will not change these facts, but rather will put them under pressure by admitting them to a type of education that is not appropriate given their learning skills (Teacher A3).

Commercial school teachers presented different perceptions of the reform. They supported the reform's objective of having equal enrolment rates in academic and vocational schools, though they considered the reform as reinforcing the poor governmental and social perception of commercial schooling and perpetuating the hierarchal nature of education system, with commercial schools at the bottom. The four commercial school teachers believed that the admissions policy of restricting enrolment of students with lower exam scores to commercial schools should be changed. They added that equal educational and occupational opportunities would be achieved by providing equal access to higher education to both vocational and academic graduates and by restructuring secondary education. The quotations below represent the perceptions of this group of teachers:

Converting hundreds of commercial schools into academic school is an advancement toward not only educational but also social and economic equality. ... Though the reform may promote a kind of equality, it will not change the social perception of vocational [commercial] school as a second-class education. To be realistic, educational equity and quality within and between academic and vocational schools would be achieved through restructuring secondary education and changing its admission policy. It is not just increasing the enrolment in academic schools or integrating technology (Teacher C1).

Even under the reform students of lowest grade will enrol in vocational schools. The 50% of graduates from preparatory school, who under the reform will enrol in vocational schools, will continue to be the poorest academic and economic students, particularly in commercial school (Teacher C3).

Academic subject teachers, currently working in academic schools but who had previously taught in commercial schools, agreed with their colleagues that the reform would not reduce students' reliance on tutoring, which is a "parallel school" in a barren education system characterized by rote learning at all levels. They believed the reform would not promote educational equality unless the curriculum content and assessment method are redesigned in order to develop student creativity, critical thinking, and problem-solving. Otherwise, the unfair competition between poor and rich students would continue under the reform because there would continue to be only limited places at the university. Private tutoring would continue to be necessary in the academic schools, and students from lower socio-economic families would still not be able to afford to pay the cost of private tutoring. To illustrate:

[Because the] curriculum depends on textbooks and memorization based assessment method, reclassifying the academic courses in both types of secondary schools or using technology in the classroom practice will not improve educational quality or reduce students' reliance on private tutoring (Teacher AC2).

Even if some students from lower class families enrolled in academic schools, they will not be able to compete for a place in the university, because the majority of students in academic schools depend on tutoring to obtain high grades and there are limited places available at the university (Teacher AC3).

9.4 Teachers' Ideology of Social Mobility/Reproduction as an Explanation of Their Perceptions of the Reform

The previous discussion indicates that all academic and commercial secondary teachers interviewed doubted that the 1997 educational reform and the 1999 SEEP would equalize educational opportunities in Egypt. The different groups of teachers articulated their dubiousness in different ways. Part of the differences can be explained in terms of the type of institutions in which they work and the perceived background and ability of the students with whom they interact. For example, academic secondary school teachers perceived that on average 70% of their students were from "upper class", "upper-middle class", or "middle class" families, while commercial secondary school teachers reported that on average 85% of their students were from "lower-middle class" or "lower class" families. With respect to academic ability, academic school teachers on average characterized 68% of their students as being "outstanding", "above average", or "average", while commercial school teachers on average categorized 80% of their students as being "below average" or "weak".

Such differences in perceptions of (or even actual differences in) socio-economic status backgrounds and academic abilities of their students cannot account for the differences in views expressed, particularly between those academic school teachers who had previously taught in commercial schools and those who had not. What seems to be important in explaining how different categories of teachers analysed the impact of the proposed reform are the differences in their ideologically informed views about the functioning of the education system in terms of promoting social mobility or reproducing social inequalities.

Some teachers viewed the stratification within the education system (i.e., the hierarchical arrangement of academic and vocational/commercial schools) as necessary because there are real—and significant—differences among students with respect to learning abilities and future career potentials. From their "functionalist" perspective, they viewed schools as institutions through which upward or downward social mobility occurred depending on students' ability and effort. Furthermore, they perceived students in the academic secondary schools as having higher levels of ability and exerting more effort than their commercial school peers. Note that the following statements representing this perspective are all made by academic school teachers who have no experience working in commercial schools:

> Most students in vocational schools are careless about their educational progress. They did not concentrate on their schoolwork from the time they were in the preparatory schools; therefore, they did not enrol in academic [secondary] school. Whereas most students in academic schools are more responsible for their school work, concerned about their future and eager for entering the university (Teacher A1).
>
> Students in vocational schools [generally] do not have the learning skills that would qualify them to enter an academic school or to continue into post-secondary education... [although] there are a few vocational students who enter the university (Teacher A2).

In addition, it is worth highlighting that private tutoring was viewed by the five academic teachers as a form of "external academic assistance for their students" (Teacher A2), especially for those who were unable to understand and comprehend the subject matter in the classroom. One academic school teacher mentioned, for example, that "students have different learning skills and abilities. Thus many students ask me for tutoring, so they can obtain better grade and make progress" (Teachers A3).

In contrast, all other teachers in the study perceived the educational system as structured in ways that basically insure that inequalities in students' socio-economic background are reproduced as disparities in educational and occupational attainment. They saw family socio-economic status, more than student ability or motivation, as the primary determiner of a student's success. This is especially the case, they argued, because the strong emphasis on exam performance—for entry into academic secondary school and into higher education institutions—make private, out-of-school tutoring (and being able to pay for it) a requirement for academic success. The following statements represent the ideas expressed by all of the former and current commercial school teachers:

The curriculum [and assessment system] promote inequality. ... Beginning in preparatory school [grades 7 to 9] students realized that without tutoring they could not compete for a place in the academic secondary school and then in the university. ... Students of parents with higher socioeconomic status are able to enrol in academic schools and then universities. I believe the reason is not only because of their learning skills but also because of their parents' abilities to pay more than £E 8,000 per year in tutoring fees (Teacher AC2).

Students from lower income families cannot pay for tutoring, improve their exam performance, and get good grades. Consequently, they are not qualified academically or economically for academic [secondary] schools and, of course, the university (Teacher C3).

9.5   Discussion

During an implementation period of the 1997 educational reform and the 1999 SEEP in Egypt, 12 teachers working in academic and commercial schools were interviewed and were asked about their views on the secondary and post-secondary educational and occupational opportunities for their students and the quality of secondary education provided to students from different socio-economic backgrounds, during both the pre-reform and post-reform periods. It was found that neither teachers in academic nor teachers in commercial schools were optimistic that the reform would enhance the quality of education or would provide more equal educational opportunities for students. Their explanations for their pessimism varied, however, and such differences in teachers' perspectives were associated, at least in part, with whether they primarily perceived of schooling as promoting social mobility or as reproducing social inequalities.

All five teachers who had only worked in academic secondary schools exhibited an ideology of schooling as promoting social mobility. They explained why they perceived the reform negatively in terms of students being responsible for their attainments and opportunities. Thus, according to these teachers, increased opportunities to enrol in academic schools for students who do not have the requisite abilities would probably harm or at least not really benefit these students. It would also reduce the quality of education in academic schools. These teachers seemed to draw upon a functionalist perspective, in that stratification within the education system (i.e., the hierarchical arrangement of academic and vocational/commercial tracks) was viewed to be a necessity because not all students have the same level of learning abilities. From this perspective, schooling provides a meritocratic mechanism for allocating individuals to occupations and allows for upward social mobility of capable, motivated children of parents with lower socio-economic status.

In contrast, three academic teachers, who had previously worked in commercial schools, and four commercial teachers articulated an ideology of schooling as reproducing social inequality. They explained their negative perceptions of the reform in terms of systemic features, such as the tracking system of secondary education, admissions policy, rote learning, memorization based-assessment method, costs associated with academic schools including private tutoring and additional books. For these teachers, the stratified secondary school system, which hierarchically differentiates academic and commercial/vocational secondary school programmes and makes it more likely that academic school students who can pay for private, out-of-school tutoring can succeed on high-stakes exams, perpetuates and legitimates social inequalities through schooling. These teachers seemed to draw upon a conflict perspective, emphasizing that inequalities in wealth and power among social classes are reproduced through tracking, curriculum differentiation, and testing in schools.

9.6 Conclusion

In this study teachers who previously taught or who were teaching in commercial schools tended to have views that were more in line with a conflict perspective, while teachers whose experiences were limited to academic schools articulated more functionalist-oriented viewpoints. This raises the question of whether the type of students one teaches influences one's conception of schooling and society, or whether individuals with particular conceptions are more likely to pursue teaching in certain types of institutions. In either case, however, it indicates how teachers' personal ideologies and their particular occupational characteristics framed their perceptions of the reform and directed their responses to the reform in schools and communities.

Acknowledgements I would like to thank Mark Ginsburg, Administrative and Policy Studies Department, School of Education, University of Pittsburgh, for his comments on this manuscript. I would also like to thank the 12 teachers who participated in the study.

References

Acedo, C. (Ed.). (2002). Case studies in secondary education reform. *Improving Educational Quality (IEQ) Project*. American Institute for Research in collaboration with: Academy for Educational Development, Juárez and Associates, Inc., Education Development, and University of Pittsburgh. USAID.
Al-Ahram Daily Newspaper. (1999, July 24). Retrieved June 21, 2001 from http://www.al_ahram.org
Ali, S. (1989). *Hemum al-Taleem al-Misrey* [Concerns of Egyptian education]. Cairo, Egypt: Al_Ahram.
Al-Mashat, R. Grigorian, D. (1998). *Economic reforms in Egypt: Emerging patterns and their possible implications*. World Bank Document.
Arum, R. & Beattie, I. (2000). *The structure of schooling: Readings in the sociology of education*. California: Mayfield.
Bogdan, R. & Biklen. S. (1998). *Qualitative research for education: An introduction to theory and methods* (3rd Ed.). Boston, MA: Allyn & Bacon.
Bourdieu, P. (2000). Cultural reproduction and social reproduction. In R. Arum & I. Beattie (Eds.). *The structure of schooling: Reading in the sociology of education* (pp. 56–68). California: Mayfield.

Bowles, S. & Gintis, H. (1976). *Schooling in capitalist America*. New York: Basic Book Co.
Bray, M. (1999). *The shadow education system: Private tutoring and its implications for the plan-
ner*. Paris: UNESCO, International Institute for Educational Planning.
Bray, M. & Kwok, P. (2003). Demand for private supplementary tutoring: Conceptual considera-
tions, and socio-economic patterns in Hong Kong. *Economic of Education Review*, 22,
611–620.
Chew, S. & Leong, Y. (Eds). (1995). *Private tuition in Malaysia and Sri Lanka: A comparative
study*. Kuala Lumpur: Department of Social Foundations in Education, University of
Malaysia.
Collins, R. (2000). Functional and conflict theories of educational stratification. In R. Arum &
I. Beattie (Eds.). *The structure of schooling: Reading in the sociology of education* (pp. 94–112).
California: Mayfield.
El-Shikhaby, A. (1983). Socioeconomic status and students' placement in public secondary
schools in Egypt. *Dissertation Abstracts International*, 2593 (University of Pittsburgh, No.
DAI-A 44/08).
Fawzey, F. (1994). *Al-Deruss al-Khosusseiah: Tahleel We Tasseel* [The private tutoring: Analysis
and foundation]. Tanta, Egypt.
Gill, I. & Heyneman, S. (2000). Arab Republic of Egypt. In Gill. I, et al. (Eds.), *Matching skills
to markets and budgets* (pp. 401–429). New York: Oxford University Press.
Ginsburg, M. (1988). *Contradictions in teacher education and society: A critical analysis*. New
York: The Falmer Press.
Ginsburg, M. (Ed.). (1991). *Understanding educational reform in global context: Economy, ideol-
ogy and the state*. New York: Garland.
Hallinan, M. (2000). Tracking: From theory to practice. In R. Arum & I. Beattie (Eds.). *The struc-
ture of schooling: Reading in the sociology of education* (pp. 218 – 224). California:
Mayfield.
Heeti, A. & Brock, C. (1997). Vocational education and development: Key issues, with special
reference to the Arab world. *International Journal of Educational Development*, 17,
373–389.
Life at the bottom: Where reforms aren't working. (1999, March 20). *Economist*, 350 (8111,
Egypt survey), p. 3–13.
Martin, D. (1991). The political economy of school reform in the United States. In M. Ginsburg
(Ed.). *Understanding educational reform in global context: Economy, ideology and the state*
(pp. 341–368). New York: Garland.
Megahed, N. (2002). Secondary education reforms in Egypt: Rectifying inequality of educational
and employment opportunities. In C. Acedo (Ed.). *Secondary education reform case studies*
(pp. 44–71). Washington, DC: American Institutes for Research (USAID-funded Improving
Educational Quality Project).
Megahed, N. & Ginsburg, M. (2003). Stratified students, stratified teachers: Ideologically
informed perceptions of educational reform in Egypt. *Mediterranean Journal of Educational
Studies*, 8(2).
Megahed, N. (2004). *Stratified students, stratified teachers: Ideologies of social mobility/repro-
duction, ideologies of professionalism, and teachers' perceptions of secondary education
reform in Egypt*. Unpublished doctoral dissertation, University of Pittsburgh.
Ministry of Education, Arab Republic of Egypt. (1999). *Secondary education reform program*.
Cairo, Egypt.
Ministry of Education, Arab Republic of Egypt. (2000). *Ehssaat al-Taaleem Qabel al-Gamayi*
[Statistics of pre-university education 1999–00]. Cairo, Egypt.
Morrow, R. & Torres, S. (1995). Social theory and education: A critique of theories of social and
cultural reproduction. Albany, NY: State University of New York Press.
Popa, S., & Acedo, A. (2003, March). *Redefining professionalism: Romanian teachers and the
private tutoring system*. Paper presented at the annual conference of the Comparative and
International Education Society. New Orleans, LA.

Program Planning & Monitoring Unit, Arab Republic of Egypt. (1998). *Secondary Education Reform Program: Preparation for a national conference on secondary education*. Cairo, Egypt.

Richards, A. (1992). Higher education in Egypt. World Bank working Paper.

Sayed, A. & Diehl, M. (2000). *Egyptian-German technical cooperation promotion of technical education and vocational training (TEVT) system: Mubarak-Kohl initiative: A program on the TEVT-reform of Ministry of Education and Economy*. Cairo, Egypt.

Sedere, U. (2000). Globalisation and the low income economies: Reforming education, the crisis of vision. USA: Universal.

Shaban, A. (1981). *Social justice and efficiency in Egyptian education: A critical investigation of the bases of the Egyptian educational philosophy, 1952 to the present*. Unpublished doctoral dissertation, University of Pittsburgh.

Sorokin, P. (2000). Social and cultural mobility. In R. Arum & I. Beattie (Eds.). *The structure of schooling: reading in the sociology of education* (pp. 19 – 21). California: Mayfield.

World Bank. (1999a). Egypt-secondary education enhancement project.

Project Information Document.

World Bank. (1999b). *Secondary education enhancement project in Egypt*. Project Appraisal Document.

World Bank. (1991). Egypt: alleviating poverty during structural adjustment. World Bank Country Study.

World Development Indicators Database. (2002, April). *Egypt, Arab Republic: Data Profile*. Retrieved June 5, 2002 from http://devdata.worldbank.org/

USAID/EGYPT. (2003). *Program description of EQUIP2 – Basic Education USAID EGYPT*. USAID Document.

USAID/EGYPT. (2000). *Economic growth activities*. Retrieved October 25, 2000 from http://www.usaid.gov/eg/index.htm

Chapter 10
Cultural Capital: What Does It Offer Students?
A Cross-National Analysis

Gillian Hampden-Thompson[1], Lina Guzman[2], and Laura Lippman[3]

10.1 Introduction

Education and social inequality are inextricably linked. While educational success is a vehicle for social mobility for both individuals and groups, children's success in school is largely dependent upon their social origins and the nature of the relationships between families and schools. A number of factors influence the relationship between family background characteristics and educational outcomes. The possession of cultural capital is one such factor that may assist in the reproduction of social inequality or, in contrast, may mitigate the effects of social origin on educational outcomes. Interest in the effects of cultural capital on educational outcomes has grown considerably in recent years (Kingston, 2001). Despite the growing volume of research, no consensus has been reached as to the benefits, if any, possessing cultural capital offers students. While some studies have found a significant and positive relationship between various measures of cultural capital and educational outcomes (DeGraaf et al., 2000; DiMaggio & Mohr, 1985; DiMaggio & Useem, 1978; Dumais, 2002), other studies conclude that no such relationship exists (Katsillis & Rubinson, 1990; Robinson & Garnier, 1985). In addition, though, one might expect the magnitude of the relationship itself to differ across cultural and national contexts; cross-national analyses have been scarce (Buchmann, 2002), with most studies focusing primarily on single countries (DeGraaf et al., 2000; Katsillis & Rubinson, 1990; Robinson & Garnier, 1985). Consequently, there is little understanding of how the effects of cultural capital vary across countries (Buchmann, 2002).

This study continues the refinement of the cultural capital concept, addressing gaps in existing scholarship by analyzing data from two major international datasets: the Program for International Student Assessment (PISA) and the Third International Math and Science Study (TIMSS). Using these datasets, the relationship between student participation in culturally enriching activities and the possession

---

[1]University of York

[2]Child Trends

[3]Child Trends

of cultural resources and student academic outcomes across nine western industrialized countries is examined. This study focuses on European and North American countries that share a Western cultural history for several reasons. First, much of the literature and, in particular, the theoretical frameworks, on this topic have been dominated by studies on Western cultures. Second, the conceptualization and measurement of cultural capital have been largely influenced by a Western cultural perspective. Thus, it is unclear the extent to which the theoretical perspectives (i.e., social mobility versus social reproduction) that form the basis of this study can be applied to non-Western countries. Third, the datasets and measures used in this study are a reflection of Western cultures. Caution is warranted in generalizing the literature or results summarized below to countries that have not been shaped by a similar cultural history due to this sampling limitation. This study provides a basis on which to measure the extent to which the effect of cultural capital differs across national borders, even those that share common cultural histories.

10.2 Literature Review

10.2.1 Home Background and Educational Achievement

Despite the burgeoning amount of research on school effects, children's home background characteristics continue to overshadow extra-familial resources in explaining many outcomes, including educational achievement (Alexander & Entwisle, 1988; Coleman, et al., 1966, 1982; Jencks, et al., 1972; White, 1982). The relationship between home background characteristics and educational outcomes is well established, particularly in the United Kingdom and the United States with the publication of the *Plowden* and *Coleman* reports, respectively. The *Equality of Educational Opportunity* report published in 1966 (Coleman et al., 1966) drew significant attention to the effect of family background characteristics on educational outcomes.

While the relationship between social origin and achievement is well established, there remains a substantial debate as to which aspects of family background characteristics are most important for children's academic success. A substantial amount of research has clearly indicated that socioeconomic factors such as parental education and family income are significant predictors of children's academic success (Katsillis & Rubinson, 1990; Lockheed & Longford, 1991; Lockheed et al., 1989; Riddell, 1989; Shavit & Blossfield, 1993). Children from families with higher income or other physical resources have, among other things, greater access to educational materials, richer educational experiences, and better quality schools. Among the number of intervening factors thought to explain the relationship between a family's socioeconomic status (SES) and children's educational achievement are parental involvement in the home (e.g., monitoring homework and discussing social issues), parental involvement at school (e.g., involvement with parent–teacher organizations and volunteering at school), and the possession of cultural capital (e.g., appreciation of cultural experiences).

Coleman's theory (1988) of social capital suggests that intra- and inter-household relations may affect the transmission of familial resources (human and social capital) to children. Inter-household linkages such as parental involvement in school activities, contact with school personnel, and knowledge of other children's parents allows the family to embed itself in valuable social networks and, in turn, benefit children's educational outcomes (Coleman, 1988; Schneider & Coleman, 1993). Intra-household linkages (relations between children and parents) are equally important. Coleman and Hoffer (1987) suggest that a family can have very little human capital, yet offer children educational advantages if they possess a high level of social capital. The case of the Southeast Asian refugees is one example of how the potentially negative effects of low human capital can be diminished by high levels of social capital. Research on Southeast Asian refugee families living in the United States revealed high levels of parental involvement in children's schooling and found that many families purchased two textbooks for each school subject, one for the children and one for parents (Coleman & Hoffer). This practice enabled parents to maximize the amount of assistance they were able to provide their children on homework and school projects.

Along with social capital, cultural capital has also been shown to play a salient role in explaining the relationship between a family's socioeconomic status and children's educational achievement. Available data on the benefits that art and cultural programs offer students, in particular low-income students, provides evidence to suggest that exposure to culturally enriching activities may mitigate the effects of low SES (Clawson & Coolbaugh, 2001). In addition, Kalmijn and Kraaykamp (1996) find that the integration of African-Americans into traditional Euro-American high-status cultures has contributed to black–white convergence in schooling. The role of cultural capital and its relationship to SES and educational success forms the basis of this study. As Coleman et al. (1966) state, the sources of educational disparity can be found in both the child's home and the child's cultural surroundings.

10.2.2 Cultural Capital and Educational Outcomes

Theory of cultural reproduction Social class reproduction has long been the focus of much research interest. Several studies of social reproduction—the child's inheritance of the parent's social class—have shown a positive association between the educational success of parents and their children. The mechanisms of social reproduction have been studied by many sociologists (Bourdieu, 1977; Bowles & Gintis, 1976; Giroux, 1983; Willis, 1977), perhaps the most prominent of which is Bourdieu who posited that the transmission of cultural capital from parent to child was a mechanism through which social reproduction occurred.

Though the concept of cultural capital plays an important role in Bourdieu's theory of social reproduction and has been studied for several decades, defining what constitutes *cultural capital* is no easy task. For Bourdieu, cultural capital consists of three forms: objectified, institutionalized, and embodied cultural capital. The first refers to cultural objects such as paintings, operas, or ballets, which require special skills and knowledge to appreciate; the second to the institutions, primarily the school system, which provide the credentials that signal attainment in the dominant culture; and the last to the ability to appreciate and understand cultural goods. It is through the possession of embodied cultural capital that the other forms of cultural capital are obtained (Dumais, 2002). Since Bourdieu himself constantly modified the concept throughout his writings, it is necessary to draw upon interpretations used by other scholars in order to clarify what is meant by cultural capital. According to Lamont and Lareau (1989), cultural capital is "institutionalized, i.e., widely shared, high status cultural signals (attitudes, preferences, formal knowledge, behaviors, goals, and credentials) used for social and cultural exclusion" (p. 156). In short, cultural capital consists of cultural, behavioral, and linguistic proficiency in the dominant or elite culture (Dumais, 2002). Cultural capital provides students a mastery or fluency in, and access to, what is culturally valued in society. This fluency, in turn, facilitates and enhances students' ability to master their curriculum and perform well in school (DeGraaf et al., 2000). This fluency shapes the way students are perceived by teachers and others who bestow rewards and credentials.

Despite the great regard that schools may have for high levels of cultural capital among its students, the institutions themselves do not usually provide this form of capital; rather, it is typically transmitted through the students' families (Bourdieu, 1977; 1979). Although schools may not manufacture cultural capital, they are one of several key institutions that help turn cultural capital into profits for those who possess it. Bourdieu argued that schools are not the great equalizers, but rather help to reaffirm and reproduce social class and privilege by valuing the preferences, behaviors, and attitudes of the dominant class over those of the non-dominant groups. Cultural capital contributes to social inequality and helps to reproduce social stratification across generations. Members of the dominant groups are able to maintain their hold on rewards and benefits by minimizing access to cultural capital for members of the lower and working classes while maximizing access for its own members.

Theory of social mobility Education is seen by many as an important factor in the process of social mobility (Blau & Duncan, 1967). It remains an intervening link between ascribed status and occupational achievement/attainment. The ability to move across social class boundaries is dependent on a number of factors including educational attainment and a family's human, social, and cultural capital. Social mobility in an upward direction can be greatly assisted when children from lower classes tap into those resources that are available to their counterparts from more fortunate social origins. In the absence of human capital within the home, children may still be able to achieve social mobility through other factors, such as the possession of cultural resources.

Although access to cultural capital is greater for those with high levels of socio-economic resources, it is not impossible for those with fewer resources to possess such capital. For DiMaggio (1982) the acquisition of cultural capital may help to overcome the disadvantages associated with fewer socioeconomic resources. In short, parents and students "may see the accumulation of cultural capital as a way to overcome the obstacles that are typical for those in their class position" (Dumais, 2002, p. 47). Thus, for DiMaggio and others, "cultural capital facilitates the [success] of anyone who has it and is not the resource of a particular class" (Kingston, 2001, p. 92). Accordingly, a student from a lower social class may use the accumulation of cultural capital as an instrument for social mobility (DiMaggio). It is important to note, however, that in response to policies and educational systems that seek to increase social mobility and decrease social inequities, members of the elite class may develop strategies that enhance their positions and lead to greater, not less, exclusivity (DeGraaf et al., 2000).

Measures of cultural capital Ever since Bourdieu introduced the concept of cultural capital, researchers have used a variety of measures to explore this idea. Typical measures include participation in cultural activities, such as attending a concert, and being involved in other "highbrow" extracurricular activities, such as art and ballet classes (DeGraaf, 1986; DiMaggio, 1982; Katsillis & Rubinson, 1990). Sullivan (2001), for example, surveyed students' reading, music listening, and television viewing preferences, as well as their knowledge of various well-known cultural figures. Similarly, DeGraaf et al. (2000) measured parents' beaux arts participation and reading habits. Other measures of cultural capital have focused upon families' household educational resources, such as computers and books, and how access to these resources in the home are essential in moulding a student's orientation to school and are associated with various educational outcomes (Lareau, 1989; Teachman, 1987). Despite the large body of research on this topic, there is little consensus in the field as to which set of measures best captures the concept of cultural capital and who (the child or parent) should be surveyed. Despite the variability, each approach appears to be tapping into the concept of cultural capital as defined by both Bourdieu and DiMaggio.

Empirical findings As previously noted, just as the measures of cultural capital have varied across studies, so too have their findings. On the one hand, several studies have found that the possession of cultural capital and engaging in culturally enriching activities is positively related to school performance (DeGraaf et al., 2000; DiMaggio & Mohr, 1985; DiMaggio & Useem, 1978; Dumais, 2002). DiMaggio (1982) reinforces the finding that students who possess significant amounts of cultural capital benefit from open channels of communication with their teachers. According to DiMaggio, "teachers … communicate more easily with students who participate in elite status cultures, give them more attention and special assistance, and perceive them as more intelligent or gifted than students who lack cultural capital" (p. 190). DiMaggio's findings suggest that the educational return of cultural capital is higher for boys from working-class families than for sons of college graduates. DiMaggio's research demonstrates a significant relationship between students' cultural capital and their school grades and finds that teachers tend to reward students who they perceive to possess high levels of cultural capital (DiMaggio & Useem, 1978). These findings suggest that schools do not necessarily reinforce status structures, as theorized by Bourdieu, instead they reward the possession of cultural capital. Additionally, in a cross-national study of the effects of parental SES on schooling, Mateju (1990) found that cultural capital accounted for some of the effects of SES in three European countries–Czechoslovakia, Hungary, and the Netherlands. Yet, others have found no relationship between high levels of cultural capital and educational outcomes (Katsillis & Rubinson, 1990), especially once family (e.g., fathers' education) and individual level (e.g., race and marital status) background characteristics are controlled. Two significant international studies, conducted in Greece and France respectively, for example, found no support for a cultural capital effect (Katsillis & Rubinson, 1990; Robinson & Garnier, 1985). Bourdieu's theory of cultural reproduction and DiMaggio's theory of social mobility form the foundation of the study's research questions. As suggested by the literature review, the concept and educational effects of cultural capital are in need of further investigation and refinement, particularly cross-nationally. It should be noted, that while these two theories have each been supported by empirical research, determining the factors that influence children's literacy and school achievement remains a complex task. It is important to acknowledge the limitations to these two theories in explaining the inequality of educational outcomes for children from different SES backgrounds. It is also important to note that to-date there is little empirical data to indicate whether these theoretical perspective are applicable to non-Western countries.

10.3 Methodology

10.3.1 Principal Research Questions

The current study is premised on five research questions, with particular emphasis placed on the following overarching issue: To what degree is cultural capital a vehicle of social reproduction (as suggested by Bourdieu) or a mechanism for social mobility (as suggested by DiMaggio)? If Bourdieu's theory of social reproduction is to be supported by the findings, the results of the analyses will show that children from high SES backgrounds benefit more from the possession of cultural capital than their lower SES counterparts. In contrast, if DiMaggio's theory of social mobility is to be supported, the results will indicate that children from lower SES backgrounds benefit more from the possession of cultural capital than those from higher SES backgrounds. The research questions included in this study are:

1 What is the relationship between cultural capital and student literacy and achievement?
2. To what extent is the relationship between cultural capital and student literacy similar to that between cultural capital and student achievement? Does the relationship vary across domains of student literacy and achievement?
3. To what degree is cultural capital a vehicle of social reproduction or a mechanism for social mobility (overarching research question)?

4. Does the relationship between cultural capital and student literacy and achievement vary across countries?
5. How does the relationship between cultural capital and student literacy and achievement in the United States compare to the relationship in other countries?

These last two research questions are informed by the cross-national relationship between cultural capital and educational achievement. If a significant amount of cross-national variation is observed, the data would suggest that the relationship between cultural capital and educational achievement is defined, at least in part, within each country and is likely less susceptible to Western cultural shifts. On the other hand, similarities in the relationship cross-nationally may indicate that the countries in this study have been influenced by one or several foreign and/or dominant cultures. In addition, the last two research questions may provide some indication as to how cultural globalization may in the future affect the educational rewards of participating in highbrow activities. Caution is warranted, however, when considering these possible explanations for any cross-national variations. Though additional research is required, the results of these last two questions may shed light on the relationship between cultural globalization and shifts in the status of highbrow activities.

10.3.2 Data and Sample

As stated previously, two large-scale international datasets—PISA and TIMSS — are used to determine the relationship between cultural capital and student literacy and achievement. Sponsored by the Organization for Economic Cooperation and Development (OECD), PISA is a unique international survey, carried out in 32 countries in 2000. Participating countries in the first PISA assessment consisted mainly of OECD countries and a small number of non-OECD countries. In addition to assessments of student literacy, PISA includes data on student and family-level background characteristics. For the majority of countries, students in the sample were enrolled in the United States equivalent of the ninth grade.

Conducted in 1995 by the International Association for the Evaluation of Educational Achievement (IEA), TIMSS is an extensive, large-scale assessment of student mathematics and science achievement. The nationally representative data provide student mathematics and science achievement scores, as well as information on students' backgrounds, attitudes, and activities. Students included in this analysis are from the middle school population. In the majority of countries, this represents the equivalent of American seventh- and eighth-grade students; for the most part these students are 13 years of age.

The main goal of PISA is to provide student assessments in reading, mathematics, and science literacy, as well as to provide measures of general and cross-curricular competencies, in order to enable participating countries to gauge their success at meeting their educational yield, at both a national and international level. The reading, mathematics, and science literacy of students was measured using multistep reasoning and real-world situational items. A central goal of PISA was to assess the educational yield of countries—how well the educational system of countries has prepared their student population for the adult world and labor force. Accordingly, the test items measure the extent to which students possess the knowledge and skills needed to function outside of the school environment. In contrast, TIMSS measures student achievement in the areas of mathematics and science. More specifically, it assesses students' knowledge of mathematics and science that has been delivered in the classroom as part of a curriculum. As such, student performance is closely related to their exposure to curriculum in their schools.

In order to account for factors related to economic development, the sample was limited to developed industrialized countries. Countries that maximized geographic and cultural representation were selected; nine countries met these criteria. They are the North American countries of Canada and the United States; the West and South European countries of Germany, Greece, and Portugal; the Nordic countries of Norway and Sweden; and, finally, the East European countries of the Czech Republic and the Russian Federation. It should be noted that while countries that varied culturally were selected, all the countries in this study are Western countries. As such, these countries are representative of a dominant Westernized culture in which participation in various cultural activities, such as attending an opera, are typically regarded as a highbrow activity. Moreover, because both the PISA and TIMSS survey items reflect Western culture, it was thought prudent to restrict the countries to those that clearly mirror this cultural bias. Hence, countries from such regions as Southeast Asia are excluded.

10.3.3   Variables

Reading, mathematics, and science literacy, as measured by assessment scores, are the dependent variables for the PISA analysis. The dependent variables in the TIMSS analysis are mathematics and science achievement, also measured by test scores. In PISA, the cultural activities index—one of two independent variables of interest in this study—is constructed using students' responses to four questions. Students were asked to report how often they go to the movies, visit a museum or gallery, attend an opera, ballet, or classical concert, and watch live theater. The four-point response scale included: never or hardly ever, once or twice a year, about three or four times a years or more than four times a year. A final cultural activities scale was constructed by summing student responses to all four items; thus, scores ranged from 0 (low frequency) to 16 (high frequency). In TIMSS, the cultural activities index was constructed in a similar manner as PISA. Students were asked how often they visited a museum or art exhibition, attended a concert, went to the theater, and went to movies. Respondents were asked to indicate the frequency of their participation in these cultural activities on a four-point scale. The scale included rarely, about once a month, about once a week, or about every day. As in PISA, an index was created by summing scores to each of the four items.

The second independent variable of interest is the availability of books in the home. Students were asked to indicate how many books were in their homes. The response categories in PISA included none, 1–10 books, 11–100 books, 101–250 books, 251–500 books, and more than 500 books. The response categories in TIMSS were identical to those in PISA, with the exception of the last two categories, which were 101–200 and 200+ books, respectively.

Seven student level and family background control variables are included in all multivariate analyses. Table 10.1 contains the descriptions of these variables, along with their means and standard deviations. Previous research has shown a strong link between parental education and student achievement (for non-US studies see Katsillis & Rubinson, 1990; Lockheed et al., 1989; Lockheed & Longford, 1991).

Table 10.1 Description of variables, means, and standard deviations

TIMSS			
Variable	Description	Mean	SE
Girl	0 = boy, 1 = girl	0.50	0.50
Upper	0 = 13 and below, 1 = 14 and above (upper age)	0.67	0.47
Foreign stock	0 = parents and child born in the country, 1 = parents born outside the country	0.05	0.22
Native language speaker	1 = official language speaker (language of math and science test), 0 = other (other "official" or national dialect)	0.93	0.26
Lives in two-parent family	0 = family other than two-parent family, 1 = two-parent family	0.82	0.38
Parents' education			
Primary	Received a primary and possibly some secondary education	0.04	0.21
Secondary	Graduated/finished high school	0.46	0.50
Tertiary	College-educated	0.50	0.50
Number of books in home	0 = 0–10, 1 = 11–100, 2 = 101–200, 3 = 200+	1.75	0.96
Educational resources in the home index	0 = no items, 1 = one item, 2 = two items, 3 = 3 items, 4 = four items (min. = 0, max. = 4)	3.45	0.84
Cultural activities index	0 = rarely attend…16 = very high frequency of attendance	4.58	2.25
PISA			
Girl	0 = boy, 1 = girl	0.51	0.50
Upper	0 = less than 9th grade and below, 1 = 10th grade and above (upper grade).	0.67	0.47
Foreign stock	0 = parents & child born in country, 1 = parents born in other country	0.05	0.22
Native language speaker	0 = other language spoken at home, 1 = language of reading test spoken at home	0.93	0.25
Lives in two-parent family	0 = other, 1 = two-parent family	0.83	0.38
Parents' education			
Primary	Received a primary and possibly some secondary education	0.04	0.20
Secondary	Graduated/finished high school	0.46	0.50
Tertiary	College-educated	0.50	0.50
Number of books in home	0 = 0–10, 1 = 11–100, 2 = 101–250, 3 = 250+	1.77	0.93
Educational resources in the home index	0 = no items, 1 = one item, 2 = two items, 3 = 3 items, 4 = four items. (min. = 0, max. = 4)	3.45	0.83
Cultural activities index	0 = never attend these events…16 = high frequency of attendance	4.54	2.29

Note: All means are unweighted.

Parents' education is included in this analysis, not only to act as an indicator of SES, but also to determine whether the impact of cultural capital is determined, in part, by SES. To address the third research question, an interaction between parents' education and the two measures of cultural capital was specified. The direction and statistical significance of the interactions will lend support to either Bourdieu's theory of social reproduction theory or DiMaggio's theory of social mobility. Parent education refers to the highest level of education completed by either parent, and is measured through students' reports.

Several other control variables may also tap into family resources and as such are included as additional proxy variables for SES. We include family structure, as it is known to be associated with SES and child poverty (Bradbury & Jantti, 1999; McLanahan & Sandefur, 1994). The educational resources variable is an index constructed from students' self-reports of whether they have a calculator, dictionary, desk, and computer in their homes. Last, we control for a student's gender, whether the student's parents were born in another country, and whether the student is a native language speaker at home.

10.3.4 Analyses

Parallel analyses were conducted with the PISA and TIMSS datasets. A two-stage strategy was employed to determine the relationship between cultural capital and student literacy and educational achievement. In stage one, the first four research questions were addressed at the individual country level. The relationship between the two measures of cultural capital—participation in cultural activities and availability to book in the home—and the five dependent variables were modelled using Ordinary Least Square Regression (OLS) for each of the nine countries. In stage two, OLS regression was used to build a fixed effects model, in which each country was represented by a dummy variable with the United States as the reference group. The country dummies are used to absorb all observed and unobserved characteristics of each country and allow the random error to be independent of the observed variables. In addition, by allowing the magnitude of the relationship between student participation in cultural activities among the nine countries to be compared, the fifth and final research question—how does the relationship between cultural capital and student literacy and achievement in the United States differ from that of other countries—is addressed.

10.4 Results

10.4.1 Descriptive Analysis

Means for the main variables of interest for both PISA and TIMSS across the entire sample, as well as by individual country, are included in Table 10.2. In PISA, the mean literacy scores across the nine countries for reading, mathematics, and science

Table 10.2 Descriptive statistics for PISA and TIMSS by country

| | Means | | | | | | | | | |
| | All Countries | | Canada | | Czech Republic | | Germany | | Greece | |
Variables	PISA	TIMSS	PISA	TIMSS	PISA	TIMSS	PISA	TIMSS	PISA	TIMSS
Student assessment scores										
Reading literacy	504.02	–	524.21	–	497.51	–	497.68	–	472.13	–
Mathematics literacy	501.79	–	524.93	–	499.19	–	500.10	–	446.92	–
Science literacy	500.73	–	520.79	–	512.65	–	495.55	–	459.53	–
Mathematics achievement	–	496.02	–	505.66	–	539.10	–	497.77	–	466.78
Science achievement	–	507.93	–	506.48	–	551.53	–	516.31	–	477.15
Cultural activities	4.58	1.73	4.72	1.95	5.12	1.16	4.49	1.27	4.93	2.39
Number of books in the home	1.76	1.77	1.80	1.86	1.97	1.95	1.75	1.71	1.39	1.39
Number of cases	61,791	75,712	29,687	16,437	5,365	6,567	5,073	5,621	4,672	7,535

| | Means | | | | | | | | | |
| | Norway | | Portugal | | Russian Federation | | Sweden | | United States | |
Variables	PISA	TIMSS	PISA	TIMSS	PISA	TIMSS	PISA	TIMSS	PISA	TIMSS
Student assessment scores										
Reading literacy	505.37	–	476.53	–	461.67	–	515.86	–	495.97	–
Mathematics literacy	497.97	–	458.50	–	478.63	–	510.07	–	482.57	–
Science literacy	498.81	–	464.36	–	459.61	–	511.48	–	490.54	–
Mathematics achievement	–	486.89	–	441.07	–	515.66	–	514.73	–	483.95
Science achievement	–	509.45	–	454.99	–	508.07	–	529.70	–	514.93
Cultural activities	4.15	1.09	4.81	1.40	3.25	1.85	4.31	1.03	5.10	2.63
Number of books in the home	1.92	2.10	1.33	1.38	1.83	1.73	1.93	2.05	1.51	1.68
Number of cases	4,147	5,630	4,585	6,637	6,438	7,840	4,416	8,636	3,846	10,809

Note: All means are unweighted.

are 504, 502, and 501, respectively. In five out of the nine countries (Greece, Norway, Portugal, Sweden, and the United States), the mean reading literacy scores are higher than those for mathematics and science literacy. Across all nine countries, Canada has the highest scores in all three domains.

In TIMSS, the mean achievement scores, across all nine countries, for mathematics and science are 496 and 508, respectively. This represents approximately an 11-point difference in the mean achievement scores between the two subjects. In all but the Russian Federation, the mean science achievement scores are greater than those for mathematics. Across both subject areas—mathematics and science— the Czech Republic has the highest score and Portugal the lowest. Overall, there is a high degree of parity in the mean scores for the two datasets.

The cultural activities index ranges from zero to 16; thus, it is interesting to note the relatively low average levels of participation in both PISA (4.58) and TIMSS (1.73). Not only are the average levels low, but there is also a notable difference between the two datasets. This difference is due in part to variations in the response scales across the two datasets. Although the activities and questions were similar across the two studies, the response options differed significantly. Specifically, PISA asked students to report the frequency in which they engaged in cultural activities on a scale ranging from never or hardly ever to more than four times a year. In contrast, the scale used in TIMSS ranged from rarely to about once a day. Since few students attend the opera, visit the museum, go to a movie, or attend live theater on a daily or weekly basis, students' reports are highly clustered in TIMSS around the lower bound response categories.

As illustrated in Table 10.2, in the PISA sample, average levels of participation in cultural activities ranged from a low of 3.17 in the Russia Federation to a high of 5.12 in the Czech Republic. It is worth noting that the mean for cultural activities in the United States is 5.05, only fractionally lower than the mean for the Czech Republic. In TIMSS, average levels of participation for students range from a low of 1.02 in Sweden to a high of 2.63 in the United States.

Turning to the second measure of cultural capital, number of books in the home, students in both datasets reported having somewhere between 11 to 100 books in their home on average. Students in the Nordic countries of Sweden and Norway reported having the most books available to them at home and students in the Mediterranean countries of Greece and Portugal reported having the least. In contrast to cultural activities, there is a great deal of parity in students' reports of books across the two datasets. For example, in Greece the mean in both samples is 1.39, which equates to somewhere between 11 to 100 books.

10.4.2   Multivariate Analyses

The overarching research question, as well as the additional research questions, is examined through a multivariate analysis. Tables 10.3, 10.4, and 10.5 present the results for the three literacy-dependent variables found in PISA. Tables 10.6 and 10.7 illustrate the results for TIMSS.

Table 10.3 OLS regression of reading literacy by country (PISA)

Variables	Countries								
	Canada	Czech Republic	Germany	Greece	Norway	Portugal	Russia	Sweden	United States
Cultural activities	5.81*	2.77*	4.02*	3.00*	4.78*	5.96*	2.81*	1.95+	5.26*
Number of books	15.81*	34.08*	32.00*	22.14*	26.00*	17.57*	25.63*	27.76*	26.96*
Parent and family characteristics:									
Highest education of parent: (ref: Tertiary)									
Primary	-9.36	-41.80	-32.48	-4.37	-12.91	27.28+	-32.88	-53.87+	20.30
Secondary	-10.80+	-11.30	-13.06	1.17	11.38	20.61#	14.57+	20.14*	-2.24
Interactions:									
Highest education of parent: (ref: Tertiary)									
Primary*cultural activities	-4.94	5.57	-0.64	-2.63	-6.53	-3.77*	-12.85#	5.24	-12.01#
Secondary*cultural activities	-0.75	1.56	1.69	-1.53	-1.98	-3.18+	-1.67#	-1.97	-2.29
Highest education of parent: (ref: Tertiary)									
Primary*number of books	-10.71	-18.47	-21.79	-13.11#	-11.06	-8.28#	2.25	-3.16	-6.68
Secondary* number of books	-3.79+	-13.93*	-8.50+	-9.40#	-6.98#	-6.09	-7.30#	-7.16+	-3.29
Intercept	386.38*	372.46*	325.31*	275.49*	288.95*	287.73*	305.18*	380.19*	325.95*
R^2	0.21	0.41	0.47	0.25	0.21	0.50	0.23	0.19	0.32
Number of observations	29375	5345	5010	4635	4080	4550	6685	4380	3845

* indicates significance at the 0.01 level; + indicates significance at the 0.05 level; # indicates significance at the 0.10 level.

Table 10.4 OLS regression of mathematics literacy by country (PISA)

Variables	Countries								
	Canada	Czech Republic	Germany	Greece	Norway	Portugal	Russia	Sweden	United States
Cultural activities	4.06*	1.24	2.39#	3.71+	2.58#	4.71*	2.48+	−0.47	5.76*
Number of books	12.74*	30.91*	34.12*	21.99*	25.63*	16.49*	25.80*	30.44*	27.58*
Parent and family characteristics:									
Highest education of parent: (ref: Tertiary)									
Primary	−24.98	−93.59	−45.75	−10.65	13.06	21.05	−31.9	−21.79	−25.31
Secondary	−10.82#	−25.90#	−7.39	−20.04	20.20#	18.73	7.84	26.03+	3.04
Interactions:									
Highest education of parent: (ref: Tertiary)									
Primary*cultural activities	2.04	11.98	1.96	−4.57	−7.85	−2.85	6.43	3.99	−0.97
Secondary*cultural activities	0.11	1.46	1.68	0.03	−2.52	−2.37	−1.64	0.52	−2.53
Highest education of parent: (ref: Tertiary)									
Primary*number of books	−11.65	−18.10	−26.61	−4.21	−13.43	−8.28	−19.70	−13.59	−7.31
Secondary* number of books	−5.64+	−9.30#	−11.57+	−1.82	−8.56#	−9.13#	−5.02	−14.68*	−7.59
Intercept	452.14*	394.66*	345.72*	236.95*	305.19*	313.3*	358.56*	383.64*	332.58*
R^2	0.15	0.29	0.40	0.26	0.16	0.46	0.16	0.16	0.33
Number of observations	16310	3055	2790	2580	2265	2520	3710	2445	2135

*indicates significance at the 0.01 level; + indicates significance at the 0.05 level; # indicates significance at the 0.10 level.

Table 10.5 OLS regression of science literacy by country (PISA)

					Countries				
Variables	Canada	Czech Republic	Germany	Greece	Norway	Portugal	Russia	Sweden	United States
Cultural activities	3.97*	3.08+	4.89*	2.04	3.08+	5.49*	2.29+	0.59	5.06*
Number of books	13.93*	42.92*	26.74*	25.39*	26.28*	19.4*	27.29*	24.33*	27.84*
Parent and family characteristics:									
Highest education of parent: (ref: Tertiary)									
Primary	−13.27	66.55	−32.35	−15.13	−29.22	33.16#	−115.19#	−60.37+	22.11
Secondary	−15.47+	4.41	−18.68#	0.61	7.03	30.94#	16.67	4.65	−4.36
Interactions:									
Highest education of parent: (ref: Tertiary)									
Primary* cultural activities	−1.19	−7.86	−2.53	0.93	−2.55	−3.51	−11.26	11.47*	−17.77+
Secondary* cultural activities	−0.59	1.70	−0.29	−1.54	−0.94	−2.87	−1.29	−0.58	−1.29
Highest education of parent: (ref: Tertiary)									
Primary* number of books	−13.4	−36.92+	−8.81	−13.13	−12.6	−10.82#	29.62	−5.77	9.29
Secondary* number of books	−3.02#	−20.86*	−2.13	−11.96+	−8.30#	−8.06	−11.86*	−5.49	−7.40
Intercept	428.18*	392.74*	348.2*	289.19*	358.78	282.49*	334.34*	413.31*	355.87*
R²	0.16	0.32	0.40	0.18	0.32	0.44	0.15	0.14	0.29
Number of observations	16320	3050	2820	2575	2260	2530	3710	2425	2125

* indicates significance at the 0.01 level; + indicates significance at the 0.05 level; # indicates significance at the 0.10 level.

Table 10.6 OLS regression of mathematics achievement by country (TIMSS)

Variables	Countries								
	Canada	Czech Republic	Germany	Greece	Norway	Portugal	Russia	Sweden	United States
Cultural activities	-7.52*	-10.34*	-8.07+	-7.54*	-7.37*	-1.36	-6.76*	-3.66+	-9.84*
Number of books	2.84	22.28*	29.72*	22.76*	22.56*	9.24+	20.77*	25.47*	24.67*
Parent and family characteristics:									
Highest education of parent: (ref: Tertiary)									
Primary	-17.37#	-20.96*	-19.15	-24.30*	0.50	-39.66*	-26.23+	4.15	-8.95
Secondary	-6.09	-6.96	-6.34	-2.22	15.55+	-25.49+	-16.37+	12.64	-1.32
Interactions:									
Highest education of parent: (ref: Tertiary)									
Primary* cultural activities	-1.84	2.78	0.88	2.23	6.70	-1.97	3.84#	-5.87+	2.71#
Secondary* cultural activities	-0.94	3.09	1.60	-0.43	0.42	-0.08	1.28	-4.95*	0.67
Highest education of parent: (ref: Tertiary)									
Primary* number of books	-3.30	-14.16#	-8.08#	-17.48*	-14.68+	0.93	-22.49*	-12.35*	-21.97*
Secondary* number of books	-1.61	-4.00	-7.37#	-11.28*	-10.52*	2.00	-5.18#	-7.57+	-11.42*
Intercept	463.98*	461.86*	440.02*	387.11*	378.31*	431.51*	458.01*	422.21*	402.93*
R²	0.11	0.15	0.18	0.18	0.17	0.11	0.12	0.21	0.22
Number of observations	16000	6540	5545	7520	5600	6605	7815	8555	10655

* indicates significance at the 0.01 level; + indicates significance at the 0.05 level; # indicates significance at the 0.10 level.

Table 10.7 OLS regression of science achievement by country (TIMSS)

Variables	Countries									
	Canada	Czech Republic	Germany	Greece	Norway	Portugal	Russia	Sweden	United States
Cultural activities	−7.35*	−7.22*	−5.74#	−6.44*	−7.80*	−3.11	−5.12*	−3.87+	−11.24*
Number of books	12.93*	21.08*	34.25*	22.39*	23.58*	11.72*	15.70*	26.34*	26.13*
Parent and family characteristics:									
Highest education of parent: (ref: Tertiary)									
Primary	−15.21	−10.54	−3.26	−11.87	16.69	−42.98*	−32.06+	8.78	−17.26
Secondary	−13.21	1.93	13.50	4.45	16.83	−31.94+	−16.28+	11.78	−1.04
Interactions:									
Highest education of parent: (ref: Tertiary)									
Primary* cultural activities	−1.68	1.90	−2.57	1.05	0.44	−0.32	2.38	−7.79#	4.18#
Secondary* cultural activities	−0.31	0.76	−1.24	0.11	0.72	0.30	0.81	−4.49+	0.13
Highest education of parent: (ref: Tertiary)									
Primary* number of books	−8.10#	−12.63+	−9.63	−16.45*	−18.80*	0.34	−9.11	−13.52*	−15.58*
Secondary* number of books	0.05	−6.13	−12.66+	−11.79*	−10.71*	4.33	−1.93	−8.76+	−9.06*
Intercept	438.54*	467.13*	435.74*	391.03*	389.43*	440.37*	442.99*	436.27*	430.47*
R^2	0.14	0.14	0.18	0.15	0.17	0.11	0.11	0.21	0.20
Number of observations	16000	6540	5545	7520	5600	6605	7815	8555	10655

*indicates significance at the 0.01 level; + indicates significance at the 0.05 level; # indicates significance at the 0.10 level.

Research questions 1 and 2:What is the relationship between cultural capital and student literacy and achievement? To what extent is the relationship between cultural capital and student literacy similar to that between cultural capital and student achievement? Does the relationship vary across domains of student literacy and achievement? As seen in all of the preceding tables, the answer depends on the country and student outcome in question, as well as the dimension of the student outcome being considered. Frequent involvement in cultural activities is positively associated with higher levels of student literacy in all nine countries and across the three domains of student literacy. While the direction is positive and statistically significant for reading literacy in each of the nine countries, the same is not true for mathematics and science literacy, however. Specifically, frequent involvement in cultural activities is significantly related to higher levels of mathematical literacy among students in Canada, Greece, Portugal, Russia, and the United States. Involvement in cultural activities is also significantly related to higher levels of science literacy for students in seven of the nine countries (the exceptions being Greece and Sweden). In contrast to the positive, but not always significant, relationship between cultural activities and student literacy observed in the PISA data, we find a negative relationship between the frequency of participation in cultural activities and TIMSS assessments of curriculum-based achievement in mathematics and science. Student involvement in cultural activities is significantly associated with lower levels of mathematics and science achievement in eight of the nine countries (the exception being Portugal). The relationship between students' access to books at home and the five dependent variables appears to be more uniform than that observed for cultural activities. With only one exception (Canada mathematics achievement), the relationship between the availability of books in the home and student literacy and achievement is both positive and significant.

Together our results suggest that the effect of participation in cultural activities differs across outcomes and, to a lesser extent, across countries. While participation in cultural activities may help to enhance student literacy, frequent participation in culturally enriching activities appears to be non-beneficial, and possibly counter-productive, for curriculum-based learning. The results also indicate the importance of considering multiple domains of student literacy and achievement. While the benefits of participating in cultural activities for reading literacy are apparent across all nine countries in this study, for example, the benefits for mathematics and science literacy are limited to a smaller number of countries. The results also suggest that across multiple countries and cultures, children's access to books at home promotes both student literacy and educational achievement.

Research question 3: To what degree is cultural capital a vehicle of social reproduction or a mechanism for social mobility? Two prominent theories—Bourdieu's theory of social reproduction and DiMaggio's theory of social mobility—have driven much of the research conducted on cultural capital. The main research question attempts to investigate these two theories further by including interaction between parents' education, a key indicator of students' socioeconomic background, and the two measures of cultural capital in the analyses. If Bourdieu's theory is to be supported by the analyses, the interaction terms should be negative in direction. If DiMaggio is correct, and students from low SES benefit more from increased participation in culturally enriching activities and availability of books in the home (i.e., social mobility), the opposite would be true. In general, the results suggest that higher levels of cultural capital—as measured either through cultural activities or books— results in smaller benefits, in general, for reading literacy among students in lower SES groups. Just over a third of the interaction terms in this study are significant and an even smaller proportion reached significance at the 0.05 level or below.

The results for mathematics literacy provide a slightly different picture. Overall, the findings indicate that students whose parents have lower levels of educational attainment benefit more in mathematics literacy from frequent participation in cultural activities than students whose parents are college-educated. None of the interaction terms reach significance, however. In contrast, increased access to books at home is associated with significantly smaller benefits in mathematics literacy to students of lower SES groups in several countries. Specifically, students in Canada, the Czech Republic, Germany, Norway, Portugal, and Sweden, whose parents have at most received a secondary level education, experience significantly smaller gains in mathematics literacy from increased access to books than students whose parents are college-educated. The results for science literacy, again, suggest fewer rewards to cultural capital for students in lower SES groups.

Research question 4: Does the relationship between cultural capital and student literacy and achievement vary across countries? As demonstrated in Tables 10.6 and 10.7, the interaction terms between participation in cultural activities and parental education are a mixture of positive and negative coefficients in both the mathematics and science achievement models, suggesting that the relationship varies across countries and within countries by outcome. In the previous models, however, few of the coefficients are significant. The results also suggest that in all but one country (Portugal), students whose parents have lower levels of educational attainment benefit less from increased access to books at home than students whose parents are college educated. The difference in benefits between those with parents who have lower levels of educational attainment and those with college-educated parents is significant in many countries.

Viewed together the results provide moderate, though limited, support for Bourdieu's theory of cultural reproduction. More specifically, the results appear to suggest that students from higher SES backgrounds enjoy, in general, greater benefits with respect to both student literacy and achievement from increased access to books at home. The results also indicate however, that the benefits to participation in cultural activities are unlikely to depend in large part on SES.

Research question 5: How does the relationship between cultural capital and student literacy and achievement in the United States compare to the relationship in other countries? The results of the fixed effect model, which allows for comparisons of the effect of cultural capital across countries and addresses the fifth and final research question, are summarized in Tables 10.8 (cultural activities) and 10.9 (access to books). For clarity of presentation, only the interaction effects are presented.

The interaction between the country dummy and cultural capital measure indicates whether cultural capital has a greater or lesser effect on student literacy and

Table 10.8 OLS regression analysis including cultural activities and country interactions for all nine countries combined

Countries	Literacy			Achievement	
	Reading	Mathematics	Science	Mathematics	Science
Cultural activities × Country (ref. United States)					
Canada	0.09	−2.68*	−1.69	0.89	3.19*
Czech Republic	0.09	−1.84	0.61	1.66	4.67*
Germany	1.68#	−0.36	1.75	1.64	2.76*
Greece	−2.32+	−1.04	−3.05+	3.13*	5.26*
Norway	−0.38	−4.32*	−1.92	2.25#	3.23+
Portugal	−0.47	−2.68+	−1.24	5.75*	7.22*
Russian Federation	−2.31+	−2.9+	−2.64#	3.4*	6.33*
Sweden	−3.54*	−5.98*	−4.54*	2.74*	4.44*
Intercept	353.58*	367.89*	382.58*	430.55*	453.48*
R^2	0.29	0.24	0.25	0.22	0.21
Observations	67920	37830	37385	74850	74850

*indicates significance at the 0.01 level; + indicates significance at the 0.05 level; # indicates significance at the 0.10 level.

Table 10.9 OLS regression analysis including books and country interactions for all nine countries combined

Countries	Literacy			Achievement	
	Reading	Mathematics	Science	Mathematics	Science
Books × Country (ref. United States)					
Canada	−12.12*	−16.72*	−12.7*	−16.15	−8.27*
Czech Republic	4.57#	3.85	6.12*	0.40	−6.69*
Germany	10.57*	8.39*	7.97*	3.91#	2.20
Greece	−8.63*	−1.71	−5.87#	−3.05	−7.83*
Norway	−3.83	−6.31#	−3.78	−5.11+	−8.00*
Portugal	−9.08*	−11.31*	−10.17*	−6.91*	−8.50*
Russian Federation	−7.07+	−4.07	−6.90#	−1.57	−9.18*
Sweden	−4.24#	−4.60#	−5.10	−0.37	−4.00+
Intercept	353.22*	371.69*	383.46*	415.24*	433.15*
R^2	0.30	0.24	0.25	0.23	0.21
Observations	67920	37830	37835	74850	74850

*indicates significance at the 0.01 level; + indicates significance at the 0.05 level; # indicates significance at the 0.10 level.

achievement, in each country, when compared to the United States. In order to obtain the effect of participating in cultural activities and the availability of books in the home, the interaction coefficient is added to the effect for the United States. For example, for the Russian Federation, the effect of cultural activities on reading literacy is 2.12 (i.e., 4.43 + −2.31). For illustrative purposes, we have calculated the cultural capital coefficients for both measures and produced two graphs that reveal the variation in the effects of cultural capital across all nine countries in this study.

Figure 10.1 illustrates the coefficients for participation in cultural activities for literacy and achievement outcomes. As the graph indicates, there is variation in the effect sizes across countries and between the literacy and achievement outcomes. In Sweden, there is a much smaller effect of participating in cultural activities on literacy than in both Germany and the United States. When we turn to two measures of student achievement, however, the greatest negative effect of participating in cultural activities appears to be in the United States, followed by Canada and Germany. In the United States, participating in cultural activities, such as going to the theater or gallery, has a strong positive relationship with student literacy, and an equally strong negative relationship with student achievement, when compared to the other countries in this study.

The coefficients for the availability of books in the home are illustrated in Fig. 10.2. In contrast to participation in cultural activities, the more books in a student's home, the greater are the literacy and achievement scores. In terms of student literacy, Germany, followed by the Czech Republic and the United States, has the strongest relationship between the availability of books and all three literacy outcomes. In terms of student achievement, the largest coefficients across both measures can be found in Germany, followed by the United States. Students in these three countries, Germany, the Czech Republic, and the United States, seem to benefit the most from the availability of books in the home when we consider literacy and achievement outcomes.

In summary, students in the United States, compared to their counterparts in the other eight countries in this study, appear to benefit significantly in both literacy

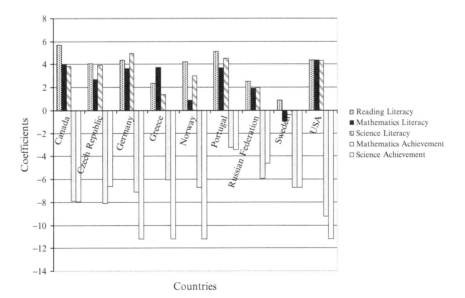

Fig. 10.1 A graph illustrating the variation in the relationship between participation in cultural activities and student literacy and achievement across nine countries

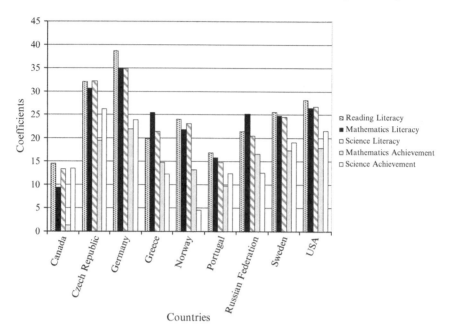

Fig. 10.2 A graph illustrating the variation in the relationship between availability of books in the home and student literacy and achievement across nine countries

and achievement scores when books are available to them at home. For literacy outcomes, the same is also the case for participating in cultural activities; however, the relationship is negative in terms of mathematics and science achievement.

10.5 Discussion

While the results of this study remain fundamentally associative in nature and, as such, causal inferences cannot be made, consistent patterns have emerged that warrant both exploration and interpretation. Moreover, because the countries included in this analysis share a similar cultural milieu, the extent to which these findings apply to other countries, in particular non-Westernized countries, is unclear. And, in fact, a different set of countries may likely have produced a different set of results.

The main research question centered on exploring the extent to which DiMaggio's or Bourdieu's theories were correct. The results provide less than conclusive evidence to suggest whether cultural capital is a vehicle of social mobility or an instrument for social reproduction. The analyses indicate that the benefits of engaging in cultural activities for students are not shaped in large part by their socioeconomic background, at least as measured by parental education. That is, contrary to both Bourdieu's and DiMaggio's arguments, students from different socioeconomic backgrounds experience similar gains or losses (as in the case of educational achievement and student literacy) from participation in culturally enriching activities. While the interaction effect between students' access to books and parental education is consistent with Bourdieu's theory of social reproduction, these results should be interpreted with caution since many of the interaction terms did not reach significance. In short, while there is some support to suggest that the benefit of having books in the home is smaller for students from low SES backgrounds, the difference appears to be small and limited to a few countries. It is important to note that the lack of conclusive support for either theory may be the result of the nature of the survey questions used in both the PISA and TIMSS instruments. In addition, parental reports may provide more valid data of the amount of cultural capital available to children. Specifically, parental reports may include less measurement error, and may be better measures of the intervening relationship of cultural capital on SES and educational achievement.

More generally, the analysis indicates a positive relationship between participation in cultural activities and student literacy (reading, mathematics, science), and a negative relationship between participation in cultural activities and student achievement in mathematics and science. The results also confirm the importance of cross-national studies. While the relationship of cultural activities and access to books with student educational outcomes is similar across countries, the magnitude of the relationship varies significantly.

The study of cultural capital has indeed been the topic of many sociological studies in recent years. Still, as highlighted by Kingston (2001), many studies have failed to make the link between social privilege and educational outcomes or social mobility. In this chapter, we attempted to extend previous research by studying the relationship across both multiple countries and multiple student outcomes. While the strength of the relationship varied across the nine countries in this study, the direction remained consistent. Overall, participation in cultural activities and the access to books in the home both have a positive relationship with student literacy. For mathematics and science achievement, participation in cultural activities was negative in direction, but there was a positive relationship with the number of books in the home.

10.6 Conclusion

The results indicate that despite the cultural differences that exist across these nine countries, the direction of the relationships is similar. In addition, the results generally failed to support conclusively either the theory of social mobility or the theory of social reproduction. Further research that is able to collect data pertaining to the possession of cultural capital from both parents and students is needed. The advantages of large-scale international surveys are well documented (Porter & Gamoran, 2002); however, further advances need to be made in the collection of family background data. Large-scale datasets would benefit greatly from more specific and multidimensional measures of cultural capital.

It is important to recognize that cultural codes that are valuable in one society can and do vary from one country to the next (DeGraaf et al., 2000). The variation found between the nine countries in this study may reflect how these highbrow cultural activities are institutionalized within each nation. As Buchmann (2002), DeGraaf et al. (2000), and Farkas (1996) have all suggested, an emphasis on participation in highbrow activities may overlook other aspects of a country's culture, which are beneficial to children's academic success. In this study, two distinct measures of cultural capital (beaux arts participation and books in the home) were included in order to account for some of this cross-national variation.

These cross-national differences may also give us an indication of the possible effect of cultural globalization on the relationship between educational achievement and cultural capital. While other foreign cultures have and will continue to infiltrate other countries, what is deemed to be highbrow may be more rigidly defined and less subject to change. It is possible that cultural globalization will influence popular culture more than it will affect high culture. In conclusion, while this study has fallen short in supporting either DiMaggio's theory of social mobility or Bourdieu's theory of social reproduction, the findings provide additional evidence that cultural capital is indeed related to children's educational achievement cross-nationally.

Acknowledgments Research for this project was made possible by the generous support of the National Institute Child Health and Human Development through the Family and Child Well-being Research Network Grant 1U01 HD37558-01. This research was completed while the first author was employed as a research intern by Child Trends.

References

Alexander, K. L. & Entwisle, D. R. (1988). *Achievement in the first two years of school: Patterns and processes.* (Vol. 46). Ann Arbor, MI: Society for Research in Child Development.

Blau, P. M. & Duncan, O. D. (1967). *The American occupational structure.* New York: John Wiley.

Bourdieu, P. (1977). Cultural reproduction and social reproduction. In J. Karabel & A. H. Halsey (Eds.), *Power in education* (pp. 487–511). New York: Oxford University Press.

Bourdieu, P. (1979). *Outline of a theory of practice.* Cambridge, UK: Cambridge University Press.

Bowles, S. & Gintis, H. (1976). *Schooling in capitalist America.* New York: Basic Books.

Bradbury, B. & Jantti, M. (1999). *Child poverty across industrialized nations.* (Innocenti Occasional Papers No. EPS 71). Florence, Italy: UNICEF.

Buchmann, C. (2002). Measuring family background in international studies of education: Conceptual issues and methodological challenges. In A. C. Porter & A. Gamoran (Eds.), *Methodological advances in cross-national surveys of educational achievement.* Washington, DC: National Academy Press.

Clawson, H. & Coolbaugh, K. (2001). The YouthARTS development project. OJJDP. *Juvenile Justice Bulletin*, May.

Coleman, J. S. (1988). Social capital in the creation of human capital. *American Journal of Sociology, 94*, S95–S120.

Coleman, J. S., Campbell, E. Q., Hobson, C. J., McPartland, J., Mood, A. M., Weinfeld, F. D., et al. (1966). *Equality of educational opportunity.* Washington, DC: US Government Printing Office.

Coleman, J. S. & Hoffer, T. (1987). *Public and private high schools.* New York: Basic Books.

Coleman, J. S., Hoffer, T., & Kilgore, S. (1982). *High school achievement: Public, Catholic, and private schools compared.* New York: Basic Books.

DeGraaf, N. D., DeGraaf, P. M., & Kraaykamp, G. (2000). Parental cultural capital and educational attainment in the Netherlands: A refinement of cultural capital perspective. *Sociology of Education, 73*, 92–111.

DeGraaf, P. M. (1986). The impact of financial and cultural resources on educational attainment in the Netherlands. *Sociology of Education, 68*, 753–778.

DiMaggio, P. J. (1982). Cultural capital and school success: The impact of status culture participation on the grades of U.S. high school students. *American Sociological Review, 47*, 189–201.

DiMaggio, P. J. & Mohr, J. (1985). Cultural capital, educational attainment, and marital selection. *American Journal of Sociology, 90*, 1231–1261.

DiMaggio, P. J. & Useem, M. (1978). Social class and arts consumption: The origins and consequences of class differences in exposure to the arts in America. *Theory and Society, 5*, 141–159.

Dumais, S. A. (2002). Cultural capital, gender, and school success. The role of habitus. *Sociology of Education, 75*, 44–68.

Farkas, G. (1996). *Human capital or cultural capital? Ethnicity and poverty groups in an urban school district.* New York: Aldine de Gruyter.

Giroux, H. (1983). Theories of reproduction and resistance in the new sociology of education. *Harvard Educational Review, 53*, 257–293.

Jencks, C., Smith, M., Acland, H., Bane, M. J., Cohen, D., Ginitis, H., et al. (1972). *Inequality: A reassessment of the effect of family and schooling in America.* New York: Harper & Row.

Kalmijn, M. & Kraaykamp, G. (1996). Race, cultural capital, and schooling: An analysis of trends in the United States. *Sociology of Education, 69*, 22–34.

Katsillis, J. & Rubinson, R. (1990). Cultural capital, student achievement, and educational reproduction: The case of Greece. *American Sociological Review, 55*, 270–279.

Kingston, P. W. (2001). The unfulfilled promise of Cultural Capital Theory. *Sociology of Education, 74*(Extra Issue), 88–99.

Lamont, M. & Lareau, A. (1989). Cultural capital: Allusions, gaps, and glissandos in recent theoretical developments. *Sociological Theory, 6*, 153–168.

Lareau, A. (1989). *Home advantage: Social class and parental intervention in elementary education.* New York: Falmer.

Lockheed, M. E. & Longford, N. T. (1991). School effects on mathematics achievement gain in Thailand. In R. S. Willms & J. D. Willms (Eds.), *Schools, classrooms and pupils: International studies of schooling from s multi-level perspective* (pp. 131–148). San Diego, CA: Academic.

Lockheed, M. E., Fuller, B., & Nyirongo, R. (1989). Family effects on student's achievement in Thailand and Malawi. *Sociology of Education, 62*, 239–255.

Mateju, P. (1990). Family effect on educational attainment in Czechoslovakia, the Netherlands, and Hungary. In J. L. Peschar (Ed.), *Social reproduction in Eastern and Western Europe.* Groningen, The Netherlands: Oomo.

McLanahan, S. S. & Sandefur, G. (1994). *Growing up with a single-parent: What hurts, what helps?* Cambridge: Harvard University Press.

Porter, A. C. & Gamoran, A. (2002). Progress and challenges for large-scale studies. In A. C. Porter & A. Gamoran (Eds.), *Methodological advances in cross-national surveys of educational achievement.* Washington, DC: National Academy Press.

Riddell, A. R. (1989). An alternative approach to the study of school effectiveness in third world countries. *Comparative Education Review, 33*, 481–497.

Robinson, R. V. & Garnier, M. A. (1985). Class reproduction among men and women in France: Reproduction theory on its home ground. *American Journal of Sociology, 91*, 250–280.

Schneider, B. & Coleman, J. S. (1993). *Parents their children, and schools.* Boulder, CO: Westview.

Shavit, Y., & Blossfield, H. P. (1993). *Persistent inequality: Changing educational stratification in thirteen countries.* Boulder, CO: Westview.

Sullivan, A. (2001). Cultural capital and educational attainment. *Sociology*, *35*(4), 893–912.

Teachman, J. D. (1987). Family background, educational resources and educational attainment. *American Sociological Review*, *52*, 548–557.

White, K. R. (1982). The relationship between socioeconomic status and academic achievement. *Psychological Bulletin*, *91*(3), 461–481.

Willis, P. E. (1977). *Learning to labor: How working class kids get working class jobs*. New York: Columbia University Press.

Chapter 11
The Institutionalization of Mass Schooling as Marginalization or Opportunity in Islamic Nation-States

Alexander W. Wiseman

11.1 Introduction

By adapting standard models of schooling, Islamic nation-states have raised basic levels of educational attainment, established largely undifferentiated curricula, and encouraged resource availability to schools. Yet, Islamic nation-states are still marginalized within the global community of nations. This chapter asks if the institutionalization of mass schooling in Islamic nation-states contributes to the social construction of marginalization. It further asks if educational and social inequality (i.e., marginalization) is an international process occurring between Islamic and other nation-states or an intra-national process occurring within individual Islamic nation-states. The evidence for Iran, Jordan, Morocco, and Tunisia presented in this chapter suggests that while the adoption or imposition of schooling modelled on Western educational models may contribute to the marginalization of Islamic nation-states, economic stratification and social inequality are intra-national processes contributing to this marginalization as much as, or more than, international ones.

In his opening address to the 46th session of the International Conference on Education, the Minister of Education of Argentina, Delich (2001), emphasized that

> [c]ountries with a medium and low level of economic development experience great difficulties in ensuring the universal provision of quality basic education while adopting the same parameters and the same strategies as the main developed countries. ... It seems clear, however, that the less developed countries' policies to promote inclusion and increase opportunities in basic education should pay closer and more systematic attention to the school system's non-traditional institutional resources and technologies.

Mr. Delich's point is important—especially in an era when education is increasingly used as a tool for the political, economic, and social development of nations (Chabbott, 2003).

By adapting standard models of schooling, both developed and developing nations have raised basic levels of universal or mass educational attainment,

Lehigh University

established largely undifferentiated school curricula, and encouraged reasonably high levels of resource availability to schools (Baker et al., 2002; Meyer et al., 1992). Indeed, schools everywhere in the world continue to look more and more alike. Yet social and educational inequalities persist and are even used to differentiate or categorize some communities as marginalized within nations and some nation-states as marginalized within the world society (Boyle, 2002; Carnoy, 2000; Crossley & Watson, 2003; Marginson & Mollis, 2001; Meyer et al., 1997).

There is a strong argument that the globalization of mass educational systems has contributed to the marginalization of people groups defined by ethnic, cultural, and national identities (Astiz et al., 2002; Carnoy, 2000; Morrow & Torres, 2000). The prevailing perspective suggests that Western models of education clash with indigenous cultural models (Boyle, 2002). Through this clash the social order of the indigenous culture is artificially stratified and social castes are produced that marginalize or disenfranchise their indigenous population (Carnoy, 1985). Through this process individuals are alienated from their indigenous culture by the imposed Western system (Mazrui, 1999).

An alternative perspective suggests that social stratification is inherent in cultures regardless of educational model or origin. Although reproduction of social stratification does occur through the Westernization of social systems and cultures, and through the adoption of Westernized mass education systems in particular, stratification and inequality are not artefacts of Western imposition alone (Inkeles, 1969). Indeed, Westernized models of mass education are often imposed or adopted without adjustment for local cultures or traditions, but over time they are often adapted to the cultural mores and specifications of the indigenous society (Spindler, 1987). Instead of promoting inequality, it is the mass and universal components of Westernized models of schooling that frequently promote educational equality. Similar arguments have been made regarding gender differences in education (Adely, forthcoming; Baker & Wiseman, 2005). Therefore, social stratification linked to schooling is often a product of local adaptation of the mass educational model rather than an inherent aspect of mass education.

In debating whether the globalization of mass schooling has marginalized whole nations within the international community, of particular social and political interest are Islamic states or nations. The terrorist events of September 11, 2001, and the aftermath in Afghanistan and Iraq only served to intensify and focus this interest, although the claim that the social construction of marginality in Islamic nation-states is the result of hegemonic Western influence is not new (Mazrui, 1997; 1999). Long before the events of 9/11, there have been reasons to look specifically and critically at Islamic nation-states, their school systems, and the effects or existence of social stratification and marginalization of opportunities (Mazawi, 1999). Little research, however, has investigated these concerns and phenomena related to education in Islamic nation-states (Wiseman & Alromi, 2001, 2003).

In order to investigate these concerns and phenomena, this chapter will ask if educational and social inequality (i.e., marginalization) is an *international* process occurring between Islamic and other nation-states or an *intra-national* process occurring within individual Islamic nation-states. The evidence presented in this chapter suggests that while the adoption or imposition of schooling modelled on Western educational models may contribute to the marginalization of Islamic nation-states, economic stratification and social inequality are intra-national processes contributing to this marginalization as much as, or more than, international ones.

11.2   A Contested Marriage of Institutions

In recent years there has been a renewed interest in the socio-educational characteristics of Islamic nation-states (Mazawi, 1999; Talbani, 1996). Many studies have focused on the unique relationship between religion and culture in the Middle Eastern region, and to some degree the impact this relationship has on schooling (Shorish, 1988). This focus has been for good reason.

In most Islamic nation-states, the schooling process overtly points toward Islam and its prophets as the ultimate guides for social values and authority. And, although predominantly Islamic nations have been frequently characterized as authoritarian in both political and educational structure, many within the worldwide Islamic community believe that Islamic ideology stresses equality for all, the blending of religious and political ideology, and the value of commitment (Alromi & Wiseman, 2003; Massialas & Jarrar, 1991). In other words, Islamic educational principles suggest broad educational opportunity through closely guided schooling processes. This ideology is intricately woven together with the social traditions of these predominantly Islamic nations, and has been emphasized by Islamization movements since the 1970s.

A question that remains unanswered is whether or not globalization of Westernized mass educational systems contributes to the social construction of marginalization in Islamic nation-states. The impact that this fusion of Islamic ideology and traditional culture has on educational opportunity structures in these nations at an organizational level of analysis is still a relatively unexplored phenomenon (Wiseman & Alromi, 2001). The blending of traditional religious and cultural institutions with the modern institution of mass schooling, therefore, presents a unique opportunity to empirically investigate the structure of educational opportunity that accompanies this seemingly contested marriage of social institutions: religion, culture, and education.

The religious and cultural context of education in Islamic nation-states suggests that schools as government institutions should support the national religion, educational resources should be equally and justly distributed, and academic commitment should be valued as much as, or more than, academic competency (Wiseman & Alromi, 2003). Yet the clash of traditional and modern institutions in predominantly Islamic nations' educational systems may create educational opportunity structures unique to that nation or region apart from, or in addition to, any Western influence inherent in the schooling system.

Not surprisingly, the dynamism that makes the conventional point of view suspect is also a problem for this sort of institutional approach. Newer institutional approaches to schooling, however, suggest that schooling structures and processes may separate from classroom teaching and student performance. This is called *decoupling* or *loose coupling* (Meyer & Rowan, 1977). Loose coupling of formal schooling structures from local or individual outcomes is a frequent characteristic of both non-Western and decentralized (or decentralizing) nations (Astiz et al., 2002).

The contested marriage of religious, cultural, and educational institutions shapes the organizational contexts of schooling in Islamic nation-states. In turn, the organizational contexts of schooling in these nations are characterized by an intersection between strong religious ideology, rapid economic change, and developing educational infrastructures (Wiseman & Alromi, 2001).

Conventional approaches to the comparative analysis of education suggest that schooling is a technical process that follows a rational logic of development and participation leading to logically appropriate outcomes (Baker & LeTendre, 2005; Ball, 1998). The decisions and recommendations of educational policymakers often reflect technical-rational perspectives of schooling in which the purpose is to prepare students to be productive citizens (Alromi & Wiseman, 2003). Research from the conventional perspective tends to focus on unidirectional, functional processes of reform rather than socially dynamic schooling processes nested within broader contexts of schooling. In other words, the conventional approach to education suggests that local level conditions and needs either drive or influence national and global educational processes and systems.

The reality is that there are often fewer rational decisions made by educational policymakers than is assumed (Wiseman & Baker, forthcoming). The conventional approach to educational policymaking suggests that policymakers rationally approach an ongoing or potential problem, carefully consider the reasons for the problem, and then sensibly debate the information and research on this problem. The final stage of this "simple, technocratic view of knowledge utilization" is that the policymakers decide how to solve specific problems based on their consideration of all the relevant data and possible options (Vickers, 1994). This is rarely the case.

For example, Mazawi (1999) suggests that "communities as social actors ... generate their own educational settings and resources" separate from nation level organizational contexts (p. 346). As a result, "community-based processes constantly [mediate] broader systemic policies and educational outcomes" (p. 347). One consequence of this phenomenon is that even when educational resources are abundant and centrally available to schools, each student's ability to take advantage of these resources varies considerably. In addition, schools' access to, and opportunity to use, national resources for school-level programs and instruction is limited by the organizational contexts of schooling unique to individual communities within Islamic nation-states.

The organizational contexts of schooling in Islamic nation-states pose a challenge to conventional approaches to schooling because of the dynamic intersection between religious ideology, economic development, and educational infrastructure. Some scholars suggest that while technical-rational processes exist as conventional perspectives suggest, organizational processes are subject to *bounded rationality* (Fligstein, 1991, p. 315). In other words, although the curriculum and teaching in schools follow rational and logical paths, these processes are also bound to a shared logic or shared rationality with other nations outside of their religious and economic milieu.

The religious principles of Islam are strong influences on the training and socialization of children in Islamic nation-states (Massialas & Jarrar, 1991). In fact, schools in these nations bear much of the responsibility for upholding these Islamic principles. Schooling in Islamic nation-states, in particular, is based on the premise that a body of knowledge exists that is divinely inspired (Massialas & Jarrar, 1987). Religious principles wield such strong influence on the schooling of students in these nations because they are fundamental components of popular social and cultural traditions. Schools, principals, and teachers are often charged with instilling Islamic principles in students through what they teach and how they teach it (Massialas & Jarrar, 1987; Talbani, 1996).

Another intersecting element of schools' organizational contexts in Islamic nation-states is each nation's level of economic growth and development. Much work suggests that student achievement associates with school resources by level of national economic development (Heyneman & Loxley, 1982, 1983a, 1983b). National monopolies of rich oil reserves have made many Islamic nation-states extremely wealthy on the whole if not always at the individual level. Yet, the situation is a more complex one than this suggests because while the wealth of nations suggests that schools have ample resources available to them, school output may not validate this assumption (Baker et al., 2002; Goesling, 2001). While some Islamic nation-states post large economic growth and development potential, their domestic investment in education and educational infrastructure remains at levels comparable to those of developing nations. For example, even though the Islamic Revolution in Iran renewed interest in education as a way to emphasize, strengthen, and encourage faith in Islam, the percentage of Iranian resources dedicated to education has dropped since the revolution.

Instead, it is often the organizational contexts of schools at both the national and school levels that have the greatest influence on students' academic performance. Although Islamic nation-states are steeped in Islamic ideology that both prescribes and proscribes certain social and educational activities, these nations also seek political and economic legitimacy in the international community beyond the boundaries of their geographic region and even the larger Islamic community. Multinational and nongovernmental organizations frequently look to education as an indicator of economic and political status and development potential. Thus, many nations, including Islamic nation-states, borrow from other nation's educational structures and ideologies in order to gain legitimacy in the world society. Often these models from which legitimacy-seeking nations borrow are western in origin and are steeped in the rhetoric of universal equality of access and opportunity. If this argument is true, then schooling structures and processes are institutionalized across many nations (including Islamic nation-states) to fit models for education that have legitimacy in the international community and with influential international organizations such as the United Nations and the World Bank.

11.3   Does Mass Education Lead to Global Marginalization or Opportunity?

Al Heeti and Brock (1997, p. 374) argue that

> issues of development, modernization and related phenomena … tend to be grounded in …
> Western paradigms … and are concerns of the macro realm, while cultural imperatives are
> essentially local (p. 374).

Consequently, education is mediated through culture even when the institutionalized system of education is modelled on Western paradigms.

Prevailing cultural perspectives on education are generally sensitive to issues of cultural mismatch. In fact, culturally sensitive perspectives often emphasize the stratifying effects of schooling and the labor market (Carnoy, 1994). Participation in the labor market often reflects culturally embedded ideas about gender, status, and society. Some assert that "work provides identities as much as it provides bread for the table" and "participation in markets is as much an expression of who one is as what one wants" (Friedland & Alford, 1991, p. 234). These perspectives further suggest that the interaction of schooling and labor market institutions is detrimental to society—that each is separately a source of both cultural conflict and the reproduction of inequality. Yet, the question remains how these arguments specifically speak to the global institutionalization of mass schooling as marginalization or opportunity.

Although social and economic class hegemony in Western nations such as the United States has long been discussed (Meyer & Baker, 1996), the West's hegemonic influence on non-Western nations, regions, and cultures is not new to educational debates and policy reform arguments (Bowles & Gintis, 1976; Friere, 1970). For instance, education has been called a form of cultural imperialism, and, therefore, by extension educational curricula or programs are influential cultural predictors or determinants (Carnoy, 1994; Carnoy & Levin, 1985; Said, 1993). Even institutional perspectives suggest that culture and education overlap in important ways (LeTendre, 1996). In truth, many argue that educational systems are organized to maintain the cultural system they represent (Apple, 1982; Bourdieu, 1977; Spindler, 1987). Arguments about world systems and globalization have suggested that schooling is both a carrier of culture and a socializing agent and, as such, is closely connected to economic and political globalization forces (Astiz et al., 2002; Meyer et al., 1997).

Therefore, if the dominant global model for schooling comes out of Western cultural traditions and encourages its own cultural philosophy, educational programs and curricula should inculcate students to some degree with the values, attitudes, and beliefs of the West even in Islamic nation-states (Wiseman & Baker, forthcoming). This is an example of the *"complexity of cultural identity"*, which emphasizes the importance of the relationship between culture and curriculum (Yates, 1987). For instance, traditionally non-Western Asian nations like China have purposely sought to gain Western-influenced knowledge through schooling while also fostering continuity in traditional values (Cummings, 1995; Hayhoe,

1992). Likewise, although "Western liberal democracy has enabled societies to enjoy openness, government accountability, popular participation, and high economic activity", the particular cultural and moral vices which often accompany an infusion of Western values or culture are strongly opposed by some communities, especially in Islamic nation-states (Mazrui, 1997, p.131).

The imposition of Western rationales for educational systems and curricula also creates cultural discontinuity and may lead to generational conflicts rather than between-culture conflicts per se (Spindler, 1987). Therefore, even in regions or nations characterized by specifically non-Western cultures, schooling predicated on distinctly Western models recruits students into emerging systems that do not reinforce traditional values but instead become agents of modernization and cultural bias. In such cases, schooling is characterized by intergenerational cultural conflict resulting from modernization. As agents of modernization under the influence of the West, therefore, school-based programs may reinforce the Western notion that economic and social "disequilibria are inherent in the process of modernization" (Schultz, 1981, p. 45). From this perspective, the hegemonic influence of the dominant western culture on schooling and the seeming inevitability of social and economic inequality determined either through explicit training or general education suggest that the global institutionalization of mass schooling is more marginalization than opportunity.

On the other hand, an alternative to prevailing cultural arguments suggests that discontinuity and even cultural conflict may maintain the dominant cultural ideology and model, but disconnect the content and skills imparted by Western educational programs and curricula from what is learned outside of schools in, for example, Islamic family and community contexts. Most societies and cultures have been overwhelmed by input from nonindigenous cultures, especially Western culture (Spindler, 1987). This input includes determinants of schooling systems such as curricular content and achievement standards. Therefore, if the influence of the West is replete throughout the world, how can Islamic nation-states avoid incorporating Western values and models of stratification into their own cultural considerations and understandings of education and society?

The answer to this question is complex, and there are little international data to support an analysis of trends in educational and social inequality both between and within Islamic nation-states. But, recent international studies of educational achievement administered under the auspices of the International Association for the Evaluation of Educational Achievement (IEA) have collected background information for nationally representative samples of students and their teachers and school principals in a few Islamic nation-states. The 1999 Repeat of the Third International Mathematics and Science Study (TIMSS 1999) included a wide variety of information about the schooling process in a number of countries, including several nations whose political and legal system are based at least in part on Islamic law.

It is important to distinguish between Islamic nation-states and Muslim countries. Muslim countries are countries that have a high percentage of Muslim citizens, whereas Islamic nation-states are countries that base either all or part of their political and legal government on Islamic law or principles. The countries that participated in TIMSS 1999 and are not Islamic nation-states, but that have high Muslim populations are Indonesia, Malaysia, and Turkey (Central Intelligence Agency [CIA] World Factbook, 2004a, 2004d, 2004g). The Indonesian legal system is based on Roman–Dutch law, with some modifications based on indigenous concepts, and the population is 88% Muslim. The Turkish legal system is derived from various European continental legal systems, and the population is 99.8% Muslim. The Malaysian legal system is based on English common law, and the percent of the population that is Muslim is above 90%.

The Islamic nation-states that participated in TIMSS 1999 were Iran, Jordan, Morocco, and Tunisia. In the Islamic Republic of Iran the constitution closely follows Islamic principles of government, and the population is 98% Muslim. The Jordanian legal system is based on Islamic law and French codes, and the population is 94% Muslim. Morocco's legal system is based on Islamic law and French and Spanish civil law, and the population is 98.7% Muslim. The Tunisian legal system is based on French civil law and Islamic law, and the population is 98% Muslim. While Western culture and Western social institutions still largely influence Jordan, Morocco, and to a lesser degree Tunisia, Iran provides an example of an Islamic nation-state that is the most closely aligned with fundamental Islamic principles (CIA World Factbook, 2004b, 2004c, 2004e, 2004f).

11.4 The Institutionalization of Schooling in Islamic Nation-States

The origins and institutionalization of mass schooling in Iran, Jordan, Morocco, and Tunisia follow similar trajectories. As former colonies of Western nations (Alkadry, 2004), many Muslim countries' educational systems have formed out of this colonial heritage. In many cases, there are still vestiges of colonial educational systems in place (Boyle, 2002). But, as these nations develop and especially since the 1990 Education for All conference in Jomtien, Thailand, schooling in most Muslim nations has expanded (Benoliel, 2003).

In Islamic nation-states, there are generally two types of schools available to children: public and Islamic schools (Benoliel, 2003). The public schools are largely secular although Islamic study is usually a part of the formal required curriculum. The Islamic schools are primarily focused on religion, but some also teach the public school curriculum. All public schools are government-sponsored, and in many instances the Islamic schools are government-sponsored as well, which emphasizes the importance that Islamic nation-states place on education. In fact, as Boyle (2002) explains:

> Education has always been very important in Islamic traditions. Muslims are exhorted in the Qur'an to learn and seek knowledge, both men and women alike. Knowledge (*'ilm*) is referred to in the Qur'an 750 times, ranking it the third most used term, behind God (*Allah*—2,800 references) and Lord (*Rabb*—950 references) and thus testifying to its centrality and importance in the religious tradition. In addition, sayings of the Prophet

Mohammed contain numerous references to the importance of seeking and acquiring both knowledge and education (p. 4).

Even with this traditional emphasis on education, the dual schooling options available (public and Islamic) and the overall increase in enrollment and access to schooling in Islamic nation-states, educational access and school enrollment rates in Islamic nation-states remain relatively low compared to other nations (Benoliel, 2003). In addition, the quality of education in Islamic nation-states has declined since the 1990 Education for All conference as schooling has simultaneously expanded, albeit at a lower rate than in other non-Islamic nations. The drop in educational quality is most apparent at the secondary level where educational enrollment is also below that at the primary level.

Iran, Jordan, Morocco, and Tunisia all follow these general trends for Muslim countries: (1) slow, but eventual expansion of educational access and opportunity as indicated by enrollment levels, and (2) simultaneous deterioration of educational quality as suggested by school shortage indicators. School expansion in developing countries is often measured by the percentage of the primary school-age population that is enrolled in public schools. In the four Islamic nation-states indicated earlier, enrollment in school is relatively high. As Fig. 11.1 shows, Tunisia and Jordan have both had 90% or more of the primary school-age population enrolled since 1998, and that percentage has continued to grow. And Iran and Morocco have climbed from about 80% and 70% of the primary school-age population enrolled, respectively, in 1998 to about 87% of the primary school-age population enrolled in both nations in 2001.

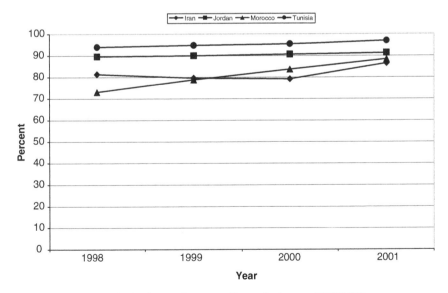

Fig. 11.1 Percentage of school-age primary enrollment, both sexes (UNESCO)

Table 11.1 Percentage of students affected by shortages in general school facilities (TIMSS 1999)

Country	Instructional materials	Budget for supplies	School building or grounds	Heating, cooling & lighting	Instructional space	National shortage average
Iran	26	61	68	50	54	52
Jordan	74	64	75	74	69	71
Morocco	59	77	58	45	45	57
Tunisia	83	77	87	48	76	74
Islamic nation-state Shortage average	61	70	72	54	61	
International average	45	47	50	36	47	

Table 11.1 shows the percentage of students reported by school principals as having been affected by shortages in general school facilities in these four Islamic nation-states. This table shows the percentage of students affected by shortages in instructional materials, budgets for supplies, school buildings or grounds, heating and lighting, and instructional space. Approximately, 50–70% of the student population in each of these individual nations is affected by these shortages on average. And, the overall average in all of these Islamic nation-states shows that 50–70% of students are affected by shortages in each of these categories of general school facilities. This is, on average, 19% more students affected by shortages in general school facilities in Islamic nation-states than in all of the other countries that participated in this study. So, as school-age enrollment is high and continues to rise in Islamic nation-states, the availability of school resources lags far behind most other nations. This poses a serious dilemma for Islamic nation-states.

11.4.1 A Model Islamic Nation-State: The Case of Iran

Although classified as Islamic nation-states because of the direct influence of Islam on their political and legal systems, Jordan, Morocco, and Tunisia provide examples of nations that have varying degrees of both Western influence and Islamic penetration into official government policy. For example, former Tunisian president Habib Bourguiba formed a one-party state after Tunisia won independence from France in 1956, and for 31 years he contained Islamic fundamentalism and established women's rights in a fashion "unmatched by any other Arab nation" (CIA World Factbook, 2004f).

By contrast, Iran's social and political organization is the most strictly tied to Islam of the four Islamic nation-states for which data are available and, therefore, serves as the model Islamic nation-state in discussing the institutionalization of schooling in Islamic nation-states.

The case of Iran provides a foundation for exploring the educational traditions and influences on education in all Islamic nation-states, including Jordan, Morocco, and Tunisia. Like Iran, most Islamic nation-states are steeped in strong religious ideology, which permeates all political, economic, and social institutions in these countries.

Following the Islamic Revolution in 1979, Iran's social, political, and economic institutions came under the auspices of an Islamic regime dedicated to the support and spread of conservative Islamic principles (Mehran, 1990; Mohsenpour, 1988; Shorish, 1988). Iranian schools became particular targets of these ideological reforms due to their close contact with, and influence on, future generations of Iranian citizens and legitimization of power (Aziz-zadeh, 1994; Massialas & Jarrar, 1987; Mehran, 1992; Talbani, 1996).

Like many other Islamic nation-states, the Islamic Republic of Iran is a surprisingly young, multilingual, and culturally diverse community in spite of its portrayal in contemporary Western media (Barber, 1996; Cohen, 2003; Encyclopaedia Britannica Online, 2001; Lewis, 1990). Yet, the Islamic Revolution of 1979 continues to be an important ideological marker in the development of Iranian society. Prior to 1979, the Iranian monarchy was relatively progressive and tolerant or even accepting of Western cultural ideals, models, and behaviors. All that dramatically changed during the revolution. Iran is now guided predominantly by Islamic principles and leaders and, although infrequent, any challenges to Islamic authority are firmly denounced.

Iran's national education system is based on the centralized French model and was introduced in 1894. After the Islamic Revolution of 1979, the French model was adjusted so that all curricula and teaching instills and encourages Islamic principles (Aziz-zadeh, 1994). In keeping with these principles, coeducational schools have been eliminated so that only single-sex schools remain. In addition, schools and universities are required to "reflect the Islamic system of beliefs" so much so that students' admission to university is in part dependent on their Islamic beliefs (Encyclopaedia Britannica Online, 2001).

In spite of these religious requirements, most education is free or at least access is facilitated for Iranian citizens. Yet the percentage of Iranian resources dedicated to education dropped during the 1980s from 3.8% in 1982 to 3.2% in 1990 (Aziz-zadeh, 1994). One of the most important resource shortages in Iran, however, concerns teachers. There is a significant crisis regarding a shortage of qualified teachers, especially in rural areas and vocational secondary schools. As a result, rural and less-developed areas of Iran sometimes see military conscripts teaching in schools in these areas (Aziz-zadeh, 1994). In addition, Iran's national system of education continues to struggle to find adequate resources to expand upper-secondary and post-secondary education. Even in modern times, Iran struggles to provide facilities and equipment for education, whether adequate or not. Thus, Iran's educational context is guided and bounded by strong religious ideology, but limited in its scope and provision through a very weak schooling infrastructure.

Given these challenges, the growth of educational opportunity and curriculum in Islamic nation-states beyond religious and traditional education is due in part to the Western influence of global policy proclamations like the 1990 Education for All statement. In this case, the input from Western nations emphasizes equality, rather than marginalization in education. This suggests that international inequality may not be as much of a factor in the marginalization of Islamic nation-states in the global community as is intra-national inequality in the access to, or provision of, educational opportunity within individual Islamic nation-states.

On the other hand, intra-national educational inequality that exists in Islamic nation-states is often due to factors that can be influenced by the general political status and economic resources that each nation has, and these status and resource factors are often largely influenced by international relationships. For example, USAID found that poor educational quality in Muslim countries was largely due to "inadequate government investment, a shortage of qualified teachers, limited and ineffective teacher training, outdated curricula, inadequate supply and poor quality of learning materials and textbooks, and weak institutional capacity at the central and local levels" (Benoliel, 2003, p. 3).

11.5 Evidence for Marginalization and Opportunity

The TIMSS 1999 provides data on educational resources and opportunities from these four Islamic nation-states and as many as 35 other nations. These data provide evidence that indicates the level of social and educational inequality both within and between nations. In other words, using TIMSS 1999 data the debate over international versus intra-national inequality or marginalization can be empirically investigated. To do so, several elements related to inequality were measured. First, social inequality related to education is measured by variation in an index of home educational resources including number of books in the home, educational aids in the home, and parents' education level. Second, formal schooling inequality is measured by variation in an index of reported availability of school resources for mathematics instruction.

International educational inequality trends are illustrated for the three Islamic nation-states and the other nations in the international sample in Fig. 11.2. To get at these notions of international inequality versus intra-national inequality, a comparison of these student and school educational inequality trends within Iran, Jordan, Morocco, and Tunisia would be helpful. In the Islamic nation-states in these data, eighth-grade students on average reported that they have access to between low and medium levels of home educational resources. Of the participating nations in this sample, Moroccan and Iranian students reported the lowest levels of home educational resources of any of the countries. Jordan and Tunisia, while significantly higher than Iran and Morocco, reported home educational resource levels significantly below the international mean. Eighth-graders' school principals in the Islamic nation-states in these data reported on average that the availability of school resources for mathematics instruction was significantly below the international mean for three of the four participating Islamic nation-states (Tunisia being the exception).

While both students and principals reported that educational resources (at home and at school, respectively) were below the international mean, it is noteworthy that the home educational resource levels were lower than the school educational

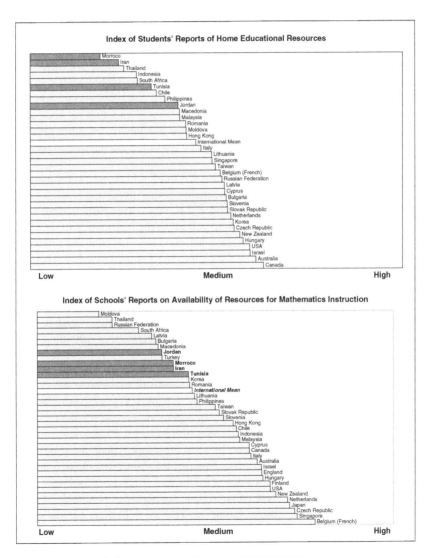

Fig. 11.2 International educational inequality trends (TIMSS 1999)

resource levels. This distinction is important because it indicates that students have more educational resources at school than in the home. If indeed the public, government-sponsored schools are modeled on Western ideology and structures, the data suggest that it is the Western-influenced schools that give students more opportunity to learn than the tradition-laden and culture-laden home, family, or local community. In other words, *inter*-national inequality among Islamic nation-states may not result from the adoption or imposition of Western models of schooling. Instead, *intra*-national inequality within Islamic nation-states may play a part in the marginalization of these nations in the global community.

Determining the level of intra-national variation in educational inequality within these nations in comparison to other nations in the international sample can be accomplished by comparing coefficients of variation for the two indexes of student and school inequality shown in Fig. 11.2. As Fig. 11.3 shows, the reports by students and school principals in these Islamic nation-states suggest that there is more variation between individual students and their families regarding home educational resources for Iran and Morocco than in all other countries, and for Jordan and Tunisia than in most other countries. And, there is more variation between schools within Iran, Jordan, and Morocco regarding the availability of school resources especially for mathematics instruction than in most other nations and, in particular, most Western industrialized countries.

Taken together, then, the evidence presented in Figs 11.2 and 11.3 suggests that intra-national variation in educational inequality both at home and at school is high in these Islamic nation-states when compared to most other participating nations. This evidence also suggests that problems related to the distribution of educational resources and opportunities *within* Islamic nation-states may contribute to the marginalization of these countries within the global community. Indeed, it is disturbing that measures of inequality in both home-based and school-based educational resources show that Islamic nation-states are significantly disadvantaged in relation to most nations sampled, and especially in relation to most other industrialized nations. But, is this international and intra-national inequality trend in Islamic nation-states somehow connected to the formal organization of schooling in these countries?

One of the most talked about effects of the institutionalization of mass schooling around the world is increased access and opportunity to receive formal school instruction, also sometimes called opportunity to learn (OTL) (Jacobson & Doran, 1988; Meyer et al., 1992; Wang, 1998). In earlier studies, enrollment was often used as an indicator of OTL, but in the latter 20th and early 21st centuries the trend towards nearly universal enrollment in most developed and many developing nations requires new measures of OTL. Figure 11.4 shows that the two indicators of educational access and opportunity used in this analysis are schools' reports on the percent of total hours spent on instruction and an index of schools' reports on good school and class attendance. Using the TIMSS 1999 data, percent of hours spent on instruction is the ratio of the number of instructional hours to the number of total hours students spend in school as reported by school principals. The index of schools' reports on school and class attendance is derived from principals'

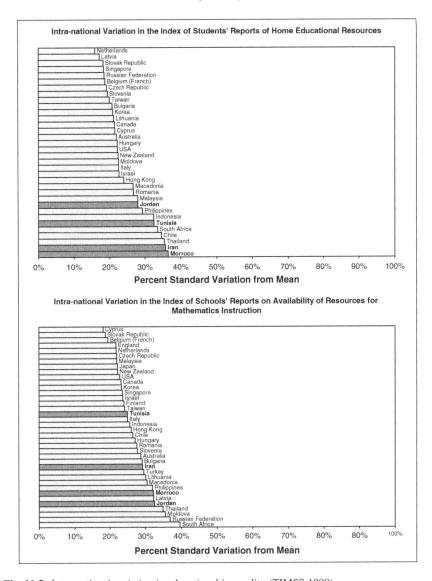

Fig. 11.3 Intra-national variation in educational inequality (TIMSS 1999)

responses to three questions concerning the severity of students' arriving late at school, absenteeism, and skipping class.

In the Islamic nation-states in this sample, school principals reported that students spent a significant amount of school time on instruction. As Fig. 11.4 shows, 82%, 83%, 87%, and 96% of the time in school was dedicated to instruction in Tunisia, Jordan, Iran, and Morocco, respectively. The percent of total school hours spent on instruction in these Islamic nation-states (except Tunisia) is significantly

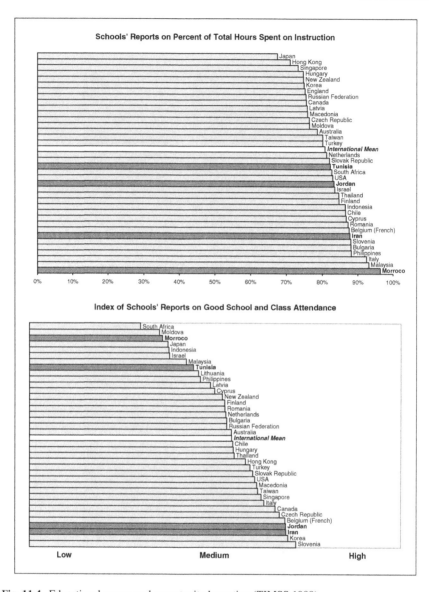

Fig. 11.4 Educational access and opportunity by nation (TIMSS 1999)

above the international mean. These same school principals differ in their reports on good school and class attendance. In particular, Jordan and Iran both reported some of the highest levels of school and class attendance while Morocco and Tunisia reported some of the lowest levels of school and class attendance in the international sample.

The evidence presented in Fig. 11.4, therefore, suggests that while instructional time in school is relatively high in these four Islamic nation-states, there is some disparity in school attendance by students in each country. In other words, the school provides ample opportunity for students to receive formal instruction (i.e., become educated), but students inconsistently take advantage of these opportunities. Based on this evidence it seems unlikely that the formal organization of mass schooling in these Islamic nation-states is a significant contributor to within-nation inequality regarding educational access and opportunities. Between the ever-rising enrollment in Islamic nation-states (and in all Muslim countries) and the high percentage of time spent on instruction when students are in school, the structure or formal organization of mass schooling seems to in fact promote equality rather than inequality. Instead, the evidence suggests that there are other factors, which may be related to local traditional or cultural influences, that may be at work.

11.6   Intra-National Versus International Inequality

How then does schooling contribute to Islamic nation-states like Iran, Jordan, Morocco, and Tunisia ending up on the political and economic fringes of the international community? The answer may be that through a society-wide reluctance to turn from traditional religious ideologies schooling is in some way hampered in Islamic nation-states. Islamic nation-states may be marginalized within the international community, but there is evidence to suggest that the educational inequality that exists in Islamic nation-states may be due to intra-national inequality in the distribution of school resources and educational opportunities rather than the hegemonic imposition of Western school models on indigenous educational systems.

Many of these nations are developing their own infrastructures. The burden that an expanding school system places on their already stretched resources means that government-sponsored public schools are often less able to meet the needs of a nation's developing economy and political establishment than they ideally would be. In addition, the pressure to develop is often heightened by Islamic nation-states' attempts to fit into the legitimate and predominantly Western model of what a modern, politically and economically competitive nation-state is. And, the provision of free, universal education is a key component of this internationally legitimate model.

Problems arise when Islamic nation-states attempt to fulfill these external expectations with only limited internal resources and support. In many cases, the traditional culture in Islamic nation-states may already emphasize education, but not the Western model of public schooling that predominantly Western, multinational organizations expect or require. As a result, community leaders and parents in Islamic nation-states may resist new forms of government-sponsored public schooling in favor of traditional schooling methods that may or may not teach an "approved" curriculum or follow standard models of schooling (Mazrui, 1999).

The combination of rapidly developing infrastructures, strong religious and cultural ideology, and a tradition of resistance to Western influences suggests that the educational delivery system in the Islamic nation-states of Iran, Jordan, Morocco, and Tunisia is loosely coupled or decoupled somewhere between the national, school, and student levels. When this happens the wealth and resources of the nation may not be distributed to the general public through the processes and outcomes of schooling. Record numbers of school-age students may be enrolled in school, but without the means to provide these students with equal educational opportunities (e.g., appropriate instructional materials, adequate supply budgets, safe buildings and grounds, adequate heating and lighting, and enough instructional space) the fact that students are enrolled in, and are going to, school may not be indicators of equality of education opportunity.

Perhaps more importantly, however, is the exclusion of traditional or culturally based ways of knowing from these "modern" schools, which is often a result of mass schooling that follows the Western model (Wiseman, 2000). Indeed, the expansion of mass schooling into previously peripheral nations and culturally or ethnically defined people groups within those nations has fostered an atmosphere of equal educational access and opportunity. But, often accompanying this environment of equality and opportunity is a clash of Western knowledge systems with traditional ways of knowing. This loose coupling of localized culture and tradition to Western educational knowledge systems can make the transition to mass schooling difficult, especially in nation-states that are officially linked to religious or cultural traditions as Islamic nation-states are.

11.7   Conclusion

Given the legitimizing capacity of education in global economic, political, and even social communities, the leveling and assimilative effects of schooling are severely tested by the institutionalization of mass schooling. It is with this institutionalization of education that loosely coupled systems can become decoupled systems, meaning that unique religious and cultural communities become further marginalized within a predominantly Western educational system. Consequently, it may not be up to education alone to either create or ameliorate the marginalization of Islamic nation-states.

In closing his address to the 46th session of the International Conference on Education, Argentinean Minister of Education Delich (2001) asserted that

[i]nstitutionalized education has a key role to play in building human coexistence. But we should not deceive ourselves. Bringing about the necessary conditions for living together in tomorrow's world does not depend only or mainly on education.

This is a lesson that is hard to learn. While the institutionalization of mass schooling may be an indicator of national political and economic development, it rarely impacts the larger national and even international community when it is separated or decoupled from the traditions and cultures that guide local communities within nations.

In Islamic nation-states, the local traditions and cultures are often dominated by strong religious ideologies first and foremost. The impact of education on social inequality in Islamic nation-states is, therefore, also largely directed by religious ideology. And, while institutionalized mass schooling has an important role to play in shaping these nations' futures, educational policymakers, teachers, students, and community members in Islamic nation-states may do better to first focus on the political and economic stratification that exists within their own societies than on the cultural or social effects of education based on Western models.

References

Adely, F. (2005). The mixed effects of schooling for high school girls in Jordan: The case of Tel Yahya. *Comparative Education Review*.

Al Heeti, A. G. & Brock, C. (1997). Vocational education and development: Key issues, with special reference to the Arab world. *International Journal of Educational Development*, *17*(4), 373–389.

Alkadry, M. (2004). Colonialism in a postmodern age: The West, Arabs and "the Battle of Baghdad". *Public Administration and Management: Interactive Journal*, *9*(1), www.pamij.com

Alromi, N. H. & Wiseman, A. W. (2003). *Schooling for individual and national development: International perspectives on school-to-work Transition*. Riyadh: King Fahd National Library.

Apple, M. W. (1982). Reproduction and contradiction in education: An introduction. In M. W. Apple (Ed.), *Cultural and economic reproduction in education: Essays on class, ideology and thestate* (pp. 1–31). London: Routledge & Kegan Paul.

Astiz, M. F., Wiseman, A. W., & Baker, D. P. (2002). Slouching towards decentralization: Consequences of globalization for curricular control in national education systems. *Comparative Education Review*, *46*(1), 66–89.

Aziz-zadeh, H. (1994). Iran: System of education. In T. Husen & T. N. Postlethwaite (Eds.), *International Encyclopedia of Education* (pp. 3007–3011). Oxford: Pergamon.

Baker, D. P., Goesling, B., & LeTendre, G. K. (2002). Socioeconomic status, school quality, and national economic development: A cross-national analysis of the 'Heyneman-Loxley Effect' on mathematics and science achievement. *Comparative Education Review*, *46*(3), 291–313.

Baker, D. P. & LeTendre, G. K. (2005). *National differences, global similarities: Current and future world institutional trends in schooling*. Stanford, CA: Stanford University Press.

Baker, D. P. & Wiseman, A. W. (2005). The declining significance of gender and the rise of egalitarian mathematics education. In D. P. Baker & G. K. LeTendre (Eds.), *National differences, global similarities: Current and future world institutional trends in schooling*. Stanford, CA: Stanford University Press.

Ball, S. J. (1998). Big policies/small world: An introduction to international perspectives in education policy. *Comparative Education*, *34*(2), 119–130.

Barber, B. (1996). *Jihad vs. Mcworld*. New York: Ballantine.

Benoliel, S. (2003). *Strengthening education in the Muslim world: Summary of the desk study, issue paper number 2*. Washington, DC: USAID, Bureau for Policy and Program Coordination.

Bourdieu, P. (1977). Cultural reproduction and social reproduction. In J. Karabel & A. H. Halsey (Eds.), *Power and ideology in education* (pp. 487–510). New York: Oxford University Press.

Bowles, S. & Gintis, H. (1976). *Schooling in capitalist America : Educational reform and the contradictions of economic Life*. New York: Basic Books.

Boyle, H. N. (2002, March). *The growth of Qur'anic schooling and the marginalization of Islamic pedagogy: The case of Morocco.* Paper presented at the annual meeting of the Comparative and International Education Society, Orlando, FL.

Carnoy, M. (1985). The political economy of education. *International Social Science Journal, 37*(2), 157–173.

Carnoy, M. (1994). *Faded dreams: The politics of economics and race in America.* New York: Cambridge University Press.

Carnoy, M. (2000). *Globalization and educational Restructuring.* Paris: International Institute of Educational Planning.

Carnoy, M. & Levin, H. (1985). *Schooling and work in the democratic state.* Stanford, CA: Stanford University Press.

Chabbott, C. (2003). *Constructing education for development.* New York: RoutledgeFalmer.

CIA World Factbook. (2004a) Indonesia Retrieved July14,2004 from http://www.cia.gov/cia/publications/factbook/geos/id.html

CIA World Factbook. (2004b). Iran. Retrieved July 14, 2004 from http://www.cia.gov/cia/publications/factbook/geos/ir.html

CIA World Factbook. (2004c). Jordan. Retrieved July 14, 2004 from http://www.cia.gov/cia/publications/factbook/geos/jo.html

CIA World Factbook. (2004d). Malaysia. Retrieved July 14, 2004 from http://www.cia.gov/cia/publications/factbook/geos/my.html

CIA World Factbook. (2004e). Morocco. Retrieved July 14, 2004 from http://www.cia.gov/cia/publications/factbook/geos/mo.html

CIA World Factbook. (2004f). Tunisia. Retrieved July 14, 2004 from http://www.cia.gov/cia/publications/factbook/geos/ts.html

CIA World Factbook. (2004g). Turkey. Retrieved July 14, 2004 from http://www.cia.gov/cia/publications/factbook/geos/tu.html

Cohen, R. (2003, July 17). Unshakeable faith. *Washington Post,* p. www.washingtonpost.com.

Crossley, M. & Watson, K. (2003). *Comparative and international research in education: Globalisation, context and difference.* New York: RoutledgeFalmer.

Cummings, W. (1995). The Asian human resources approach in global perspective. *Oxford Review of Education, 21*(1), 67–81.

Delich, A. G. (2001). Opening address by Mr. Andres G. Delich, Minister of Education of Argentina. 46th Session of the International Conference on Education.

Encyclopaedia Britannica Online. (2001). Iran. Retrieved January 31, 2001 from http://search.eb.com/eb/article?eu=109309

Fligstein, N. (1991). The Structural transformation of American industry: An institutional account of the causes of diversification in the largest firms, 1919–1979. In W. W. Powell & D. P. J. (Eds.), *The new institutionalism in organizational analysis* (pp. 311–336). Chicago, IL: University of Chicago Press.

Friedland, R. & Alford, R. R. (1991). Bringing society back in: Symbols, practices, and institutional contradictions. In W. W. Powell & D. P. J. (Eds.), *The new institutionalism in organizational analysis* (pp. 232–266). Chicago, IL: University of Chicago Press.

Friere, P. (1970). *Pedagogy of the oppressed.* New York: Continuum.

Goesling, B. (2001). Changing income inequalities within and between nations: New evidence. *American Sociological Review, 66*(5), 745–762.

Hayhoe, R. (1992). Modernization without Westernization: Assessing the Chinese experience. In R. F. Arnove, P. G. Altbach & G. P. Kelly (Eds.), *Emergent issues in education: Comparative perspectives.* Albany, NY: SUNY Press.

Heyneman, S. P. & Loxley, W. A. (1982). Influences on academic achievement across high and low income countries: A re-analysis of IEA data. *Sociology of Education, 55*(1), 13–21.

Heyneman, S. P. & Loxley, W. A. (1983a). The distribution of primary school quality within high- and low-income countries. *Comparative Education Review, 27*(1), 108–118.

Heyneman, S. P. & Loxley, W. A. (1983b). The effect of primary-school quality on academic achievement across twenty-nine high- and low-income countries. *American Journal of Sociology*, 88(6), 1162–1194.

Inkeles, A. (1969). Making men modern: On the auses and consequences of individual change in six developing countries. *American Journal of Sociology*, 75(2), 208–225.

Jacobson, W. J. & Doran, R. L. (1988). *Science achievement in the United States and sixteen countries: A report to the public*. Washington, DC: National Science Foundation.

LeTendre, G. K. (1996). Constructed aspirations: Decision-making processes in Japanese educational selection. *Sociology of Education*, 69(July), 193–216.

Lewis, B. (1990). The Roots of Muslim rage. *Atlantic Monthly*, September, 47–60.

Marginson, S. & Mollis, M. (2001). "The door opens and the tiger leaps": Theories and reflexivities of comparative education for a global millennium. *Comparative Education Review*, 45(4), 581–615.

Massialas, B. G. & Jarrar, S. A. (1987). Conflicts in education in the Arab world: The present challenge. *Arab Studies Quarterly*, 9, 35–52.

Massialas, B. G. & Jarrar, S. A. (1991). *Arab education in transition*. New York: Garland.

Mazawi, A. E. (1999). The contested terrains of education in the Arab states: An appraisal of major research trends. *Comparative Education Review*, 43(3), 332–352.

Mazrui, A. A. (1997). Islamic and Western values. *Foreign Affairs*, 76(5), 118–132.

Mazrui, A. A. (1999). Globalization and cross-cultural values: The politics of identity and judgment. *Arab Studies Quarterly*, 21(3), 97–109.

Mehran, G. (1990). Ideology and education in the Islamic Republic of Iran. *Compare*, 20(1), 53–65.

Mehran, G. (1992). Social implications of literacy in Iran. *Comparative Education Review*, 36(2), 194–211.

Meyer, J. W. & Baker, D. P. (1996). Forming American educational policy with international data: Lessons from the sociology of education. *Sociology of Education* (Extra Issue), 123–130.

Meyer, J. W., Boli, J., Thomas, G. M., & Ramirez, F. O. (1997). World society and the nation-state. *American Journal of Sociology*, 103(1), 144–181.

Meyer, J. W., Ramirez, F. O., & Soysal, Y. N. (1992). World expansion of mass education, 1870–1980. *Sociology of Education*, 65(2), 128–149.

Meyer, J. W. & Rowan, B. (1977). Institutionalized organizations: Formal structure as myth and ceremony. *American Journal of Sociology*, 83(2), 340–363.

Mohsenpour, B. (1988). Philosophy of education in postrevolutionary Iran. *Comparative Education Review*, 32(1), 76–86.

Morrow, R. A. & Torres, C. A. (2000). The state, globalization, and educational policy. In N. C. Burbules & C. A. Torres (Eds.), *Globalization and education: Critical Perspectives*. New York: Routledge.

Said, E. W. (1993). *Culture and imperialism*. New York: Random House.

Schultz, T. W. (1981). *Investing in people: The economics of population quality*. Berkeley, CA: University of California Press.

Shorish, M. M. (1988). The Islamic revolution and education in Iran. *Comparative Education Review*, 32(1), 58–75.

Spindler, G. (Ed.). (1987). *Education and the cultural process: Anthropological approaches*. Prospect Heights, IL: Waveland.

Talbani, A. (1996). Pedagogy, power, and discourse: Transformation of Islamic education. *Comparative Education Review*, 40(1), 66–82.

Vickers, M. (1994). Cross-national exchange, the OECD, and Australian education policy. *Knowledge & Policy*, 7(1), 25–47.

Wang, J. (1998). Opportunity to learn: The impacts and policy implications. *Educational Evaluation and Policy Analysis*, 20(3), 137–156.

Wiseman, A. W. (2000). Navajo transition to higher education: Knowledge systems, cultural values, and educational policies. *International Journal of Educational Research*, 33, 621–629.

Wiseman, A. W. & Alromi, N. H. (2001). *The "Gulf state phenomenon": A comparative analysis of the organizational contexts of schooling in Gulf nations*. Paper presented at the annual meeting of the Comparative and International Education Society, Washington, DC.

Wiseman, A. W. & Alromi, N. H. (2003). The intersection of traditional and modern institutions in Gulf states: A contextual analysis of educational opportunities and outcomes in Iran and Kuwait. *Compare, 33*(2), 207–234.

Wiseman, A. W. & Baker, D. P. (2005). The worldwide explosion of internationalized education policy. In D. P. Baker & A. W. Wiseman (Eds.), *International Perspectives on Education and Society*. Amsterdam: Elsevier.

Yates, P. D. (1987). Figure and section: Ethnography and education in the multicultural state. In G. Spindler & L. Spindler (Eds.), *Interpretive ethnography of education: At home and abroad*. Hillsdale, NJ: Lawrence Earlbaum.

Index

Book titles in the 12-volume series

Volume 1 *Education and Social Inequality in the Global Culture* (Karen Biraimah, *University of Central Florida*, William Gaudelli, *Teachers College Columbia University*, and Joseph Zajda, *Australian Catholic University, Melbourne Campus*)
[evaluating educational inequality in the global culture]

Volume 2 *Comparative and Global Pedagogies: Equity, Access and Democracy in Education* (Lyn Davies, *University of Birmingham*, Suzanne Majhanovich, *University of Western Ontario*, and Joseph Zajda, *Australian Catholic University, Melbourne Campus*)
[examining equality, equity and democracy in education globally]

Volume 3 *Globalisation, Policy and Comparative Research*
(Joseph Zajda, *Australian Catholic University, Melbourne Campus*, and Val Rust, *UCLA*)
[covering major discourses in comparative education research]

Volume 4 *Race, Ethnicity and Gender in Education: Cross-Cultural Understandings*
(Joseph Zajda, *Australian Catholic University, Melbourne Campus*, and Kassie Freeman, *Bowdoin College*)
[critiquing global discourses of race, ethnicity and gender in education]

Volume 5 *The Politics of Education Reforms: Comparing Educational Outcomes* (Joseph Zajda, *Australian Catholic University, Melbourne Campus*, and MacLeans Geo-JaJa, *Brigham Young University*)
[examining schooling, social stratification and inequality in intra-national education research]

Volume 6 *Nation-Building, Identity and Citizenship Education: Cross-cultural Perspectives* (Joseph Zajda, *Australian Catholic University, Melbourne Campus*, Holger Daun, *Stockholm University*, and Lawrence Saha, *Australian National University*)
[analysing dominant discourses of identity politics and nation-building in comparative education research]

Volume 7 *Global Values Education: Teaching Democracy and Peace*
(Joseph Zajda, *Australian Catholic University, Melbourne Campus*, Yaacov Iram, *Bar-Ilam University*, and Holger Daun, *Stockholm University*)
[evaluating the most effective models and curricula for teaching tolerance and peace intra-nationally]

Volume 8 *Decentralisation, School-Based Management, and Quality*
(Joseph Zajda, *Australian Catholic University, Melbourne Campus*, and David Gamage, *University of Newcastle*)
[examining key issues in decentralisation, school-based management and quality debate in schooling intra-nationally]

Volume 9 *Comparative Information Technology: Languages, Societies and the Internet*
(Joseph Zajda, *Australian Catholic University, Melbourne Campus*, and Donna Gibbs, *Macquarie University*)
[discussing the nexus between the new modes of IT and society globally]

Volume 10 *Globalisation, Education and Social Justice: New Schools for the 21st Century* (Joseph Zajda, *Australian Catholic University, Melbourne Campus*, and Val Rust, *UCLA*)
[discussing major and innovative models for tomorrow's schools in comparative education]

Volume 11 *Globalisation, and Comparative Education Research*
(Joseph Zajda, *Australian Catholic University, Melbourne Campus*, and Val Rust, *UCLA*)
[covering the evolution and current state of comparative education and policy research]

Volume 12 *Schooling for the Future: Comparative Education Policy for the 21st Century*
(Joseph Zajda, *Australian Catholic University, Melbourne Campus*, Val Rust, *UCLA*, and Birgit Brock-Utne, *University of Oslo*)
[evaluating major discourses in pedagogy, and education policy in the global culture]

Lightning Source UK Ltd.
Milton Keynes UK
UKOW06n0752030915

257965UK00001B/20/P

9 781402 069260